Praise for *The Roth Revolution: Pay Taxes Once and Never Again*

"There are few advisors as IRA-knowledgeable as Jim Lange. His book is chock full of creative Roth IRA planning ideas to help every client."

Natalie Choate, Esq.
Author, *Life and Death Planning for Retirement Benefits*, 6th Edition

"Jim Lange has done it again. In *Retire Secure!*, Jim showed how minimizing taxes and investment expenses can lead to a comfortable retirement. In *The Roth Revolution*, he clearly explains the remarkable advantages of Roth IRAs and their role in estate planning. Everyone considering conversions of traditional IRAs to Roths should read this book."

Burton G. Malkiel
Author, *A Random Walk Down Wall Street*, 10th edition

"Looking to protect your money? Read Jim Lange's *The Roth Revolution*— and you could make your financial life a whole lot less taxing."

Jonathan Clements
Author, *The Little Book of Main Street Money*
Former Personal Finance Colomnist, *The Wall Street Journal*

"An amazing, comprehensive explanation of the hows and whys of Roth IRAs with real life examples unlocked by Jim Lange who has set a new standard in retirement tax planning."

Diane McCurdy, CFP
Best-Selling Author of *How Much is Enough?*

"*The Roth Revolution* is must reading for anyone contemplating moving money into a Roth IRA, which in my opinion is everyone. Jim Lange is one of the few people who has the knowledge when it comes to IRAs and also has the ability to put this knowledge into understandable language."

Barry C. Picker, CPA/PFS, CFP
Co-Author, *100+ Roth IRA Examples & Flowcharts*

"Jim Lange hits another homerun with *The Roth Revolution*. Anyone concerned about ensuring his or her nest egg is enough for retirement needs this book … and that's just about all of us."

Lois P. Frankel, Ph.D.
Author, *Nice Girls Don't Get Rich*

"*The Roth Revolution* is an invaluable tool for any advisor assisting a client with a decision on whether to convert to a Roth IRA. With the expanded opportunity for taxpayers to take advantage of a Roth IRA regardless of their income, this is a resource that should be on every advisor's desk."

Bob Keebler, CPA
Author, *A CPAs Guide to Making the Most of the New IRAs*

"With charts, graphs, checklists and examples, Jim Lange, an advisor's advisor, presents the answers to the Roth IRA puzzle in clear, concise terms. His book is loaded with solid answers to the very questions your clients are sure to ask."

Steve Leimberg
Publisher, Leimberg Information Services, Inc. (LISI)

"This book shows you how to plan your finances so you don't run out of money in retirement—perhaps the biggest single consideration of your life."

Brian Tracy
Author, *The Way to Wealth*

"Jim's specific advice to taxpayers in different tax brackets (Chapter Thirteen) makes a complicated topic easy to understand."

Bill Losey, CFP
Author, *Retire in a Weekend!*

"Jim Lange helps people. You should read *The Roth Revolution!*"

John D Bledsoe
Author, *The Gospel of Roth*

"*The Roth Revolution* is a clear and comprehensive guide to a financial planning tool everyone should understand. I highly recommend it."

Michael T. Palmero, Attorney at Law
Author, *AARP Crash Course in Estate Planning*

"Jim Lange has done it again! *The Roth Revolution* is a worthy follow up to *Retire Secure!*, written in a highly readable style that provides an excellent guide for all of us whose clients want to know whether they should convert to a Roth IRA. We were particularly pleased to find a thoughtful discussion of combining Roth IRAs with philanthropy."

Jon Gallo, J.D.
Author, *The Financially Intelligent Parent*

THE ROTH REVOLUTION
Pay Taxes Once and Never Again

James Lange, CPA/Attorney

NEW YORK

THE ROTH REVOLUTION
Pay Taxes Once and Never Again

ISBN 978-1-60037-857-7 (paperback)
Library of Congress Control Number: 2010934448

Published by:

MORGAN JAMES PUBLISHING
The Entrepreneurial Publisher
5 Penn Plaza, 23rd Floor
New York City, New York 10001
(212) 655-5470 Office
(516) 908-4496 Fax
www.MorganJamesPublishing.com

Interior Design by:
Bonnie Bushman
bbushman@bresnan.net

In an effort to support local communities, raise awareness and funds, Morgan James Publishing donates one percent of all book sales for the life of each book to Habitat for Humanity.

Get involved today, visit
www.HelpHabitatForHumanity.org.

Acknowledgments

The Roth Revolution could not have been written without the work and dedication of many others. Their contributions were invaluable.

Steven T. Kohman, Certified Public Accountant, Certified Specialist in Estate Planning, has worked with me for over 15 years and has co-authored many articles with me. Steve is a master of making financial projections and developing recommendations for Roth IRA conversion decisions and other retirement and estate-planning issues. Steve combines his extensive tax background with his superb quantitative and computer skills. His quantitative analysis, evidenced in the graphs and charts throughout, present compelling proof of the fundamental concepts that make up the backbone of *The Roth Revolution*.

Matt Schwartz, Esq., is an exceptionally bright and gifted IRA-and estate-attorney who has worked with me for ten years. I am proud to have him as a colleague. Matt has made many original contributions to *The Roth Revolution* as well as many corrections. He works closely with our clients to strategize and develop estate plans that help optimize a family's assets. He helps implement the estate plan and completes the documentation necessary to implement our recommended planning solutions. Typically, Matt drafts wills, trusts, beneficiary designations of retirement plans, beneficiary designation of insurance policies, living wills, powers of attorneys, etc.

Both Steve and Matt bring an incredible dedication to their work. They think about IRAs and Roth IRAs and estate planning all the time. They write articles, give talks, help me with books, and read constantly to keep up with the ever changing tax laws. They are among the best in their field both academically and in practice.

Sandy Proto, our Office Manager, who has been working with me for 17 years, was particularly helpful in coordinating everyone working on the book as well as making critical editing contributions.

I would also like to thank my mother, Barnetta Lange, Ph.D., who edited *The Roth Revolution* for grammar and clarity. My mom, a Professor Emeritus of Journalism of Point Park University, is not shy with the red pen. Her edits have made the writing clear and easier to read. Plus, she is dedicated. She edited an earlier draft and after many corrections and additions, she edited a revised draft.

Cynthia Nelson, the content editor, has been working with me for over 12 years. During this period, she has had editing and writing responsibilities for many of my published works. She is a rare find. She cuts through some of the technical and legal jargon that I sometimes fall into and expresses complex thoughts in a way the lay reader can understand, and yet she allows me to express my humanity and my humor in my own voice. She has also added her own touches which makes reading *The Roth Revolution* a better experience.

I also want to thank all the pre-release readers and reviewers of *The Roth Revolution*. In particular, special thanks to Natalie Choate, Ed Slott, Bob Keebler, Steve Leimberg, Burton Malkiel, Brian Tracy, Jonathan Clements, John Bledsoe, Barry Picker, Walt Dollard, Parvin Lippincott and Bob Miller.

I must also convey my gratitude to my full-time coworkers (in addition to Steve, Matt and Sandy) who provide so much help in my practice that without them, the book could never have been written: Glenn Venturino, CPA—how can I properly thank you for 23 years of superb service to our clients and for your own contributions to the book?; Alice Davis, our client service coordinator, who is so wonderful and personable with our clients and is the first to jump on board when anything needs to be done; Donna Master, who keeps our books and so much more, and Daryl Ross, our legal administrative assistant/master tax return compiler. Special thanks to Nicole DeMartino, our Marketing Director, who has helped with the legwork needed to get this book in your hands as well as helping with text.

There are two special subcontractors who work on my behalf whom I want to thank. Stephen May—my webmaster for 14 years—how can I properly thank you? And Rich Davis who has been invaluable in producing fabulous CDs, DVDs, and YouTube files of some of my best information.

And closest to my heart, I want to thank my beloved wife, Cindy Lange, who understands me but in spite of that, still puts up with me. This book would never have happened without her help, support and love. Finally, thank you to my 15-year-old daughter, Erica, whom I love dearly. Thank you for not complaining when I worked weekends and went back to the office after dinner to work on the book.

Thank you all.

Foreword

Foreword by Ed Slott, CPA
"America's IRA Expert"

Not without cause, the past few years have provoked a profound sense of pessimism about the prospects of a carefree and comfortable retirement. Whereas retirement used to be anticipated as a time of freedom, a time to enjoy the fruits of your labor, now it seems to evoke nothing short of anxiety and dismay.

The stock market crash in 2008 changed the retirement plans of many American workers. Many people on the cusp of retirement saw their portfolios drop significantly and now must consider postponing retirement to help replenish what was lost during the market downturn. Retirees must rethink their spending. Younger workers are affected too. With guaranteed pension plans a relic of the past, a drop in retirement benefits, and Social Security a question mark, many are searching for effective strategies to make ends meet once their working years are over.

American workers, young and old, question the strength of the economy, and all are concerned with minimizing taxes and investing for a secure retirement.

As individuals, we can feel powerless when it comes to changing the economy. We can, however, be smart about protecting ourselves and our families by reducing taxes and planning for our future using the best strategies available. I have written extensively about how IRA owners and their families need to make wise decisions to avoid damaging taxes on their IRAs. But, if you take into consideration the problems with the economy, the wars, and health care, tax increases seem inevitable. Are there multi-pronged strategies that workers, retirees, and their families can benefit from? How should consumers protect themselves?

I have long been an advocate of Roth IRA conversions for many IRA and retirement plan owners, and Roth conversions should certainly be among the financial strategies you consider to protect yourself and your family.

In Jim's previous book, **Retire Secure!**, he offered exceptional advice on the myriad of considerations that come into play when planning for a secure retirement. He also included some discussion of Roth IRA conversions. In **The Roth Revolution, Pay Taxes Once and Never Again**, he analyzes Roth IRA conversions and whether they are the right choice for you and your family. He discusses why you should consider a Roth conversion, how much you should consider converting, and how to time the conversions to minimize or eliminate the tax impact. His combined analysis makes his recommendations stand out among the crowd.

Jim's work is well-respected in the IRA world and his new book only further solidifies his reputation. Jim is known for his "number crunching" so his comprehensive financial analysis of Roth conversions for IRAs, 401(k)s and 403(b) is thorough and rigorous. The book's timing is perfect. **The Roth Revolution** anticipates some of the looming challenges Americans will be facing, and hits the mark on some of the challenges we are facing right now. It offers readers proven solutions for minimizing taxes and shows, step-by-step, how to build tax-free wealth for generations.

I take Jim's subtitle **Pay Taxes Once and Never Again** to heart, and embrace his argument that millions of IRA, 401(k) and 403(b) owners will benefit from making a Roth conversion. In this time of economic uncertainty, don't let pessimism and anxiety stand in your way—take control over the things you can change. The time to do it is now.

Table of Contents

Chapter Ten
**AN AGGRESSIVE STRATEGY—THE ROTH LAUNCHER—
RECHARACTERIZING OR UNDOING A ROTH IRA CONVERSION 119**

What's New

Five new tax laws make Roth IRA conversions more compelling than ever before.

At press time the first new law was not actually passed and signed, but the likelihood of its passage was so great, and the change will be so important to so many workers that I felt compelled to include it.

Convert 401(k)s to Roth 401(k)s

If most of your retirement plans are in IRAs, you can skip this section to and go to New Tax Law #2. Also, this section is not a good starting point for readers new to Roth IRAs, Roth IRA conversions, and retirement plans.

The new law allows employees to convert dollars in their 401(k) and 403(b) plans to Roth 401(k) and Roth 403(b) plans.

Any money converted from your retirement plan to the "Roth 401(k) or Roth 403(b)" part of your retirement plan will be considered taxable income.

The old regulations limited an employee's access to his or her 401(k) or 403(b) plan; even if you wanted to make a Roth conversion, it was not permitted. If and when the new law passes, assuming employers have or add Roth designated accounts to their plans, you can make a Roth conversion or a series of Roth conversions of whatever amount is appropriate to your situation. The new law is a big deal for employees who have wanted to make a large Roth conversion but who did not have significant balances in an IRA. Now you will be able to make a Roth conversion of your 401(k) or 403(b).

Deciding how much to convert from a 401(k) or 403(b) to the Roth designated account (the official name for Roth 401(k) and Roth 403(b) accounts) requires the same analysis as deciding how much to convert from a traditional IRA to a Roth IRA. Furthermore, there is another significant benefit inherent to this law.

These new Roth designated accounts will enjoy *excellent creditor protection.* Please see Chapter Eighteen for a more complete discussion of this new law and a series of action points that many employees should consider.

No Income Limitations

As of January 1, 2010, the income limits on Roth IRA conversions are history. This law is actually more important than New Tax Law #1, but I figured you would know this one by now. Now, any IRA owner, regardless of income, is eligible to make a Roth IRA conversion. For the first time in their lives, millions of high-income taxpayers are eligible for Roth IRA conversions.

Tax Rate Increases

In 2011—as the Bush tax cuts fade into the sunset— income-tax rates are going up for middle- and high-income taxpayers. Taxpayers making Roth IRA conversions at today's lower rates will avoid the higher tax rates of the future. As of press time, President Obama indicated that he did not want to see tax increases for married taxpayers with incomes of $250,000 or less. It is also possible that the tax increases for upper-income taxpayers will not be as severe as the projections available at press time. More importantly, however, in the long run, tax rates are likely to go up and locking in Roth IRA conversions at today's rates is quite favorable.

Health Care Reform Act Surtax

In 2013, the Health Reform Act surtax kicks in, which will add an extra 3.8% on unearned income. By converting now, you pay taxes at pre-sunset (2010) rates and reduce the impact of the surtax in 2013.

Defer and Spread Income

In 2010 only, if you make a Roth IRA conversion, you will recognize half the income in 2011 and half the income in 2012. If you prefer to recognize the income in 2010 because the tax rates may be lower, you must make a special election to recognize the income in 2010.

We were a fan of Roth IRA conversions under the old laws and using old tax rates. Now that all IRA owners and many 401(k) and 403(b) owners are eligible to convert—regardless of income—Roth IRA conversions in 2010 will be extremely beneficial for many, if not most, individuals with significant IRAs and retirement plans.

Want proof? Read on. We will prove that for many IRA and retirement plan owners making a Roth IRA conversion versus not making a conversion— or perhaps a series of smaller Roth IRA conversions over a number of years— results in dramatically more purchasing power for your family.

Roth IRA conversions have always deserved much more attention than they have received. But, the income restrictions prior to 2010 severely limited eligibility for a Roth IRA conversion. Only IRA and retirement plan owners with modified adjusted gross incomes (MAGI) of less than $100,000 were eligible to make a Roth IRA conversion. I was salivating waiting for 2010 to help my high-income clients, readers and listeners. I knew that it would be a banner year for Roth IRA conversions. Many of my high-income clients were waiting too; some of them scheduled appointments several years in advance.

What I could not have anticipated was that there would be *two* tax increases, one in 2010 and one in 2013. Both of these tax increases make Roth IRA conversions even more beneficial in 2010.

The chart below summarizes tax rates at press time between 2010 and 2013 (2010 being the last year of the Bush tax cuts and 2013 being the year when the 3.8% Health Care Reform surtax takes effect).

Taxable Income – Married Filing Jointly (Years after 2010 to be adjusted for inflation)	2010	2011	Top Rate with Surtax 2013*
$0 – 16,750	10%	15%	15%
$16,750 – 68,000	15%	15%	15%
$68,000 – 137,300	25%	28%	28%
$137,300 – 209,250	28%	31%	31%
$209,250 – 373,650	33%	36%	39.8%
Over $373,650	35%	39.6%	43.4%

* Note: The 3.8% surtax will be applied to either the capital-gains tax or the income tax, but not both. Determine which is less: unearned income or the taxable income (AGI) less the $250,000 (for married). If unearned income is smaller, then it would be taxed at 20% + 3.8% = 23.8%. If the AGI minus the $250,000 threshold is less, then the 3.8% would be applied to the excess portion of the AGI (as shown for the year 2013).

Please note these are just the tax increases already set by law. At press time there was talk that many of these rates will be changed by 2011. Some say only the income brackets for taxpayers with incomes of $250,000 or above will change. The tax rates should be monitored because as we will show throughout the book, your tax rate and future tax rates are critical to the issue of whether, how much and when to make a Roth IRA conversion. On the other hand, the table does not reflect any additional tax increases that could potentially (you might say inevitably) be levied over the next 10 to 20, or even 50 years.

Likely tax increases make Roth IRA conversions that much more compelling now. They also compress the window of opportunity to make the most favorable Roth IRA conversion or set of conversions.

After completing a thorough analysis of a client's retirement and estate plan, I frequently recommend a series of Roth IRA conversions over several years. This strategy has been optimal for many middle-income taxpayers. We cover that strategy in **The Roth Revolution**. For higher-income taxpayers, with tax rates of 33% or higher, 2010 will likely be better than future years to make a Roth IRA conversion. (See Chapter Thirteen).

It is my sincere belief that almost all IRA and retirement plan owners with significant retirement plan accumulations should consider doing a Roth IRA conversion of at least a portion of their IRA or retirement plan in 2010.

If you believe that federal income tax rates will increase substantially, then the arguments for making significant Roth IRA conversions become even more compelling.

To get the most up-to-date news of this law, go to www.rothrevolution.com.

Oldies but Goodies, Classic Concepts Regarding Roth IRA Conversions

This book will explain the underlying general principles and concepts behind Roth IRA conversions. I did, however, want to make technical nit pickers happy. I often include the nitty-gritty detailed calculations for readers who are interested. For most readers, the technical parts, though helpful, aren't as necessary, and I indicate in the text portions that you can skip.

We also present complete analysis and explain our methodology in the hope it will assist you to make similar calculations and/or be in a better position if you consult a financial professional.

But the good news doesn't stop there. We also cover two additional techniques that could significantly enhance the value of Roth IRA conversions for millions of taxpayers. Though not well known, both techniques are tested, sound and extremely profitable.

The first technique involves making a Roth IRA conversion of after-tax dollars and/or non-deductible IRAs without having to pay the tax on the conversion. This technique works only if you have non-deductible IRAs or after-tax dollars inside a retirement plan. When it does work, however, it provides phenomenal value—sometimes hundreds of thousands of dollars of value—with no tax costs. Please see Chapter Nine.

The second technique offers a unique way to take advantage of existing laws that involve re-characterizing, or undoing, a Roth IRA conversion. The technique takes advantage of what I would consider a legal loophole to get the biggest Roth IRA conversion for the least amount of taxes. Granted, the number of people who will take advantage of the technique is limited, but those who go to the extra effort will be richly rewarded. It involves making multiple Roth IRA conversions in separate accounts and choosing later on which accounts get to stay Roth IRAs and which Roth IRA accounts will be recharacterized. (Please see Chapter Eight).

Finally, it is important to look at the legacy potential of a Roth IRA. It is likely that many, if not most, readers making Roth IRA conversions will not spend all of the money in their Roth IRAs during their lifetime. It is important to examine the estate-planning implications of Roth IRA conversions. We will project not only the benefit for you, but also for your spouse, your children and grandchildren.

Last, but not least, I will also recommend what I consider the best estate plan for most IRA and retirement-plan owners with traditional families.

In the real world, Roth IRA conversion strategies comprise only one part of my comprehensive set of recommendations. Furthermore, the recommendations are often interconnected. Therefore, I will include information on complementary strategies to Roth IRA conversions. Please see Chapter Nineteen.

My objective is to present my vision of how Roth IRAs, Roth 401(k)s, and Roth IRA conversions offer different ways to maximize your and your family's purchasing power over time. I think this topic is so critical to the future of so many millions of Americans that I feel a tremendous responsibility to accurately provide the best information that I have. I want to help you make the best Roth IRA decisions. Some of the advice may at first sound unattractive—like writing a check to the Internal Revenue Service (IRS) before you have to. But, for the vast majority of readers who implement the recommended strategies, the long-term benefits from the tax-free accumulations will outweigh any short-term pain.

Special Notes to the Reader
Regarding Several Technical Issues

The Use of the Phrase "Measured in Purchasing Power"

Throughout the book, I have attempted to be as intellectually and technically accurate as possible. I do not have a special agenda to get you to make a Roth IRA conversion unless it is objectively the right thing for you to do.

One issue I have wrestled with is the issue of inflation and the use of the phrase "purchasing power." Throughout financial literature, sometimes projections of future wealth are given in real dollars. Other times they are given as inflation-adjusted dollars.

If you make a Roth IRA conversion of $100,000 and wait 20 years, given certain assumptions (please see Chapter Three for details), you will be better off by $93,364 if you use purchasing power as your tool. What I mean by that is that if you compare two financially identically situated IRA owners and one makes a $100,000 Roth IRA conversion and the other one doesn't, the one who made the conversion will be better off by $93,364 in 20 years, taking income taxes into account.

In that situation, it is technically incorrect to state that "measured in purchasing power, you will be $93,364 better off." It is more technically accurate to say "measured in purchasing power but not taking into account the impact of inflation, you are better off by $93,364." I do show in that chapter that if you take inflation into account, the IRA owner who makes a $100,000 Roth IRA conversion is better off by $51,693 measured in 2010 dollars, not $93,364 measured in future dollars.

One of the reviewers suggested I not use the phrase "purchasing power" if I do not adjust that number to include inflation. In many situations throughout the book, I show the impact of making a Roth IRA conversion in both current dollars adjusted for inflation (the purists' purchasing power) and future dollars but reduced for taxes (the way I sometimes measure).

For example, the first eighteen projections are shown in both future dollars and today's dollars. Both numbers are tax-adjusted. Purchasing power, however, is easier for most people to understand than "tax adjusted" or any other phrase I could use.

Journalistic Accuracy Comment

There is an area that I could properly be accused of being inaccurate. I am the son of a journalism professor and the integrity of the reporter is a value that has been instilled in me since early childhood. I want to be objective and report facts accurately. My idea of a consummate journalist is Ed Murrow or Walter Cronkite, both of whom attempted to be objective. Therefore, when I talk about actual client stories, the journalist in me wants to depict an accurate story with accurate details.

Unfortunately, when I refer to stories about real people, there is a competing value that trumps journalistic accuracy. That value is client confidentiality. If I were to report accurately the details of someone's situation, even without saying their name, that would be a breach of confidentiality. I rejected including much compelling information and some particular stories because I did not want to risk someone figuring out the identity of the person associated with the story.

As a result, all of the stories, though inspired by real people and real situations, are made up. I could not use actual stories with actual details because that would be violating client confidentiality. And, I confess to occasionally manufacturing some of the details of a story to simplify and/or help prove the point I am trying to make.

"Get your facts first, then you can distort them as you please."

— Mark Twain

Also, most people are far more complex and multi-faceted than the characters in my stories. Usually, I include a story to clarify one or two points that I am trying to make. For a better example of an instructive situation that is closer to what we see in practice, with actual clients with multifaceted needs, please see the story of Paul and Carol in Chapter Nineteen called ***Combining Different Strategies***. Even that story, however, was concocted.

Investment Rate

When making financial projections, you have to assume some interest and/ or growth rate. Back in the late nineties, I wanted to use 8%. Most readers told me I was being way too conservative. I tried to remind them that most of these projections were for a long period of time, and they should not let the temporary investment mood distort the long-term projections. They yelled, protested and wanted me to use 10% or higher. To be fair, the conservative engineers never wanted me to use 10%.

Today, when I use 8%, the same people submit that I am being overly optimistic. I agree that getting an 8% return is a challenge in today's investment environment, but hopefully that will change. The S&P average for the last 84 years, even taking into account the downturn in 2008, has been 9.8%. The small cap stocks have averaged 11.9% in that same period (Ibbotson SBBI 1926-2009). I don't think 8% is way out of line historically. If you consider that these are usually long term projections, then if the rate is lower for a few years that will not tremendously skew the advice. If there is another big downturn after the conversion, and the market never recovers or takes many years to recover, that will skew the advice.

But higher investment rates do not distort the recommendations to make a Roth IRA conversion or not make a conversion. It might influence how much to convert. If actual investment results are lower, say 6% or even 4% or even 2% (I hear the engineers yelling, use 2%) over a long-time period, the Roth IRA conversion would still be favorable. It would, however, not be nearly as favorable as if the investment rate was higher.

Topics that are Not Covered
in *The Roth Revolution*

There is obviously quite a bit of information that could be relevant to readers interested in Roth IRA conversions that is not included in this book. Though I tried to include many complementary strategies to Roth IRA conversions, there are a number of other areas that I could have chosen to cover.

For example, calculating the safe withdrawal rate is an important factor in a client's long term planning. This is not covered, even though it is a critical variable in helping determine spending, gifting and even Roth IRA conversion decisions.

Another area I could have covered would have been combining commercial annuities and Roth IRA conversions. There are some extremely interesting strategies combining commercial annuities and Roth IRA conversions. I did not cover commercial annuities in *The Roth Revolution*. I also didn't cover the new rule that is also part of the proposed law that is part of the Small Business Act. That law will allow current commercial or tax deferred annuity owners greater opportunities to annuitize their annuity in a favorable manner.

Roth IRA Conversions and Non-traditional Investments

We also do not cover Roth IRA conversions using non-traditional investments. If you have an asset that you think is going to skyrocket in value, purchasing that asset in your IRA and making a Roth IRA conversion before the value increases could be a splendid strategy.

For example, let's say you want to buy a piece of real estate for $100,000, or for that matter any investment that you think is going to rapidly appreciate. Let's assume you aren't making this investment for a tax deduction. It would be fine, assuming you meet all the rules and requirements, to make this investment in your IRA. You will likely need to find a different trustee than your current IRA trustee. While the value of the investment is still low—say $100,000— you could buy it in your IRA and get an appraisal of $100,000. Then, you could make a Roth IRA conversion and pay taxes on $100,000. Please assume that five years later, the investment is worth $500,000. You could withdraw it tax-free or better yet allow it to keep growing tax-free. You just saved tax on $400,000 of income.

There are certainly fine opportunities in purchasing certain assets in your IRA, making a Roth IRA conversion, and taking advantage of the tax-free growth. On the other hand, there are many pitfalls in this area that you should be aware of before embarking on this strategy. Most conservative Roth IRA conversion experts would put a capital C with caution for this strategy, but in the right situation, it could work out very well.

Many readers are mesmerized by this concept and don't dot their "i's or cross their t's"—and they could get in serious hot water.

I have not covered this concept (other than this brief mention) because it would be difficult to do it justice and to properly explain the rules and the risks involved.

Planning for Long-Term Care

The field of elder law is booming as our population ages. There are many strategies that many readers could consider to protect their assets from a nursing home in the event of their incapacity and need for long-term care.

A Roth IRA conversion is often an effective technique when trying to preserve assets for the independent spouse and the children after the second death. I do not specialize in elder law and we have not covered some of the techniques of combining asset protection and Roth IRA conversions. It's not that we don't like these strategies, but again, the complexities of this topic go beyond the scope of *The Roth Revolution*.

We also did not include two chapters I originally wanted to include but attempted to respect the publishers wish to try to keep the book to 300 pages.

One chapter I did not include covers the math behind Roth IRA conversions. That chapter, though not necessarily practical, would be of interest to readers who really want to understand some of the nitty gritty reasons why the numbers work the way they do. If that section is of interest to you, you can find it posted it on our website, www.rothrevolution.com.

I have also not included a very technical chapter on determining the true marginal tax rates of different Roth IRA conversions in different situations. Again, if you are either a detail oriented engineer or if you are a financial professional willing to roll up your sleeves, please see www.rothrevolution.com.

Good luck. Keep an open mind. Here we go. I hope you have a great ride.

Chapter One

Roth IRA Conversions and the Dream of Tax-Free Income for Generations

"If you don't know where you are going, you will wind up somewhere else!"
— Yogi Berra

Main Topics

- The importance of measuring the value of your retirement plan in purchasing power, not in total dollars

- How to measure your IRAs purchasing power

- The advantages of the Roth IRAs—no required minimum distributions (RMDs) for you and your spouse

- Why Roth IRA conversions are not just for the young

Key Idea

The "secret" to understanding IRAs and Roth IRAs conversions is to measure your wealth in terms of purchasing power. Having $1 million in your IRA does not mean you can buy $1 million worth of goods and services.

—— **$$$** ——

Albert Einstein said that the most powerful force in the universe was compound interest. Einstein also said the hardest thing in the world to understand was the income tax. If you combine understanding the best tax strategies with the power of long-term compound interest, you unleash a tremendous force that will dramatically increase wealth for you and your family.

Do you like the idea of a one-time tax payment and "then you are done?" After you make the conversion, your Roth IRA will grow tax-free for you, your spouse, your kids, and your grandkids. *The Roth Revolution* will help you understand the power of Roth IRAs, Roth 401(k)s, Roth 403(b)s and Roth IRA conversions. It will also help you determine if Roth IRA conversions are a good idea for you and your family. If they are a good idea for your family, then we will offer insight on how much to convert and when to convert.

A Quick Review of Traditional Tax Planning

Traditionally, tax planning has revolved around optimizing strategies to defer or delay paying your taxes. That is why most financial advisors, CPAs in particular, and other retirement-planning experts, including me, have traditionally recommended maximizing contributions to your IRAs, 401(k)s, 403(b)s, SEPs, and other types of traditional retirement plans while you are working. This strategy offers you a tax deduction when you make the retirement-plan contribution. The invested money grows tax deferred and eventually, either you and/or your heirs pay taxes on the distributions. Hence, the sub-title of my last book, *Pay Taxes Later*.

In the same spirit, after you retire, we recommended spending after-tax assets before your IRAs, 401(k)s, etc. The logic was, by deferring taxes on withdrawals from your retirement accounts, when you finally do take out money and owe taxes, your accounts would have accrued additional interest, dividends, accumulations and capital gains. *Paying taxes later,* or deferring taxes, is a bedrock principle of financial planning, leading to a secure retirement. Jane Bryant Quinn once quipped that my mantra was "pay taxes later." But…there is a major exception to the general rule of "pay taxes later." A more precise summary of my tax philosophy would be: "pay taxes later…*except for a Roth.*"

> After making hundreds of financial projections since 1998 when the Roth IRA law was established, it has become apparent to us that, in general, Roth IRAs, Roth 401(k)s, Roth 403(b)s and Roth IRA conversions that create tax-free growth, usually result in more purchasing power for IRA owners and their families.

After making hundreds of financial projections since 1998 when the Roth IRA law was established, it has become apparent to us that, in general, Roth IRAs, Roth 401(k)s, Roth 403(b)s and Roth IRA conversions that create tax-free growth, usually result in more purchasing power for IRA owners and their families. And, recent changes in the tax laws offer superior opportunities for both retirees and workers in the Roth IRA or Roth 401(k) or Roth 403(b) environment. For many—if not most—readers, Roth IRA conversion and contribution opportunities have the potential to help your family realize the dream of tax-free income over three generations. The key to unlocking the tax-free dynasty treasure chest lies in Roth IRA conversions.

As I see it, there are some things you can't control, such as how the market will do over time. There are, however, things you can control, which include getting the best tax planning available to you, and taking advantage of available opportunities. Now, more than ever, Roth IRA conversions represent one of those opportunities.

The Roth IRA Conversion Rationale

A traditional retirement plan, whether it's an IRA, a 401(k) 403(b), KEOGH, SEP, or a 457, is funded with tax-deferred contributions from both you and/or your employer. Once you reach retirement, you will either need to take money out of the account to meet your living expenses and/or you will be required to begin withdrawing money from your IRAs and retirement plans when you reach age 70 and ½. In general, the distributions from your IRA and retirement plan are added to your existing income and you pay taxes on the total. You will have to pay income taxes on the withdrawals at your existing tax rate; or possibly a higher tax rate if the additional income pushes you into a higher tax bracket.

Through a Roth IRA conversion, you can convert a traditional plan, or a portion of a traditional plan, into a Roth IRA. When you make the conversion, you have to add the amount of the Roth IRA conversion to your income, and pay the taxes on the amount of additional income from the Roth IRA conversion. You are, in effect, paying income tax *now*. After paying the taxes upfront, you will have converted your traditional IRA, or a portion of your traditional IRA, to a Roth IRA. Why would anybody want to do that?

The reason you might be willing to pay income taxes now is because the growth on the original investment and all withdrawals by you and/or your family members, will be tax-free (after certain conditions are met). The less attractive alternative is doing nothing (the status quo) and paying taxes at future ordinary income tax rates on the traditional IRA withdrawals and taxes now and annually on investment income of the money that you would otherwise pay in taxes to make the Roth IRA conversion.

A further advantage of Roth IRAs is that, unlike with a traditional IRA, there are no required minimum distributions (RMD) for you or your spouse. With good planning, this will give you years of tax-free growth on the total investment. After you and your spouse die, it is likely that Roth IRA dollars will be part of your estate. At that point, your children and/or trusts for grandchildren will be required to withdraw money from the inherited Roth IRA. But those distributions will be tax-free.

You may still be asking, "Who in their right mind would write the government a check when they don't have to?" The answer is me, many of the readers and clients I have advised over the years, and I hope, after reading this book—you will be one too. The reason bears repeating: the Roth IRA will grow income-tax-free for the rest of your life, income-tax-free for the rest of your spouse's life, and income-tax-free for the lives of your children, your grandchildren (or trusts for your grandchildren), and potentially even your great grandchildren.

To use an agricultural analogy, a Roth IRA conversion requires you to pay tax on the seed. In this case the seed is the amount of the IRA you are converting to a Roth IRA. Then you plant the seed (invest your Roth IRA) and over many years, it blossoms and grows. Then when either you, or your heirs, harvest the crop (the original investment and the growth on the investment), the harvest is income-tax-free. But, the advantages of the Roth conversion, when circumstances warrant one, should not be under-estimated; it could mean hundreds of thousands of dollars—sometimes millions of dollars of additional purchasing power to your family. And it even offers significant advantages for the Roth IRA owner.

The Secret—Measuring Wealth Using Purchasing Power Instead of Total Dollars

Please note that in some sections I get fairly quantitative, but I will try to let you know what's coming and give you the option to skip ahead. The following section is a little bit technical, but it is the key to understanding Roth IRA conversions.

If, however, you don't want to deal with even a little bit of nitty gritty, and you want to get "the answer" of the advantage of making a Roth IRA conversion, please go to Figure 1.

Please bear with me for one relatively simple example that will, I hope, switch on a light of new understanding. I'm about to reveal the secret to understanding Roth IRA conversions and even the nature of IRAs and retirement plans. I call it "the secret" because very few people, including CPAs, financial planners, financial advisors, attorneys, and even Roth IRA commentators, know it. I believe understanding the secret is the first step in understanding Roth IRA conversions and the nature of IRAs and retirement plans in general.

Usually, in the world of money, whoever has the most wins! Right? We want the most money. What I'm going to suggest is that having the "most money" is not the best way to measure affluence or wealth. Don't panic, I am not getting metaphysical with you and say people with a wonderful family but no money are rich.

I think the best way to measure wealth or affluence is by assessing your *purchasing power*, not your total dollars. If you have a $1 million in an IRA, or any amount for that matter, you don't have a million dollars of purchasing power because when you cash in that IRA, you have to pay taxes because your funds are tax deferred, not tax free. So, someone who has a million dollars in an IRA is not worth a million dollars measured in purchasing power—even though the face amount of their investment is a million dollars. Understanding the concept of purchasing power is critical to truly understand the benefits of a Roth IRA conversion.

The Key to Unlocking the Secret

The Simple Math (Arithmetic) Behind the Secret

Let's assume for discussion's sake that you have $100,000 in a plain old traditional IRA or 401(k), 403(b), etc. I typically refer to the money in those accounts as *pre-tax dollars*. Let's also assume you have $25,000 outside of the IRA in other investments; I refer to that money as *after-tax dollars*. For this simple example, I am also going to assume that you are in the 25% tax bracket. For this example, the $100,000 in the IRA and the $25,000 outside the IRA is all the money you have.

The way we traditionally measure money we would say you have a total of $125,000 total dollars: $100,000 of IRA or retirement plan funds (pre-tax) and $25,000 outside of IRAs or retirement plans (after-tax). That is all well and good and I concur that $125,000 does represent the total number of dollars you have in this simple example. I, however, submit that the more appropriate measuring tool is purchasing power.

Continuing with the previous scenario, ($100,000 IRA and $25,000 of after-tax), let's assume you want to buy something for $100,000. (Not a wise decision, but this is only an example!) You would have to cash in the IRA and pay taxes on the IRA withdrawal. Assuming a flat income tax rate of 25%, the tax on the $100,000 IRA withdrawal is $25,000. And in this example, you conveniently have the $25,000 in after-tax dollars to pay the income taxes on the IRA withdrawal. After you pay the $25,000 in taxes, you are left with $100,000 that you need to make your purchase.

So what does that mean? Well, if you have $100,000 in your IRA, $25,000 outside the IRA, and you are in the 25% tax bracket, you have only $100,000 of purchasing power. Do you see why I would consider the $125,000 total dollars to be valued at $100,000 if our measurement is purchasing power? In contrast, if you had $100,000 in after-tax dollars or $100,000 in Roth IRAs, you would not have to suffer a tax hit on the withdrawal of those funds (except perhaps capital gains tax on the appreciation of the after-tax dollars). Therefore, the purchasing power of either after-tax dollars and/or Roth IRA dollars is equal to the face amount of the investment. So, $100,000 in after-tax dollars equals $100,000 of purchasing power. $100,000 in IRAs *plus* $25,000 in after-tax dollars also provides you with $100,000 of purchasing power if we assume a flat 25% tax rate. But if you just look at the numbers on paper, you might think that the guy with the $125,000 is richer.

Now let's compare Mr. Status Quo, who sits there with his $100,000 IRA and $25,000 after-tax, to Mr. Roth IRA Conversion, who converts his $100,000 IRA to a Roth IRA and uses the $25,000 outside the IRA to pay the taxes. On day one, he has the same purchasing power as Mr. Status Quo.

Roth IRA Value after conversion		**$100,000**
Traditional IRA	**$100,000**	
Other non-IRA funds*	**25,000**	**-0-**
Total dollars	**$125,000**	**$100,000**
Less taxes paid on IRA (if distributed)	**(25,000)**	**-0-**
Purchasing power	**$100,000**	**$100,000**

*(Non-IRA funds of $25,000 used to pay tax on conversion)

For this example, we assume the liquidation rate (which is the rate of tax we have to pay when we withdraw our traditional IRA) is equal to the conversion rate, (the rate of tax we have to pay to make

> On day one, measured in purchasing power, Mr. Status Quo and Mr. Conversion are equals.

a Roth IRA conversion) then the breakeven point is day one (no time needed to break even). On day one, measured in purchasing power, Mr. Status Quo and Mr. Conversion are equals.

Now take this concept and apply it to you. Let's assume that you want to make a Roth IRA conversion. Now consider using purchasing power instead of total dollars as your measurement tool. You and/or your advisor complete the appropriate paper work and what used to be $100,000 in a traditional IRA is now a $100,000 Roth IRA. Please note in most cases, you don't even have to change investments to convert your traditional IRA to a Roth IRA. Then, sometime in February of the year following the year you make the conversion, you will receive a Form 1099 that in effect says, "Please add $100,000 to your taxable income for the year you made the Roth IRA conversion." Continuing with our simple example, you are taxed at the 25% rate. You pay your 25% tax on the additional $100,000 income. Conveniently, you have the $25,000 of after-tax money to pay the income taxes. You send the $25,000 of after-tax money to Uncle Sam. (Please note the analysis is much different if you don't have the $25,000 of after-tax money to pay the tax on the Roth IRA conversion).

So what do you have now? You have $100,000 in your Roth IRA. If you cash in your $100,000 Roth IRA, how much tax do you have to pay? None. You have $100,000 of purchasing power. Without the Roth IRA conversion, you would have a total of $125,000, but only $100,000 of purchasing power because of the taxes that would be due if you cashed in your IRA.

Can we agree that, if your measurement tool is purchasing power rather than total dollars, and the tax rate is constant, making a Roth IRA conversion will not diminish your purchasing power as of day one?

This is a critical concept. Traditional wisdom holds that Roth IRA conversions are great for young people because young IRA owners have so many years for tax-free growth. Traditional thinking also holds an IRA owner who is 60, 70, or 80+, a Roth IRA conversion is not such a good idea because the IRA owner won't have enough years of tax-free growth to make up for paying the income tax on the conversion. That's what most financial writers think. Measuring in total dollars is a common flaw with many software programs (including software programs from huge companies that should know better). I take great exception to this traditional thinking.

I believe they are not measuring the most important element which is *purchasing power*. Measuring in *total dollars* in my view leads to incorrect and overly conservative Roth IRA conversions. When you use purchasing power as your standard for measurement, it is clear, from day one, that the conversion makes the individual no better off, but also no worse off.

Does this suggest to you that perhaps, even for an older individual, a Roth IRA conversion could be an acceptable transaction? You could be 90 years old, do a Roth IRA conversion and given the previous assumptions, you would have a level of purchasing power equivalent to your pre-conversion purchasing power. You could be 110 years old and it might be very appropriate to make a Roth IRA conversion. You can't be too old to do a Roth IRA conversion. Admittedly, it would be more beneficial for a younger person to make a Roth IRA conversion than an older IRA owner. The younger IRA owner will likely have more years to enjoy tax-free growth. But, just because it is better for a younger person doesn't mean it is bad for an older IRA owner. Furthermore, while older IRA owners are likely to derive some benefits from the conversion, their heirs might enjoy life changing increases in wealth.

Please note all this analysis is the same for employees who have 401(k) or 403(b) balances and have access to a Roth Designated Account. Please see "What's New" before Chapter One.

—— $$$ ——

Key Lesson for this Chapter

Paying taxes now and converting a portion or all of your traditional IRA to a Roth IRA creates tax-free growth. This tax-free growth can last through three generations, creating a tax-free dynasty for you, your children, and your grandchildren.

Chapter Two

Measuring the Benefits
of a Roth IRA Conversion

"Make crime pay – become a lawyer."

—Will Rogers

Main Topics

- Calculating your increased purchasing power with Roth IRA conversions

- Why it is likely that at least part of your Roth IRA will remain unspent and will pass to your heirs through your estate

- What is an inherited Roth IRA?

- Principal differences between inherited Roth IRAs and inherited traditional IRAs

- How life expectancy determines RMDs for beneficiaries of inherited Roth IRAs

Key Idea

To Roth or Not to Roth? It depends, but more often than not, the answer is "Roth."

—— $$$ ——

Thus far all I have tried to prove is that on day one, in terms of purchasing power (given that you have the after-tax dollars to pay the tax on the conversion), if you make the conversion to a Roth, your purchasing power is equivalent to what it was without the conversion.

Well, that is all fine and good, but our concerns extend further than day one. We want to know the impact of a Roth IRA conversion in year one, year ten, and maybe even year sixty-five.

What I will do next is compare the long-term results for Mr. Status Quo and Mr. Roth IRA conversion. Our measurement tool will be purchasing power, not total dollars.

In the first scenario, Mr. Status Quo has $100,000 in an IRA that is growing income tax-deferred. That is to say, currently, he is not paying income taxes on the dividends, interest, capital gains, or growth of his traditional IRA. Eventually, the IRA owner, or his or her heirs, will have to withdraw at least a portion of that IRA. When they do, they will have to pay ordinary income tax on the entire withdrawal, including the growth from the original $100,000.

To arrive at purchasing power of Mr. Status Quo, we are going to subtract the taxes that would be due on the IRA if it were withdrawn. The purchasing power of Mr. Status Quo over time will be measured by taking the hundred thousand dollars in the IRA and growing the $100,000. Then, at each measuring point, whether it is one year, ten years, or 50 years later, we will subtract the taxes that would be due on an IRA withdrawal to arrive at purchasing power. Once again, we will assume that Mr. Status Quo has the money to pay the taxes on the IRA withdrawal from outside the IRA.

But, don't forget that Mr. Status Quo also has the $25,000 outside the IRA which is also growing. Assuming the $25,000 is invested in after-tax investments it will earn dividends, interest, and capital gains that will be subject to tax.

In this slightly more comprehensive measure of Mr. Status Quo's purchasing power, we combine the purchasing power of the IRAs after adjusting for taxes, and the purchasing power of the after-tax dollars to determine his true purchasing power over time. Then, we graph the results measured in purchasing power of what happens if Mr. Status Quo just sits on his money and fails to make a Roth IRA conversion.

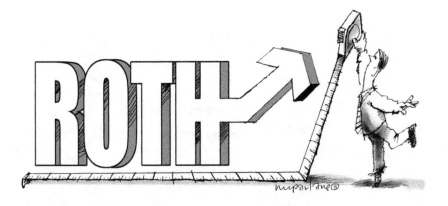

Measuring the Benefit

Now, to determine if a Roth IRA conversion makes sense, we will compare the projections of Mr. Status Quo with his hundred thousand dollars in the IRA and $25,000 outside the IRA, to projections for Mr. Roth IRA Conversion who started with the same assets as Mr. Status Quo. Mr. Roth IRA Conversion, however, chose to make a Roth IRA conversion of his hundred thousand dollar IRA. He paid the income tax on the conversion with the $25,000 that he had outside the IRA. So, Mr. Roth IRA has only his $100,000 Roth IRA. He, however, will never have to pay income taxes either currently or in the future on any growth or appreciation in the converted Roth IRA.

The results from projecting both sets of numbers and plotting the results on a year-by-year basis are shown below in Figure 1 (assumptions that are somewhat more comprehensive are listed below the graph[1]).

---

1 Please note that the methodology used to make these calculations is identical to the methodology we used in 1998 when we published our first peer-reviewed article in *The Tax Adviser*, the tax journal of The American Institute of CPAs. For our original publication we wanted a journal that would thoroughly scrutinize our numbers, and our methodology for arriving at our numbers. We passed scrutiny. While the methodology for our current analysis is the same, the assumptions are different. Our updated analysis includes current tax rates and a more conservative interest rate.

Figure 1

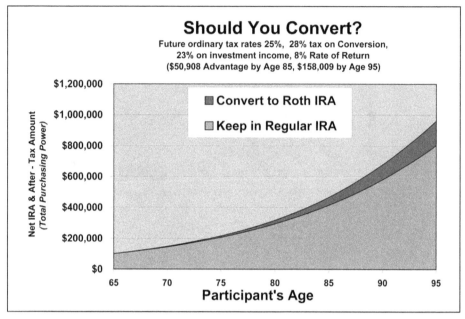

Should You Convert?

Future ordinary tax rates 25%, 28% tax on Conversion,
23% on investment income, 8% Rate of Return
($50,908 Advantage by Age 85, $158,009 by Age 95)

Assumptions for Figure 1

- 65-year-old with $100,000 regular IRA and $28,000 after-tax funds also available $100,000 IRA converted

- 25% federal tax bracket on RMDs from regular IRA

- 28% tax bracket for Roth conversion amount & taxes on total regular IRA balances for comparisons

- Federal and state taxes of 23% on after-tax investment income based on 20% capital gain and qualified dividend rules, 3% state tax rate and other factors

- 8% rate of return on investments

- Takes only RMDs, reinvested in after-tax funds

- Measured in total purchasing power that subtracts accrued income taxes from traditional IRA

- Numbers are actual dollars not adjusted for inflation

A common objection that comes up when I recommend Roth IRA conversions is, "Why should I pay the income taxes so my heirs can enjoy the benefits of the Roth IRA conversion?" But look at the graph. Even without taking into consideration the benefits to the surviving spouse, children, or grandchildren, or any other heirs, at age 85, Mr. Roth IRA Conversion is better off than Mr. Status Quo by $50,908. Yes, you are writing a check for the taxes on the additional income from the Roth IRA conversion. By doing so, you actually increase (not decrease) your own purchasing power. During your lifetime, you gain an additional $50,000+ worth of purchasing power. Let that sink in for a while. Granted these assumptions oversimplify most individuals' circumstances, but they get to the heart of the advantages of a Roth IRA conversion.

So, if you told me that you could not care less about what your kids inherit from you, but you do care about how much you and your spouse will have to spend during your lifetimes, I would still recommend a Roth IRA conversion.

> So, if you told me that you could not care less about what your kids inherit from you, but you do care about how much you and your spouse will have to spend during your lifetimes, I would still recommend a Roth IRA conversion.

Please note all this analysis is the same for employees who have 401(k) or 403(b) balances and have access to a Roth Designated Account. Please see "What's New" before Chapter One.

Measuring the Benefits of Your Roth IRA Conversion for your Children and Grandchildren

Why You Will Likely Die with a Roth IRA

Many couples do care about leaving their kids with a bit of extra security, but not necessarily at the expense of their own interest and comfort. But, what if you could leave your children some money and not compromise your purchasing power? Imagine that you have been persuaded to follow through, potentially with the help of an advisor who understands Roth IRA conversions, on the recommendations in this book. If you did, you would end up with at least three different types of assets.

1. After-tax dollars
2. IRA or retirement plan dollars
3. Roth IRA dollars

In ***Retire Secure!,*** (Wiley, Feb., 2009) I went to great lengths to prove that, in general, the optimal order to spend assets in your portfolio is: after-tax dollars, then IRA dollars, and finally your Roth IRA dollars. You could also read that analysis in a reprint from an article published in ***Bottom Line Personal*** by going to www.rothira-advisor.com/articles/BottomLineArticle.pdf.

From my experience with my clients, and based on what I would consider prudent spending order recommendations for both your IRAs and your Roth IRAs, it is highly unlikely that you will spend all your money before you and your spouse die.

Most of my clients have fairly conservative spending habits relative to how much money they have. If you are like most of my clients, you are by nature better at saving than spending. Perhaps you feel that you have everything you want right now and you take satisfaction in getting great value for your money. Maybe you are saving for nursing home coverage. You may just say you are saving money for a rainy day. It may be that saving gives you a sense of security in an uncertain world. Perhaps you are just a creature of habit and you keep spending (adjusted for inflation) what you have always spent. Or maybe, you are just being prudent in the face of the unknown—since you don't know how long you are going to live, you want to be secure for the longest time frame.

My point is that I don't think you are going to die broke. If you follow my spending order, you will likely die with a Roth IRA.

The Unique Features of an Inherited Roth IRA

The section that follows is an explanation of what happens to your Roth IRA when you die. Most workshop attendees love this explanation because it was something they never really understood and wanted to understand. If you don't feel like grinding through the explanation and want to skip to the results, please see Figure 2.

For our purposes for this chapter, I am going to assume if you die with a Roth IRA, that you will leave it to your spouse. Your spouse will be able to do a trustee to trustee transfer into their Roth IRA. They will have no required minimum distribution. Then, when they die and live it to your children, your children, or any non-spousal heir, now has a financially unique beast; an *inherited Roth IRA*, complete with its own rules and advantages.

Remember, that after *you* made the Roth IRA conversion, you were not required to take required minimum distributions (RMDs).

A big difference between a Roth IRA and an *inherited Roth IRA* is that the person or people (other than your spouse) who inherit your Roth IRA are not permitted to take that inherited Roth IRA and combine it with their own Roth IRA. Furthermore, owners of inherited Roth IRAs must take annual RMDs.

The RMD is based on their life expectancy. For example, please assume the child who inherits your Roth IRA is 55 and has a 29.6 -year-life expectancy (according to the IRS tables found in Publication 590 Table 1. That child would be required to take an RMD of 2.96% of the Roth IRA (the balance of the account divided by the child's life expectancy). The child is permitted to take more than the minimum, but if he or she can afford it, it would be prudent to let as much as possible of the inherited Roth IRA continue to accumulate tax free.

The good news for your heirs is that distributions from the inherited Roth IRA, whether RMDs or amounts over and above the minimum, are not subject to income tax.

Imagine that! Leaving your child an inherited Roth IRA opens a window for many more years of tax-free growth. So, there are multiple benefits to a Roth IRA conversion:

1. Since you don't have to take a RMD from your Roth IRA after the conversion, you can let the money accumulate tax free. With anything close to normal market conditions, over the long run the Roth IRA will continue to grow because of appreciation, dividends, interest and capital gains.

2. You will have much more purchasing power if you make a Roth IRA conversion; and if you don't manage to spend all your money, your heirs will have a splendid advantage in having many additional years of tax-free growth.

3. Your heirs don't have to pay taxes on their inherited Roth IRA
    distributions. The combination of no RMDs over the course of your
    and your spouse's lives, and tax-free RMDs for your heirs, make the
    value of the inherited Roth IRA tremendous compared to the value of
    the traditional IRA. (This is true even if you take into consideration
    the growth on the after-tax money that that Mr. Status Quo would
    have passed on to his heirs).

The following section is some more nitty gritty that the average reader may
not need to know, but of course would be helpful in gaining an appreciation of
how IRA and Roth IRA dollars are treated at death.

What Happens if You Die and Leave Your Roth IRA to the Next Generation?

If you die and leave either a traditional IRA or a Roth IRA to the next
generation, your beneficiaries must take a minimum distribution of the inherited
IRA or Roth IRA every year after you are gone starting the year after you die (or
the same year if you are in RMD mode and had not taken a distribution before
you died).

The RMD of the beneficiaries of your IRA or Roth IRA are based on their
life expectancy. Let's assume you die and leave a $100,000 inherited IRA to your
son who is 55 at your death. According to the IRS' Single Life Table, he has a life
expectancy of 29.6 years. To arrive at the RMD of the inherited Roth IRA, you
divide 29.6 into the balance of the inherited Roth IRA. So roughly, the child
will be forced to take a RMD of 3% of the entire inherited IRA or inherited
Roth IRA.

If the investment rate greater than 3% (hopefully) we find that the inherited
Roth IRA is actually growing after the death of the Roth IRA owner (assuming
the young beneficiary limits distributions to the RMD of the inherited Roth
IRA). The following year your son would have to use 28.6 as the factor to divide
into the balance of the inherited IRA as of December 31 of the previous year.
The following year, the factor would be reduced to 27.6 etc. etc. As your child's
life expectancy declines (the unfortunate consequence of growing older…), the
RMD of the inherited Roth IRA will eventually exceed the growth on the Roth

IRA. Eventually, assuming the child lives as long as his or her projected life expectancy, the inherited Roth IRA will be exhausted (but it will have had a good long life).

If you leave an inherited IRA, the distributions, typically the RMDs even at 3% per year and growing, will be taxable even though the growth on the account is tax deferred. If you leave an inherited Roth IRA, the distribution will be tax-free and the growth of the amount continuing to be invested in the inherited Roth IRA will grow tax-free.

As I go on, I will continue to refine the assumptions for Mr. Status Quo and Mr. Conversion—now we are looking beyond the owner's life expectancy.[2] When we continue with our projections, we find that the heirs (usually children after the surviving spouse) of Mr. Roth IRA Conversion are better off than the heirs of Mr. Status Quo by over $600,000.

"I guess the real reason that my wife and I had children is the same reason that Napoleon had for invading Russia: it seemed like a good idea at the time."

— Bill Cosby

Figure 2 shows that by the time your child is 85 years old, he or she will be over $600,000 better off from your original $100,000 Roth IRA conversion.

---

2 I will continue to use the same peer-reviewed methodology scrutinized in 1998, with adjustment to the tax rates, reduced income expectations, etc.

Figure 2

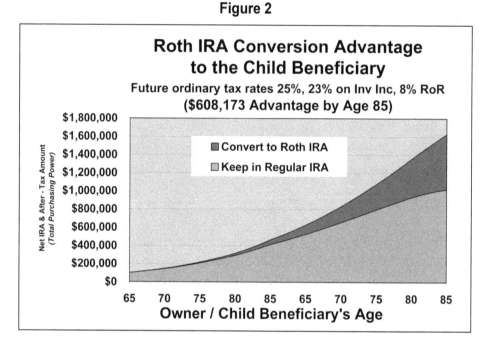

Roth IRA Conversion Advantage to the Child Beneficiary

Future ordinary tax rates 25%, 23% on Inv Inc, 8% RoR
($608,173 Advantage by Age 85)

- ■ Convert to Roth IRA
- □ Keep in Regular IRA

Net IRA & After - Tax Amount
(Total Purchasing Power)

Owner / Child Beneficiary's Age

Assumptions for Figure 2

- IRA owner and spouse die 20 years after the conversion
- Funds inherited by 55-year-old beneficiary
- Spending is equal to RMD from traditional IRA for each scenario
- Measured in total purchasing power of remaining funds after 28% income tax allowance on the balance of the regular IRA
- 8% rate of return measured in real dollars
- No inflation adjustment

Now, what if the eventual beneficiary was someone with a longer life expectancy than that of your children? What about your grandchildren—or more accurately, well drafted trusts for the benefit of your grandchildren. This is where the advantages of Roth IRA conversions get really interesting.

Your grandchildren's longer life expectancy would mean a larger factor or divisor and a longer "stretch" of the inherited IRA. If instead of leaving your Roth IRA to a 55-year-old son, what if you left it to a 25-year-old granddaughter? She would have a longer life expectancy factor and a smaller RMD and assuming she chooses (or is forced to in a trust) keep the money in the inherited IRA or Roth IRA, she will enjoy a much greater advantage than her parent.

Figure 3

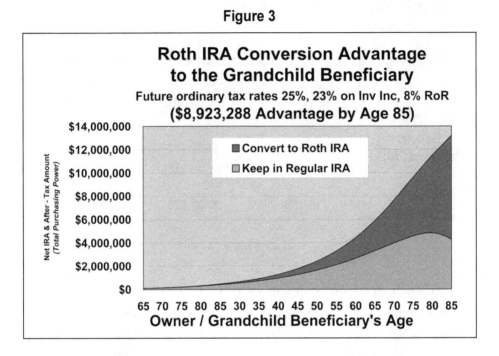

Assumptions for Figure 3

- IRA owner and spouse die 20 years after the conversion
- Funds inherited by 25-year-old beneficiary
- Spending is equal to RMD from traditional IRA for each scenario
- Measured in total purchasing power of remaining funds after 28% income tax allowance on the balance of the regular IRA
- 8% growth measured in real dollars
- No inflation adjustment

How much better off would your grandchildren be? Over $8.9 million better off. That's quite a legacy from a $100,000 Roth IRA conversion.

Now to be fair about this: I did not include inflation in the analysis above. If I had included inflation and had measured in 2010 dollars, obviously the benefits to the family would be much less. The following chart shows the benefits in both real dollars and inflation-adjusted dollars for you, your children and your grandchildren.

Advantages in Today's Dollars (assume 3% annual inflation)

	IRA Owner	Child of IRA Owner	Grandchild of IRA Owner
Total Dollar Benefit Per Graph, Age 85	$50,908	$608,173	$8,923,288
Measured in 2010 Dollars	$28,186	$160,825	$838,585

—— $$$ ——

Key Lesson for this Chapter

An objective comparison of making a Roth IRA conversion vs. retaining a traditional IRA indicates that the conversion can make an enormous difference for you and your family.

Chapter Three

Measuring the Benefits of Roth IRA Conversions in Light Of Two New Tax Increases

"If stupidity got us into this mess, then why can't it get us out?"
— Will Rogers

Main Topics

- The importance of taking action in 2010 to prepare for 2011 tax increases
- How two new tax increases are making Roth IRA conversions more urgent and attractive than ever
- The clear advantages of converting before the January 1, 2013 Health Care Reform surtax kicks in
- The benefits of Roth IRA conversions can be measured in tens of thousands for the IRA owner, hundreds of thousands for the children of the IRA owner, and millions of dollars for the grandchildren
- Why converting to a Roth IRA before taxes increase is a good decision.
- How to minimize estate-and inheritance taxes with Roth IRA conversions

Key Idea

High-income taxpayers, i.e., those in the 25% tax bracket or higher, should strongly consider a Roth IRA conversion or a series of Roth IRA conversions in

2010 to prepare for the tax increases due to take effect in 2011 and 2013. Doing a Roth IRA conversion now allows you to take advantage of the lowest tax rates and saves you from paying the 3.8% Health Care Reform surtax increase on unearned income.

—— $$$ ——

The analysis for the previous three graphs assumed an initial tax bracket of 25%. If you add another $100,000 of income, however, that would likely push you into the 28% bracket. After that one time bump into the 28% bracket, we assumed you and your heirs would revert to the 25% bracket.

Tax increases are coming for tax year 2011 and beyond for taxpayers currently in the 25% bracket and higher. The two increases are: the sunset provisions of the Bush tax cuts and the Health Care Reform surtax of 3.8%. So, if you are in the 25% or higher bracket now, the tax increases will make a Roth IRA now make the Roth IRA conversion now more desirable. The chart below shows the different tax brackets for a married couple, filing jointly, for 2010 and beyond.

Taxable Income	2010	2011	Top Rate with Surtax 2013
$ 0 – 16,750	10%	15%	15%
$16,750 – 68,000	15%	15%	15%
$68,000 – 137,300	25%	28%	28%
$137,300 – 209,250	28%	31%	31%
$209,250 – 373,650	33%	36%	39.8%
Over $373,650	35%	39.6%	43.4%

Please note this reflects current law as we go to press. President Obama has stated he does not want a tax increase for taxpayers in the 25% bracket. The chart above, however, represents the actual law at press time.

Now, the next logical step in our analysis is to assume that you are—or will be—in the 28% bracket or higher and facing higher taxes if not in short run almost certainly in the long run. If you are making $250,000 or more, then the following savings will come that much faster because we more certain that tax rates for high income tax earners will certainly be higher both in 2011 and thereafter.

Using our previous methodology, we alter the assumptions and put Mr. Roth IRA Conversion and Mr. Status Quo in the highest tax brackets. Remember this analysis accounts only for the tax increases that have already been passed and are part of existing law. There is no telling what the future might hold for tax increases.

Therefore, a Roth IRA conversion in 2010 takes advantage of the lowest tax rates. But for wealthy taxpayers, converting before 2013 also avoids the 3.8% Health Care Reform tax increase on unearned income. If we take into consideration the two additional tax increases (and assume for the moment that you are in the top tax bracket), you would find the benefit of making a Roth IRA conversion even more compelling.

New Tax

For example, when Figure 1 is recalculated, using the 35% tax bracket for 2010 and the 43.4% tax bracket for subsequent years, the benefits from the Roth IRA conversion are even greater.

Figure 4

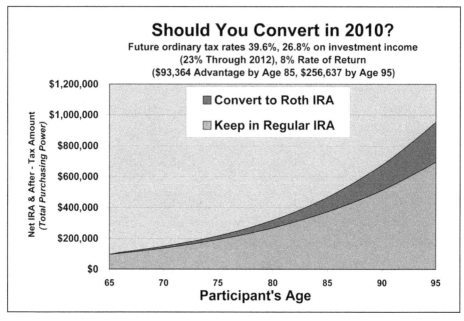

Assumptions for Figure 4

- 65 year old with $100,000 regular IRA and $35,000 after-tax funds also available

- $100,000 IRA converted

- 39.6% federal tax bracket on RMDs from regular IRA in the future & taxes on total regular IRA balances for comparisons

- 35% tax bracket for 2010 Roth conversion

- Federal and state taxes of 26.8% on after-tax investment income (23% through 2012) based on 20% capital gain and qualified dividend rules, 3% state tax rate, and 3.8% surtax starting in 2013

- 8% rate of return on investments

- Takes only RMDs, reinvested in after-tax funds

- Measured in total purchasing power that subtracts accrued income taxes from traditional IRA

- Does not take into account inflation

Please note that, under the new rates and measured in purchasing power, just 20 years after the Roth IRA conversion the benefit amounts to $93,364. At the old rates, the benefit would be $50,908. Converting in 2010 confers the greatest benefits because you have locked in the tax rates of 2010. In subsequent years, the tax rates will be higher.

Once again, without factoring in benefits to an heir, this shows that the individual who makes the conversion can benefit directly. In this instance, taxpayers in the top tax bracket could have an additional $93,364 of purchasing power by making a Roth IRA conversion in 2010 and living 20 years.

Children of High Income IRA Owners

Follow our line of reasoning, and taking into consideration the already passed tax increases for families in the top tax bracket, the chart for the beneficiaries of Mr. Roth IRA Conversion would look as follows.

Figure 5

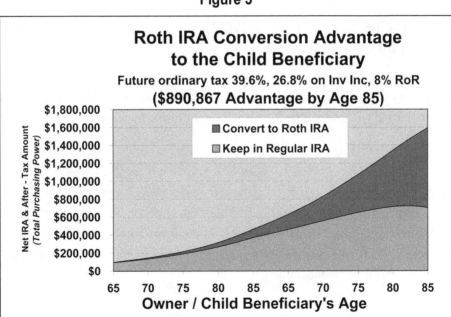

Assumptions for Figure 5

- IRA owner and spouse die 20 years after the conversion
- Funds inherited by 55-year-old beneficiary
- Spending is equal to RMD from traditional IRA for each scenario
- Measured in total purchasing power of remaining funds after 39.6% income tax allowance on the balance of the regular IRA
- 8% rate of return
- Not adjusted for inflation

As you can see, the benefits to Mr. Roth IRA Conversion's heirs compared to the benefits of Mr. Status Quo's heirs would be $890,867 over the life of the child or children. The coolest thing about a Roth IRA conversion is that it is advantageous both for the owner and the owner's heirs. The benefit to the heirs could be considered an added bonus, but the bonus will likely be life changing.

The Benefits of Roth IRA Conversions to the Third Generation of High-Income Taxpayers

The next step in our journey is to assume you make a Roth IRA conversion, live twenty years, and then pass your Roth IRA on to your grandchildren through a well-drafted trust. Once again, we will factor in the increased tax rates.

To be clear, I am assuming an investment rate of 8%. These days I hear many people squawk when I use an 8% rate of return. They used to squawk when I used 8% back in the dot com years when they wanted me to use 10 or 12%. The 8% assumption is still 1.8% less than the 84 year average of the S&P 500 index as reported by *Morningstar* for the years between 1926 and 2009. Obviously, if I used a lower interest rate, the benefits would not be as great, but they would still be considerable.

Figure 6

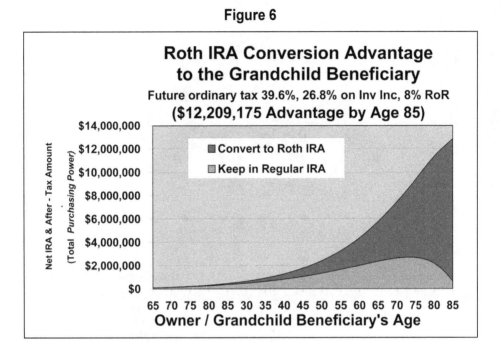

Roth IRA Conversion Advantage to the Grandchild Beneficiary
Future ordinary tax 39.6%, 26.8% on Inv Inc, 8% RoR
($12,209,175 Advantage by Age 85)

Assumptions for Figure 6

- IRA owner and spouse die 20 years after the conversion

- Funds inherited by 25-year-old beneficiary

- Spending is equal to RMD from traditional IRA for each scenario

- Measured in total purchasing power of remaining funds after 39.6% income tax allowance on the balance of the regular IRA

- 8% rate of return measured in real dollars

- Does not take inflation into account

Grandchild as Beneficiary

Even before running these numbers, I knew the differences were going to be significantly more than the differences using constant tax rates. Frankly, however, after running the numbers, I was still taken aback by how much better off you and your family will be—assuming you are in the 28% bracket or higher and you make 2010 Roth IRA conversion.

Furthermore, if we want to have a more meaningful picture of the benefits of a Roth IRA conversion, it makes sense to consider inflation. The following table, therefore, compares the actual dollar benefit measured in the purchasing power of the future which includes the impact of inflation using an inflation rate of 3%. We then compare that to the current purchasing power measured without inflation in 2010 current dollars. The revised numbers follow:

	IRA Owner	Child of IRA Owner	Grandchild of IRA Owner
Total Dollar Benefit Per Graph, Age 85	$93,364	$890,867	$12,209,175
Measured in 2010 Dollars	$51,693	$235,580	$ 1,147,383

Of course, many readers expect that there will be additional tax increases, in which case, the benefit of the Roth IRA conversion would be greater than anything even shown here.

Are these Pie in the Sky Projections of the True Value of a Roth IRA Conversion to Your Family?

Actually, for many if not most people, the numbers that I have stated are actually conservative for three major reasons.

First, I believe there will be additional tax increases, and I think I have made it clear that converting to a Roth IRA before taxes go up is a good idea. If you take into account the enormous deficits: two wars, health care, Social Security, pension guarantees, mortgage guarantees, etc., it is fairly clear we are going to need tax revenues from somewhere. Even as we speak, the 2010 tax brackets are at an historic low for top tax-bracket taxpayers. A history of top tax brackets by year that is summarized in a graph as follows:

Figure 7

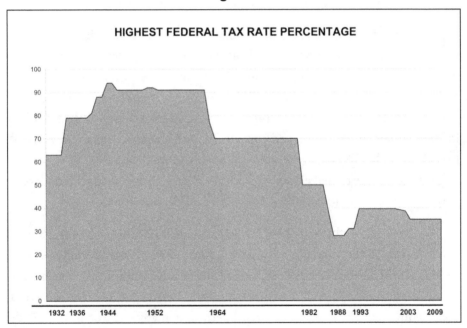

Summary of New Effective Tax Rates Comparing 2010 with 2011 Rates and 2013 when Health Care Reform Takes Effect

Top Rate with Taxable Income	2010	2011	Surtax 2013
$0 – 16,750	10%	15%	15%
$16,751 – 68,000	15%	15%	15%
$68,001 – 137,300	25%	28%	28%
$137,301 – 209,250	28%	31%	34.8%
$209,251 – 373,650	33%	36%	39.8%
Over $373,650	35%	39.6%	43.4%

(Please consider the previous caveat about future tax rates).

The second reason, and perhaps the more powerful reason, is that my previous examples assumed only a $100,000 Roth IRA conversion. In reality, there is no limit as to how much money you are allowed to convert from your traditional IRA to your Roth IRA. (In Chapter Eight, we will examine how much and when to convert). It is sufficient to say right now that in many cases, and particularly for individuals in the upper and top income-tax brackets, it may be advisable to make a Roth IRA conversion of considerably more than $100,000. In fact, it might be advisable to make a conversion of several hundred thousand dollars, or $1 million, or even multi-million dollar Roth IRA conversions.

We have made financial projections, even before factoring in the surtax, which indicated that making a Roth IRA conversion of several million dollars would put the IRA owner and his family in a better position than not making the conversion. So while all the above analysis is based on a hundred-thousand-dollar conversion, it is possible, even likely, that many—if not most—of the readers of this book could end up converting more than $100,000 during their lifetime and the benefits of the Roth IRA conversion would be much greater than the graphs above show just because of the amount converted.

The Benefits of a One-Million-Dollar Conversion

Now, let's take it to the next level for high-income taxpayers. Let's assume that our high income taxpayer makes a $1M conversion and pays taxes at the highest rate.

Figure 8

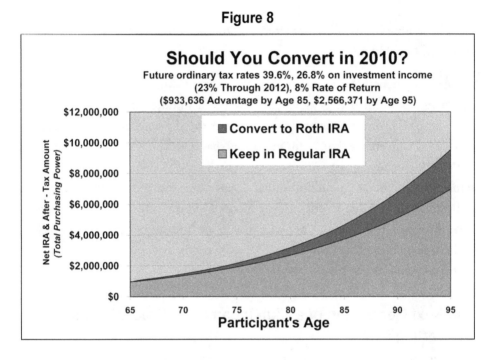

Assumption for Figure 8

- 65-year-old with $1,000,000 regular IRA and $350,000 after-tax funds also available

- $1,000,000 IRA converted

- 39.6% federal tax bracket on minimum distributions from regular IRA in the future & taxes on total regular IRA balances for comparisons

- 35% tax bracket for 2010 Roth conversion

- Federal and state taxes of 26.8% on after-tax investment income (23% through 2012) based on 20% capital gain and qualified dividend rules, 3% state tax rate, and 3.8% surtax starting in 2013

- 8% rate of return on investments in real dollars

- Takes only RMDs, reinvested in after-tax funds

- Measured in total purchasing power that subtracts accrued income taxes from traditional IRA

- Doesn't take inflation into account

Please note in just 20 years after making the conversion, the IRA owner is better off by $933,636.

Another benefit for high-income taxpayers making a Roth IRA conversion might not be immediately obvious. Lower-and middle-income taxpayers will likely trigger an increase in their marginal tax rate by adding income from the Roth IRA conversion. For example, if a taxpayer in the 25% bracket makes a $100,000 conversion, he will move into, at least, the 28% tax bracket. If the same taxpayer makes a million-dollar conversion, his or her tax bracket will jump to 35%. In other words, adding income will not only cause an increase in *taxes*, but also an increase in *tax rates*. If you are already in the top tax bracket, additional income from the Roth IRA conversion will not trigger a tax rate increase—there is nowhere to go!

The Next Generation of a High Income Tax Bracket Family Converting $1M

Following our now predictable pattern, let's look at the benefits of a $1 million conversion for the first generation heirs of the original owner and his or her spouse.

Figure 9

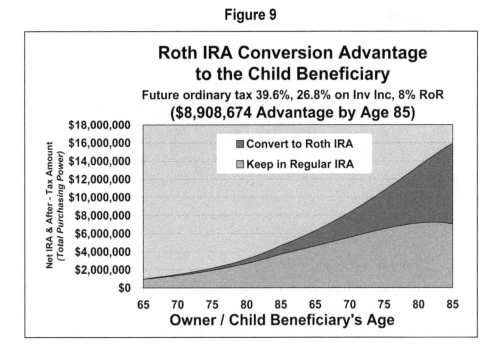

Assumptions for Figure 9

- IRA owner and spouse die 20 years after the conversion

- Funds inherited by 55-year-old beneficiary

- Spending is equal to RMD from traditional IRA for each scenario

- Measured in total purchasing power of remaining funds after 39.6% income tax allowance on the balance of the regular IRA

- 8% rate of return measured in real dollars

- Doesn't factor inflation

The Benefits to the Grandchildren of Mr. Roth IRAs $1M Conversion

Figure 10

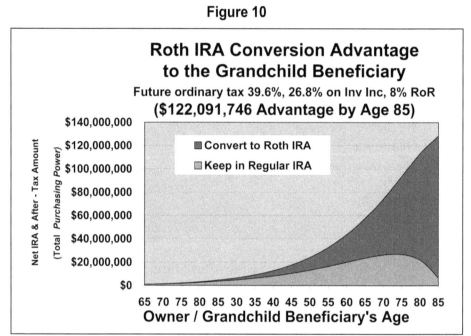

Assumptions for Figure 10

- IRA owner and spouse die 20 years after the conversion

- Funds inherited by 25-year-old beneficiary

- Spending is equal to RMD from traditional IRA for each scenario

- Measured in total purchasing power of remaining funds after 39.6% income tax allowance on the balance of the regular IRA

- 8% rate of return suing real dollars

- Not adjusted for inflation

Now, we will be fair and consider inflation. We summarize the last three graphs of a $1M Roth IRA conversion with their value in future (or real) dollars compared to dollars measured in 2010 purchasing power.

Advantages in Today's Dollars
(assume 3% annual inflation and 8% rate of return)

	IRA Owner	Child of IRA Owner	Grandchild of IRA Owner
Total Dollar Benefit Age 85	$933,637	$8,908,674	$122,091,746
Measured in 2010 Dollars	$516,932	$2,355,797	$ 11,473,828

But wait, there is more. Yes, there are even more benefits to Roth IRA conversions that have not even been accounted for in the previous analysis.

The Reduced Estate and Inheritance Taxes Associated with a Roth IRA Conversion

The other benefit of the Roth IRA conversion that hasn't been addressed in the analysis is the advantage conferred when factoring in the estate and inheritance taxes for the heirs of Mr. Roth IRA Conversion. For simplicity's sake, we will revert to the $100,000 Roth IRA conversion example. Let's go back to the chart on 40.

Roth IRA Value after conversion		$100,000
Traditional IRA	$100,000	
Other non-IRA funds*	25,000	-0-
Total dollars	$125,000	$100,000
Less taxes paid on IRA (if distributed)	(25,000)	-0-
Purchasing power	$100,000	$100,000

*(Non-IRA funds of $25,000 used to pay tax on conversion)

You'll notice that Mr. Status Quo has $125,000 in total dollars even though he has only $100,000 of purchasing power. Mr. Roth IRA Conversion on the other hand has $100,000 in total dollars and $100,000 of purchasing power. In the event that Mr. Roth IRA conversion dies one day after he makes the conversion, he has reduced his taxable estate by $25,000 dollars. In other words if he paid the $25,000 in income taxes on the Roth IRA conversion and he was subject to federal estate taxes at 40%, he would have saved $10,000 in federal estate taxes ($25,000 times 40%). Even if Mr. Roth IRA Conversion's estate is not subject to federal estate taxes, it is likely his estate will be subject to state, estate, or inheritance taxes.

One of the old strategies, before Roth IRA conversions, was for taxpayers with significant IRAs to cash in at least a portion of their IRAs before death. The benefit of cashing the IRA and paying the tax before death was that, in effect, by paying the taxes due on cashing in the IRA, you removed that money from your estate for federal estate-tax purposes, as well for state, estate, and inheritance tax purposes.

While I was never necessarily a huge fan of that strategy, it did serve to reduce federal estate and state inheritance taxes. Today with a Roth IRA conversion, you ultimately have the same benefit of reducing federal estate and state inheritance taxes by doing a Roth IRA conversion before death. Instead of being left with plain old after-tax dollars, however, you are left with Roth IRA dollars—with all the benefits mentioned earlier. Specifically the benefits of a conversion are:

- Income tax-free growth for you, your spouse, and potentially, your children and grandchildren.

- No RMDs for your Roth IRA for either you and/or your spouse.

- And, if you take into account the potential for further tax increases, the benefits of making a large conversion or a series of smaller conversion can be measured in hundreds of thousands or even millions of dollars.

—— $$$ ——

Key Lesson for this Chapter

Compare two identically situated IRA owners. One makes a Roth IRA conversion and the other one doesn't. The person who makes the Roth IRA conversion is better off by tens of thousands of dollars. When children inherit a

Roth IRA, their time horizon for tax-free growth is significantly longer. For them, the Roth IRA benefits can be measured in hundreds of thousands of dollars. Carrying this idea one step further, the potential benefit to grandchildren can be measured in seven figures.

Please note all this analysis is the same for employees who have 401(k) or 403(b) balances and have access to a Roth Designated Account. Please see "What's New" before Chapter 1. There may be some variations of what happens to these accounts when someone dies, but conceptually, I think it is the same.

Chapter Four

A Deathbed Roth IRA Conversion Story

"I'm very proud of my gold pocket watch.
My grandfather, on his deathbed, sold me this watch.

— Woody Allen

Main Topics

- A deathbed Roth IRA conversion story in detail
- Even if a Roth IRA conversion is not life changing for you, it may be for your family

Key Idea

It's never too late to do a Roth IRA Conversion.

—— **$$$** ——

I received a call from Bill, a gentleman who was literally on his death bed. Bill was going to die within the year and he knew it, I knew it, and his family knew it. He had $1 million in an IRA and $300,000 outside the IRA for a total estate of $1.3 million. This was back in the days when the federal exemption amount was $1,000,000 (meaning the first $1,000,000 was not subject to federal estate or transfer tax).

Now, I am not generally in the habit of making house calls, but in his case, I made an exception. I literally sat at the side of his bed while he told me of his hopes and dreams for his children and grandchildren. He had two children, Andy and Sarah, and each of his children had two children. Andy was a physician doing well financially. Sarah was a single mom with a job, but given just her own resources, her prospects for a secure retirement were not good.

Bill's wife had predeceased him. This meant there was no more money for Bill's family other than what Bill would leave them. Bill wanted to make sure that his family was provided for as well as possible under the circumstances. No matter what we did, it was not going to make a financial difference in his life. It was all about his family.

Some people don't want to do anything or think about anything when they are sick. I have, however, been in this business 30 years and have frequently seen terminally ill clients get a burst of energy for making last-minute financial moves for the benefit of their family. In one case I remember the wife saying to the husband who was dying, "You got it done dear, great job." You could see the relief on the man's face.

I remember my own father being completely distracted from horrendous pain when he was talking to us about his estate and making plans to provide for my mother. It was clear to all of us he was dying, but the act of planning for my Mom took his thoughts away from his own suffering and made him feel useful. I would like to think that Bill, meeting with me and thinking about Roth IRA conversion issues for the benefit of his family, was a helpful distraction from the pain he was suffering. Though he was dying, I would also like to think it gave him some hope for the future, even if not for his own future.

He was a smart old engineer, and he had attended one of my workshops before he took ill. His own advisor of many years told him not to do a Roth IRA conversion, but in his gut, he knew his regular advisor was not really qualified to give Roth IRA conversion advice.

A special note for financial advisors: It is okay not to really understand Roth IRA conversions or not know how to make financial projections to make Roth IRA conversion recommendations. If that is the case, it is fine to refer clients to a Roth IRA conversion expert for that piece of the client's financial plan. Though I prefer that Roth IRA conversions be integrated into the overall financial plan, I understand many advisors lack Roth IRA conversion expertise. It is possible, even likely, if you are a financial advisor reading this book, you will know more than most advisors, but still might not know how to make projections to help a client determine the optimal amount and timing of a series of Roth IRA conversions. You should consider referring out the Roth IRA conversion piece or working with someone who does understand these issues and can make the appropriate financial projections.

What is *not* okay is to advise clients against making a Roth IRA conversion simply because you don't understand Roth IRA conversions or you don't know how to make these projections. Do your clients a service and tell them that is not your area of expertise and help them find the help they need.

Alternately, grind through this book and after going through the entire book, including the nitty gritty sections, try to determine if you think you are qualified to make the projections and do the work and give your clients Roth IRA conversion advice. We also have supplemental material for advisors at www.rothrevolution.com. We also have a done for you Roth IRA Conversion workshop. Please see www.therothirainstitute.com.

At this point, Bill didn't want to change his investments, but he did want to bring me in for the Roth IRA conversion and estate-planning piece.

My instinct, which was confirmed after making financial projections, was to make a Roth IRA conversion of the entire $1,000,000. (We are over-simplifying the fact pattern. He actually had enormous medical bills that helped him offset some of the income from the Roth IRA conversion.)

It was his one last shot. If he made the Roth IRA conversion and paid the taxes on the conversion with most of his other non-IRA or after-tax money, he would have $1 million in a Roth IRA. The $300,000 would be used to pay the income taxes on the Roth IRA conversion. His total estate would be reduced by the $300,000 he paid in income taxes on the Roth IRA conversion. Even though the estate had the same purchasing power before and after the conversion, he reduced his taxable estate for federal estate and state inheritance tax purposes by $300,000. That would leave his taxable estate for federal estate tax purposes at $1M and since the exclusion back then was $1M, there would be no federal-estate tax.

Deathbed Conversion

We saved federal-estate tax and PA inheritance tax on $300,000 of taxable assets with the $1M exclusion. Had we done nothing and had he died with $1.3 M, his family would have had to pay federal estate tax on the $300,000 ($1.3 million estate – $1 million exclusion) and his family would have had to pay Pennsylvania inheritance taxes on an additional $300,000.

We lowered his estate tax and his inheritance taxes.[3] In addition, his children and grandchildren would be getting money income tax-free for the rest of their lives.

There is another point to this story. Before I met Bill, the beneficiary designation of his IRA was consistent with his will which said children equally. One of the problems with this language is that if one of his children died before Bill died, that child's inheritance would go to his or her sibling rather than to his or her children. That is not what Bill wanted. If his child dies before him, he doesn't want to disinherit the grandchildren. The second problem with the simple beneficiary designation was that it failed to allow for the possibility of the wealthier child not wanting to keep the entire inherited Roth IRA for himself. The wealthier child might want at least a portion of his inherited IRA or

---

3 Please note in the earlier calculations made in this book we did not factor in the estate tax savings in the graphs comparing Mr. Status Quo to Mr. Roth IRA Conversion. Had we also factored in the potential estate and inheritance taxes, the advantages of doing the conversion would have been higher.

inherited Roth IRA to go for the benefit, in well-drafted trusts, of his children, in this case his five-year-old twins.

We changed the beneficiary designation to children equally, per stirpes (actually we included well-drafted trusts for the children of his children). We added the provisions hat each of his children had a right to "disclaim" or give up their—or a portion of their—interest in favor of a well-drafted trust for the benefit of that particular child's children. In other words, if the wealthier child did not want to receive his portion of the inherited Roth IRA, we put in place a mechanism where the wealthier child could "disclaim" all or a portion of his share of the inherited Roth IRA. The portion that the wealthier child disclaimed would go into a well-drafted trust for the benefit of his children.

We had the same type of option for his daughter Sarah. Sarah, however, who was not in as strong a financial situation as Andy, appropriately figured she needed her share of the estate and chose to keep her share and not to disclaim anything to her children.

The trustee of the trust for the benefit of Andy's children was Andy, Bill's son and father of the grandchildren. That way Andy, as father and trustee, could distribute income and principal for the health, maintenance, and support of his own children, but not for his niece and nephew. The fact that any money Andy disclaimed would go to his kids and not his niece and nephew gave Andy a bigger incentive to disclaim because all the money would be in his family.

You might say that isn't fair to Sarah's children. Most clients, however, prefer to treat their children equally. In this case Bill did treat Andy and Sarah equally. He just gave them both options on what to do with their inheritance. Andy decided to disclaim half of his portion to his children and Sarah decided to keep her portion of the inherited Roth IRA.

The trust that we drafted for Andy's children, like a typical minor's trust would be something like the following: Bill's grandchildren, subject to the approval of the trustee, would be entitled to the income of the trust and the invasion of principal for health, maintenance and support. When Bill's grandchildren are age 25, the grandchildren would have access to one third of the corpus (principal). When the grandchildren are 30, they receive access to another one-third of the corpus. When the grandchildren are 35, the trust is terminated and it is divided among them. The terms of this trust are not that different from a conventional minor's trust except we took special care to include the necessary conditions in the trust in order for the individual beneficiary of the trust to qualify as a designated beneficiary. (See **Retire Secure!**, Wiley, Feb., 2009, p. 234).

Obviously, you could make the trust say almost anything you want as long as it meets the specific conditions for the individual beneficiary of the trust to qualify as a designated beneficiary.

Since Andy had a lot of money and a strong income, upon Bill's death, Andy decided to keep half of the inherited Roth IRA and to disclaim the remaining half to the trusts for his children. Sarah kept all of her share of the inherited Roth IRA. Assuming an average life span of 80 years, Andy's children, who were age five at the time of Bill's death, will enjoy around 75 years of tax-free income, assuming they live that long and assuming they don't cash in the inherited Roth IRA before they have to. Sarah, who was 55, would have about 25 years of tax-free growth assuming she lives that long. The entire inherited Roth IRA will be distributed by the end of the beneficiaries' life expectancy—not their actual life.

Please note that the rules on the RMD of an inherited Roth IRA as well as the inherited IRA are in **Retire Secure!**, (Wiley, Feb., 2009, Chapter Five, p. 85-94).

Because of Bill's pro-active Roth IRA conversion, his family will be better off by millions of dollars.

One lesson of this story is you can't be too old or too close to death for it to be extremely beneficial to do a Roth IRA conversion. To personalize the issue for many people reading this book, if one of

> One lesson of this story is you can't be too old or too close to death for it to be extremely beneficial to do a Roth IRA conversion.

your parents has a traditional IRA, it might be wise to determine whether your parent or parents should make a Roth IRA conversion.

The side benefit of the conversion was it lowered Bill's federal-estate tax and it lowered his PA inheritance tax because for estate—or inheritance tax purposes. Unfortunately, whether it's an IRA or a Roth IRA it will be taxed. But if it's a Roth IRA, the purchasing power is much greater. If I'm going to be taxed, I would rather be taxed on more purchasing power at the same rate than less purchasing power.

—— $$$ ——

Key Lesson for this Chapter

People of all ages—not just young taxpayers—can reap the benefits of a Roth IRA conversion. If you have a traditional IRA, you owe it to yourself and your family to seek expert advice and develop a long-term, Roth IRA conversion plan.

Chapter Five

My Roth IRA Conversion Story: How I Got Started with Roth IRA Conversions

"Alexander Hamilton started the U.S. Treasury with nothing,
and that was the closest our country has ever been to being even."

— Will Rogers

Main Topics

- Jim's personal Roth IRA conversion story

- The advent of Roth IRA conversions in 1998

- How Roth IRA conversions can improve quality of life

- How you can confidently rely on the analysis in this book because the methodology has been scrupulously peer-reviewed

Key Idea

The same methodology used in **The Tax Adviser's** "Article of the Year" in 1998, is used to make the Roth IRA calculations you see in this book. You can be assured that the methodology used in these examples has been reviewed with intense scrutiny by the top CPAs in the industry. Obviously, tax rates and other laws have changed so we include the updated analysis.

—— **$$$** ——

First, here is a note about the methodology of the original article and this book. To simplify the methodology is measuring IRA wealth after adjusting for income taxes, but not adjusting for inflation. Technically, that isn't measuring wealth in true purchasing power which would include inflation. We didn't take inflation into account in that peer reviewed article in 1998. In this book in most cases we try to present both the inflation adjusted and real dollars. More importantly for our purposes, we are adjusting for income taxes.

My Roth IRA Conversion Story

The laws that created the Roth IRA and Roth IRA conversions were first proposed in 1997. As a tax practitioner, I am in the habit of ignoring proposed changes to the tax law. The reason I ignore proposed legislation is that if I study proposed law, I get proposed law mixed up with what is really law, and it's just too confusing. So, usually I wait until the proposed legislation becomes actual law before I learn it and attempt to figure out a way to employ it to my clients' and readers' advantage.

But it was different with the proposed legislation regarding Roth IRA conversions. The word on the street was that this law was going to pass. When I read the proposed changes to the IRA law creating these Roth IRA conversions, I knew this was something I should not ignore—this was no ordinary proposed legislation.

I thought, "This is big!" Just from a gut instinct, I knew this was going to be a game changer for millions of IRA-and retirement-plan owners. I'm a chess player and a bridge player, and I like long-term strategies. One of the most satisfying things about my career is helping clients and readers determine and implement the best long-term strategies and, for my clients, watching our recommendations play out over the years. I particularly enjoy recommending a strategic plan and enjoy watching the advantages of the strategy unfold over time. Of course, many times adjustments are needed along the way. The important thing, however, is that it is better to have a long-term plan than to have financial drift.

Anyway, back in 1997 though my instinct was telling me Roth IRA conversions were a great thing, that wasn't enough to prove anything to me or anyone else. Our office studied the law and under the direction of a talented CPA in my office, Steve Kohman, we made the appropriate financial projections. Steve is also a Certified Specialist in Estate Planning and does masterly Roth IRA conversion and related financial projections.

One of the biggest differences between how we made financial projections and how other people analyzed Roth's, both back then and now, is that we understood the secret: measure results in purchasing power—not in total dollars.

After making the appropriate financial projections using purchasing power as our measurement tool, we found the benefits of Roth IRA conversions were astounding. I was so excited because though people knew Roth IRA conversions were coming, they didn't know how advantageous they were. I thought (and to this day still think) I can help so many people improve the quality of their lives and the lives of their children and grandchildren. Now Roth IRA conversions are better known, though still not well understood. All the projections we ran confirmed my suspicions that Roth IRA conversions were a great thing for many—if not most—IRA and retirement-plan owners.

Now I had mathematical proof that, using reasonable assumptions, Roth IRA conversions were a great thing for many, perhaps millions, of taxpayers.

> Now I had mathematical proof that, using reasonable assumptions, Roth IRA conversions were a great thing for many, perhaps millions, of taxpayers.

But knowing that people are cynical about anything a financial advisor, or worse yet, an attorney will tell them (CPAs have a little more credibility); I had to provide compelling proof that my analysis was sound. I knew people were going to say, "Who are you to recommend that I pay income tax up front?"

I knew from my academic background that the best way to prove something was to submit a paper to a peer-reviewed journal. A peer-reviewed journal is a journal that subjects your submissions to a jury of your peers. They delve into the analyses to see if it is accurate. Their reputation is on the line. If it passes muster and they publish it, you gain credibility.

The best peer-reviewed tax journal, both then and now, is a journal published by the American Institute of Certified Public Accountants called *The Tax Adviser*. It's the equivalent of *The New England Journal of Medicine*, but it's for CPAs and tax professionals. So I went to the editors of *The Tax Adviser*, and told them I think Roth IRA conversions are going to be really big. I asked if could write the article on Roth IRA conversions. If they think you can do a good job, they will reserve the topic for you, and they did. That meant if I could write an article that could get past their reviewers I would have the first peer-reviewed article on Roth IRA conversions. Though the article must be approved by a committee, usually one guy is the "primary number cruncher" who must review the analysis. The author is not permitted to meet or talk directly to the reviewer/number cruncher.

Peer Review

The primary number cruncher they assigned me was the king of the nitpickers. He not only wanted all the analysis, but he also wanted the spreadsheets and the formulas within the spreadsheets. He sent us what seemed like a zillion questions, constantly trying to probe for mistakes or weaknesses in our analysis. He was, however, asking the right questions. Then, he started with suggestions. His suggestions were excellent. By the time I answered all his objections and incorporated his suggestions, the article was much stronger than when I originally submitted it.

He also understood my estate-planning recommendation. Though it could have properly been considered a different topic for a different article, he allowed me to include it—that was fine, my favorite estate-planning strategy, Lange's Cascading Beneficiary Plan (they would only let me call it the Cascading Beneficiary Plan) also received peer review. The article was published in May, 1998, and it won "Article of the Year." The methodology that we used to make the initial Roth IRA conversion calculations is the same methodology we use today; we just update the numbers.

When the article was published, I felt confident that I was onto something significant that would benefit my clients and readers. I couldn't believe that more financial professionals were not pro-actively suggesting Roth IRA conversions to their clients and readers, but I certainly was.

A Roth IRA Conversion Douses the Impact of a Devastating Fire

On February 16, 1998, our office suffered a devastating fire. Our office was above a pizza shop that suffered an electrical fire. Never ever put your office above a pizza shop. Bad idea. Fortunately, I had appropriate insurance and backup systems, but I didn't get the insurance reimbursement until the following calendar year.

All of a sudden, my 1998 income was below $100,000 and that meant I qualified for a Roth IRA conversion. I was 42 years old at the time. My wife, Cindy, has a master's degree in electrical engineering from Carnegie Mellon University and is good at quantitative projects. Using the methodology that Steve and I developed in writing the article, we "ran our numbers." My daughter was three years old at the time. We had $250,000 in our combined IRAs. We determined the best thing to do would be to convert the entire amount. Cindy agreed, and that is what we did.

We paid taxes on $250,000 and at that point, paying those taxes really hurt. True, back then you could spread the income over a four-year period. But that was not the main advantage. The main advantage is many years, likely decades and possibly a century of tax-free growth. I will also state that if I am wrong about Roth IRA conversions, then I am going down with you.

When we made the decision to convert, Cindy' and my primary thinking was income-tax-free growth we could use as we got older. As luck would have it, and in large part due to the analysis I have done on Roth IRA conversions, business is good. I've been very fortunate and it is likely that we will not need all that money. In which case, that Roth IRA money—or at least a portion of it—will be left to our daughter when we die. It is even possible, that at least a portion of our Roth IRA could go to our grandchildren! Our family could easily enjoy 100 years of income-tax-free growth from that Roth IRA conversion. Yes, in 1998 I might have been one generation younger than a lot of you, but you can do the same thing. And even if the number of years of tax-free growth isn't as high, the concept is the same, and you and your family can benefit from you making Roth IRA conversions.

When writing this book I thought it would be instructive to measure the impact of our decision to make a Roth IRA conversion back in 1998. What follows is a chart of the impact of the status quo vs. making the conversion. The chart starts comparing my and Cindy's wealth and then at our death, the benefits for our daughter.

Figure 11

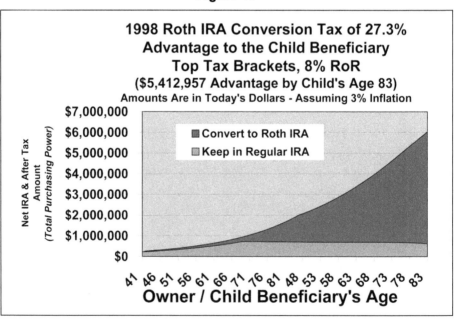

Assumptions for Figure 11

- 8% rate of return and a 3% inflation rate

- Measured in 1998 dollars

- Assumed the top tax rates starting the year after we converted until my daughter's life expectancy

- Assumed when I turn 70 that I will withdraw $78,714 which is how much I would have to take if I had not made the conversion. I then increase spending 3% per year.

- Calculated tax on $250,000 of income in 1998 and it was $68,156 = 27.2624% of the conversion

Subsequent Events

To complete my story with Roth IRAs, I will also relate some subsequent events. Despite the fact that the market had a bad decade, my wife and I did well with our investments in the Roth IRA. We didn't get 8%, but we did fairly well. I have maxed out my Roth 401(k) that I implemented at work. (More information about Roth 401(k)s, including a comparison between Roth 401(k)s and traditional 401(k)s, can be found in Chapter Sixteen). And, we maxed out the non-deductible IRA for both Cindy and me.

Now to be fair, I had the unusually favorable circumstance of being able to convert at a low rate while being relatively young. While the benefits for you and your family might not be as great, the same concepts apply and you too could be significantly better off by making a Roth conversion.

—— $$$ ——

Key Lesson for this Chapter

Jim practices what he preaches but you too can benefit from three generations of tax-free growth.

Chapter Six

The Three Buckets of Money Story

"When I was young I used to think that money was the most important thing in life and now that I am old, I know it is."

—Oscar Wilde

Main Topics

- The optimal order for spending different types of assets
- How following the optimal order makes a tremendous difference

Key Idea

Spend after-tax dollars first, IRA dollars next and Roth IRA dollars last (with some exceptions).

—— **$$$** ——

I met new clients, George and Marie, who were both 69 years old back in 1998. George and Marie had a substantial IRA and substantial money outside the IRA. They were more savers than spenders. They knew they were not likely to change their spending habits, but George still wanted to make sure he and his wife had more than enough money for their own purposes. They even wanted a buffer in case they became sick or the stock market did badly. It was extremely important to them that their children and grandchildren get the greatest benefit from their money after George and Marie were both gone.

3 Pots of Money

We made financial projections for them. In their case, we determined that the appropriate thing to do was to make a $500,000 Roth IRA conversion. We weren't licensed to sell life insurance back then but even before we were licensed, we were big fans of second-to-die life insurance for wealthy IRA owners.[4] George and Marie were working with an insurance professional who recommended a $2M second-to-die life insurance policy. We included the second-to-die life insurance analysis as an integral part of the financial projections. We determined that a $1M second-to-die policy was appropriate. Before we recommend second-to-die life insurance, we always want to make sure there are sufficient assets to cover all expenses for the husband and wife—with plenty left over. We also want to make sure that there is still sufficient money to fund other gifts to children as well as education funds, usually 529 plans for grandchildren.

The plan we determined for this particular couple was to convert $500,000 of their IRA to a Roth IRA. After the Roth IRA conversion and after paying

---

4 More information on the benefits of second-to-die life insurance and the combination of second-to-die life insurance and other forms of gifting and Roth IRA conversions can be found in **Retire Secure!**, (Wiley, Feb., 2009 in Chapter 12, pp. 203-224 and in Chapter 11, pp. 184-193).

the taxes on the conversion from outside the IRA, they would live off three pots of money. They would have after-tax dollars, IRA dollars (because we did not recommend they convert the entire amount) and Roth IRA dollars. The plan was that they would spend their Social Security and the after-tax dollars first. They would also be receiving RMDs from the remaining IRA. Eventually, if they lived long enough, depending on investment performance, their after-tax dollars would be exhausted. Once the after-tax dollars were exhausted, they were to spend their IRA and retirement-plan dollars, but not the Roth money. According to our calculations that would provide more than enough money for George and Marie to live comfortably—even better than they were living when they first came to see me. The assumption was that if they followed that plan and they exhausted all their after-tax dollars and IRA dollars, they would eventually be left with the Roth IRA dollars. And, those Roth IRA dollars will eventually go to their children and grandchildren. That family will be millions and millions of dollars better off because of the pro-active position they took, which was doing that Roth IRA conversion.

Postscript: We recently did a review (twelve years after our initial Roth IRA conversion advice). Frankly, the actual numbers were worse than the projections. That is, we did not anticipate a flat market and their assets today are lower than were our original projections. Luckily, their family, though not as much well off as we first projected, is still significantly better off than if they had not made the conversion. In addition, if the market comes back up over time, the benefits will still be tremendous.

Even though we reduced the life insurance recommendation, it turned out that investment held up better than any other investment. On the other hand, the purchasing of a two-million-dollar policy would have left them extremely cash tight.

This isn't just numbers. Making the appropriate financial decisions changes lives. It is true for this client; it was true for Bill's family when he made a $1,000,000 Roth IRA conversion on his deathbed. And, it can be true for you as well.

> This isn't just numbers. Making the appropriate financial decisions changes lives.

For many of you, being better off by $90,000 or even several hundred thousand dollars in your lifetime won't make a big difference in how much money you spend. For many of you, your spending patterns are pretty well fixed. So, let's assume you won't spend the additional money that you save as a result of making Roth IRA conversions. It is still a good thing to have more money and more purchasing power rather than less money and less purchasing power during your lifetime. The additional purchasing power can act like a buffer or a backstop in the event that you need more money than normal projections would indicate. The additional purchasing power acquired through Roth IRA conversions could be a big plus. Some people may object to making a Roth IRA conversion because they are afraid of running out of money and afraid of bad things happening to the economy. I would say the fear of running out of money and being afraid of changes in the economy (like massive income tax increases) are actually arguments in favor of making Roth IRA conversions.

You can't measure the pleasure of the added security you will have with additional purchasing power. It is still appropriate to develop a long-term Roth IRA conversion strategy because the benefits are so compelling for you, your children and your grandchildren. A Roth IRA conversion will make a tremendous difference in the quality of their lives.

Your son/daughter could be hundreds of thousands of dollars better off because you made a Roth IRA conversion. One of the beautiful things about the Roth IRA conversions is that unlike life insurance, which may be fine for your kids, but not good for you, Roth IRA conversions are good for you and fine for your kids. With life insurance, the premiums are paid out of your pocket. With the Roth IRA conversion, you are better off and the bonus is that your children and/or grandchildren will be much better off.

—— $$$ ——

Key Lesson for this Chapter

Spending after-tax dollars first, IRA dollars next and Roth IRA dollars last is the optimal order for spending assets. Following this method of spending money will make a tremendous difference in your life and in the lives of your children.

Chapter Seven

Typical Roth IRA Conversion Advice: It Is Not Usually Advantageous to Convert the Entire IRA

*"The nation should have a tax system that
looks like someone designed it on purpose."*

— William Simon

Main Topics

- The drawbacks of making a Roth IRA conversion that is too large

- How Social Security affects your tax bracket

- The sticker shock of the tax bill could dissuade you from a Roth conversion—don't let it

- How a series of partial Roth IRA conversions may be most appropriate strategy for many IRA owners

- The importance of tax brackets in Roth IRA conversion decisions

Key Idea

Comparing your regular marginal tax rate with your effective tax rate on a Roth IRA conversion is critical for the decisions of whether and how much you should convert to an IRA.

—— $$$ ——

Please note all this analysis is the same for employees who have 401(k) or 403(b) balances and have access to a Roth Designated Account. Please see "What's New" before Chapter One.

Perhaps after reading the first couple of chapters and these stories, you think I am a Roth IRA conversion maniac looking to make huge Roth IRA conversions for everyone I meet. Not so. In reality, my typical advice for middle-income taxpayers is usually to make a series of partial Roth IRA conversions over a period of years.

As a practical matter, the reduced sticker shock of writing a series of smaller checks to the IRS instead of writing one big check is much easier to take. The main reason, from a quantitative perspective, that I like a series of small conversions for lower-and middle-income taxpayers is that you can avoid a big jump in tax brackets. Ideally, you want to make a conversion in the lowest possible tax bracket. The amount to convert becomes a significant decision because if you convert too large an amount, it could result in not only paying a higher tax, which I can live with, but paying tax at a higher tax rate than you customarily pay which can be disadvantageous. Usually, in the short run, and quite often in the long run, making too large of a Roth IRA conversion may put you in a worse position than if you never made any Roth IRA conversion. On the other hand, if you don't convert enough, you could be missing a fine opportunity for tax-free growth for you and your family. In practice, we go through an involved process before we make Roth IRA conversion recommendations.

To oversimplify, however, some useful information to determining the appropriate amount to convert is to gather the relevant information:

- always keep in mind the income-tax rate on the additional income from the Roth IRA conversion

- make projections about your and/or your heirs' future tax rates

- measure results in purchasing power rather than in total dollars

Using these guidelines, we can establish a rule of thumb: limit the amount of money you convert to a Roth IRA to an amount where the extra income will be taxed at your current or future tax rate.

Let's look at a simple example. Consider a married couple, filing jointly, whose taxable income lies in the 15% bracket and can reasonably be expected to remain in the 15% bracket. Their taxable income is $40,000. If you look at the tax tables, you'll see that income for married taxpayers earning between $16,751 and $68,000 is taxed at 15%. This is known as the marginal tax bracket. The first $16,750 was really taxed at the 10% bracket. If you add one dollar of taxable income to someone who had an income of $16,750, that additional $1 of income would be taxed at 15%. Even though the actual tax rate for a married couple with taxable income of $16,751 is closer to 10% than 15%, we would say they have a marginal tax rate of 15% because every additional dollar of income would be taxed at 15%.

2010 Tax Rates for Married Filing Jointly

Taxable Income ($)	x%
$ 0 – 16,750	10%
16,751 – 68,000	15%
68,001 – 137,300	25%
137,301 – 209,250	28%
209,251 – 373,650	33%
373,651 and above	35%

For this example, we simplify by not taking into account some real world problems encountered when you are calculating marginal tax rates. For example, one problem with calculating the marginal tax rate on additional income from a Roth IRA conversion would be its effect on the taxability of Social Security income. Frequently, taxpayers in the 15% bracket are not paying any tax on their Social Security income. If you add additional income through a Roth IRA conversion, you may get taxed on your Social Security. So, the marginal tax bracket of someone who makes a Roth IRA conversion who would otherwise be in the 15% bracket would be in a higher tax bracket because of the new or increased taxability of their Social Security. Please see Chapter Twelve on strategies involving the combination of Roth IRA conversions and when to take Social Security.

Since the top of the 15% bracket is $68,000, it would be a reasonable starting point to suggest to the married couple with $40,000 of taxable income to consider making a $28,000 Roth IRA conversion for this year. The additional $28,000 will be taxed at the taxpayer's existing and predicted future tax rate of 15%. Please note this argument assumes that the taxpayer with the $40,000 income has after-tax money to pay the tax on the Roth IRA conversion. Based on measuring wealth in purchasing power, the taxpayer will break even on the first day but over time, the advantages of making the Roth IRA conversion at that level will continue to grow.

If that same taxpayer made a $500,000 Roth IRA conversion, the additional income on the conversion over $68,000 would be taxed at higher marginal rates. Much of the additional income would be taxed at the highest rate of 35%—or even higher depending on the year the conversion was made. In that situation, you would not have a break-even point of day one, and you might never reach the break-even point even factoring in the lives of your heirs. The basic problem is that you are paying 35% tax upfront to save taxes at 15% later. That just won't work.

Not quite as bad, but still bad, is a 15% taxpayer, who is likely to remain in the 15% tax bracket, makes a Roth IRA conversion that will push him into the 25% bracket. Depending on a bunch of assumptions, the breakeven point for that taxpayer would be too many years for us to recommend that strategy.

There is, however, a significant exception to the rule of trying to stay in your existing tax bracket when making a Roth IRA conversion. If the jump is slight, from 25% to 28% for example, I often recommend making a Roth IRA conversion. Assume you are in the 25% bracket and can reasonably be expected to remain in the 25% bracket. Even though your break-even point will not be day one if you measure in purchasing power, it is likely that making a Roth IRA conversion will be a good strategic decision. The same reasoning is true for someone in the 28% tax bracket whose conversion might push her into the 33% bracket. That jump in income would be significant. If you are likely to remain in the 28% bracket, we might recommend you conservatively choose to make a Roth IRA conversion that is small enough to keep you in the 28% bracket. Then, the following year you could repeat that same strategy. Depending on individual situations, interest rates, investment horizon, etc., it may be better to make a series of smaller conversions and stay in the 28% bracket than making a larger conversion that would push you into the 33% bracket.

The key is that the marginal tax brackets on the Roth IRA conversion as well as your—and possibly your heirs' future tax rates—are critical elements in deciding whether and how much and when to make a Roth IRA conversion.

The key is that the marginal tax brackets on the Roth IRA conversion as well as your—and possibly your heirs' future tax rates—are critical elements in deciding whether and how much and when to make a Roth IRA conversion.

What Happens if Your (or Your Heirs') Tax Rate Will Change?

In the first section when we talked about purchasing power, we assumed a flat income tax rate. In reality, that rarely happens. But, now that we have some of the basic concepts about marginal tax rates, we can push on to examples closer to the real world where tax rates change over the years.

For example, let's assume you have a significant IRA, are retired, but younger than age 70 and you are currently in the 15% tax bracket. Let's forget about future tax increases. You could end up in the 25% bracket or higher when you reach 70 because the income on your RMD could push you into the next tax bracket. In that case, a conversion that would put you in the higher tax bracket would not be unreasonable as that will be your future tax bracket. This scenario could apply to the millions of taxpayers whose tax bracket will increase after they start their RMDs.

Perhaps you are usually a 25% or higher taxpayer but you are laid off and now have very little taxable income. If you expect to be employed in the future, the year or years you are laid off might be an ideal time to make a Roth IRA conversion.

If you have unusually large deductible expenses, you may enjoy tremendous benefits from making a Roth IRA conversion while you are in a low tax bracket. If you are thinking of making a one-time large contribution to a charity, that might be a fine year to make a Roth IRA conversion. The combination of a significant charitable contribution and a Roth IRA conversion in the same year is a wonderful—almost like peas and carrots—combination. One way to look at the combination of a charitable contribution and a Roth IRA conversion is that you are saving so much money for yourself and your family with the Roth IRA conversion, you can afford to give a piece of that tax savings to the charity of your choice. And the greater deduction you get for the contribution, the greater the value of the conversion to your family.

I have had college professors make a large Roth IRA conversion during the year they took a sabbatical. Some of my business clients who had a tough year during the downturn took advantage of their lowered income-tax rate to make a Roth IRA conversion at all time low income tax rates.

I hate to point out opportunities you may have missed, but 2009 was an ideal year for seniors to make a Roth IRA conversion because you didn't have a RMD. And your taxable income, everything else being equal, was probably the lowest it would ever be for the rest of your life. One of the lessons to be learned is that if you think you are getting value from this book and this information, you should sign up for my free e-mail newsletter so you won't miss fine opportunities like the one you had last year. This concept of timing a Roth IRA conversion to be made in low-income tax bracket year has many applications. For example, let's say you are one or two years from retirement and you are currently in a high tax bracket, but you plan to retire before you are age 70. In that case, you may be better off waiting until after you retire to make a Roth IRA conversion. If you wait until you retire but before you turn age 70, you will no longer have the income from your job, you won't have started to receive the income from your RMD, and any income generated from a Roth IRA conversion would likely be taxed at a much lower tax rate.

Many taxpayers who plan to continue working for a long time would be advised to make the conversion while they are working anyway because of the additional benefits of having many years of tax-free growth. There is also the tough-to-measure benefit of possible tax increases as well as the possibility that the tax laws could change in a way that would reduce the tax benefits of future Roth IRA conversions.

A Surprising Pattern of Over-Converting if You are Over 70

Let's examine another surprising pattern. Let's assume you are over age 70 and you have a large RMD or you are accounting for your future RMD after you turn age 70 in determining how much of a Roth IRA conversion to make. One of the benefits of making a Roth IRA conversion is that you no longer are required to take RMDs on the Roth IRA either during your lifetime or the lifetime of your spouse. If you make a large Roth IRA conversion and reduce your future RMDs, you will also be reducing your future taxable income and might be reducing your future tax bracket. So, if you aren't careful, you could end up making too big of a Roth IRA conversion; and paying at a high-income-tax bracket to save income taxes that will eventually be taxed at a lower bracket because you will have no—or at least a reduced—RMD lowering your income and lowering your tax bracket.

This pattern is often overlooked by seniors that are in a high tax bracket because of their RMDs. Without carefully making the appropriate financial projections, seniors may conclude it is beneficial to make a large Roth IRA conversion where a more comprehensive look would reveal that a smaller conversion—or more likely, a series of smaller conversions—would be more beneficial.

The General Concern about Raising Tax Rates

Many advisors and clients are making Roth IRA conversions now because they fear tax rates are going up in the future. Please note this is different, though related, to the point proven in Chapter Three that showed it is advantageous for upper income taxpayers to convert now as *we know* those rates are going up. The readers and advisors I am talking about now are saying they have a sense that we are in an increasing tax rate environment. Since Roth IRA conversions are even more favorable considered in the light of increased tax rates, they are inclined to make Roth IRA conversions now.

It is hard to argue with that logic. I tend to be a little more conservative and have at least historically recommended converting the optimal amount according to the law that we know.

What About Changes in the Tax Law that Could Make a Roth IRA Conversion Disadvantageous?

A common concern is: what if changes in the future make converting to a Roth IRA today a mistake?

First, let's address the most common concern. What if Washington decides to tax Roth IRAs later on? Potentially, if they decided to tax Roth IRAs later on, you could be worse off by making a Roth IRA conversion now.

People who have that concern often point out there was never supposed to be tax on your Social Security. Do you remember when they promised us no tax on Social Security? What are they doing now: they are taxing our Social Security! What if we make a Roth IRA conversion, we pay our hard-earned dollars in taxes to make a Roth IRA conversion and then they turn around and say "Too bad, we decided to tax the Roth anyway?" Then you are not only not better off, you are worse off because you don't have the money you paid in taxes. That is a very good objection!

Let me answer that objection to the best of my ability: With the Social Security, we have to ask who was doing the promising about future taxation: the President and Congress. I hate to say it, but they are not very reliable sources—they can say things and mean well but what they say is not necessarily legally enforceable. The proper word describing what you may have heard or read is "dicta." Dictum is non-legally enforceable language muttered by a judge or a politician or a Congressman or even a president.

The rules on Roth IRAs, however, are part of the Internal Revenue Code. They state that if you make a Roth IRA conversion that money and the growth on that money will never be subject to income tax. Could they change the law in the future? Absolutely. Could they change it retroactively for money that is already a Roth IRA when they make a change in the law? They might try, but I would say that would be an ex post facto—after the fact law—that is unconstitutional, and a violation of due process. I believe that you would have a very well funded revolution. I can't tell you that there is zero chance of that, but I think that the odds of a tax increase which would make a Roth IRA conversion even more favorable are much more likely than an ex-post-facto law.

Another potential objection: What if they eliminate the income tax and they go to a sales tax? I think that some type of national sales tax or a value added tax or a use tax is a very real possibility. In my opinion, however, that would be assessed on top of the income tax, not instead of, the income tax.

Finally, they could try to institute a special "excise tax" on Roth IRAs. That is probably the most realistic and legitimate fear. I can't promise they won't. I do think, however, that even if they implement some type of excise tax, it may still have been favorable to make a Roth IRA conversion.

With that being said, I would envision potential changes to the tax law as more of a plus than a minus for reasons that you would want to do a conversion. Not to say there is zero risk, but I would say, that it is worth the risk.

What if You Don't Have the Money to Pay the Tax on the Conversion from Outside the IRA?

Unfortunately, an absence of money outside the IRA is a common problem for the type of readers and clients who gravitate to my material and hire me as an advisor. Many of my clients have a similar background. They married young, perhaps 30 or even 40 years ago or more. At the time they married, neither the husband nor the wife had any significant assets. But, given their work ethic, at least one spouse, historically the husband, would get a job that he stayed with for 30 years or more. Money was never easy during the early years. The salary might have been all right, but it was hard to get ahead. There was the mortgage payments, the car payments, the kids' braces, the kids' college tuition, etc. Saving money was tough. On the other hand, they were prudent people who didn't tend to spend beyond their needs. In addition, they saw the value in contributing to their retirement plan at work, and often contributed the maximum allowed. In addition, they were attracted to companies and organizations that had retirement plans where the employer also made regular contributions to their retirement plans. Thus, they had all money going into a retirement plan, but weren't able to save much money outside the retirement plan. Now they are age 65 or even older and their retirement plan has grown to $1M or more, but they don't have much money outside their retirement plan.

I sometimes joke that I have many clients with a seven-figure IRA, a house, a Honda and that's it. This pattern is especially prevalent for college professors who end up with significant balances in their TIAA-CREF accounts. TIAA-CREF is actually the largest investment provider for employees of non-profit organizations. Though the funds are usually controlled by Internal Revenue Code Section 403(b), it is conceptually similar to its counterpart in the private sector, Internal Revenue Code Section 401(k). What is particularly interesting about the college professors is that many of them did not enter the field for the money but because they wanted to work in their discipline. Their finances up to retirement were relatively simple, but now that they are approaching retirement or are already retired, they face a huge number of choices that they haven't given much thought to throughout their careers.

Though the engineers usually think about money more than do the college professors, they often end up in a similar situation. They also married young, worked hard, scrimped and saved and put in as much as they could afford into their retirement plan. Now many of them have seven-figure retirement plans, a house, and a car or two.

Illustration of the Extreme Situation when there is No Money to Pay the Tax on the Conversion

Let's take the extreme of this pattern: all your money is in the IRA or retirement plan and there is no money outside the retirement plan. If you are in this position and you want to make a Roth IRA conversion, you don't have the money to pay the taxes on the conversion unless you go into the IRA or retirement plan itself to pay the taxes on the conversion.

First let's ignore the impact of increases in the tax rate, the advantages in reducing estate and/or inheritance taxes, and the advantage of not being forced to make a RMD, and then you run the numbers. Theoretically, you should come to a break-even point. That would indicate that given those assumptions, when there is no money outside the retirement plan to pay the taxes, since there is no advantage in making the conversion, you should not do it. That has been the traditional advice and frankly that has been the advice that I usually give. In general, I don't like making a Roth IRA conversion unless we can pay the taxes on the conversion from outside the IRA.

I fear that ending the discussion there is pre-mature. All the assumptions used to get to the conclusion of "no benefit" are not realistic assumptions. If there is a tax increase, if you take into account the savings in estate-and/or inheritance taxes, and if you take into account the advantage of not being forced to take a RMD, then there are advantages to making a conversion—even if you don't have the money to pay the tax on the conversion from outside the IRA.

The right answer, as usual, has some guidelines but it is best to make financial projections on your specific situation before taking a course of action. In general I am far more reluctant to recommend a Roth IRA conversion if we don't have the money to pay the tax from outside the IRA.

A similar but easier question arises when the only money to pay the tax on the conversion comes from highly appreciated assets. You may not want to sell them to get the funds to pay for the conversion. If you do, you will incur capital gains taxes, and it seems difficult to cash in highly appreciated assets, pay capital gains, and use the remaining proceeds to pay the tax on a Roth IRA conversion. I have recommended that strategy, but *I rarely recommend converting unless you have the money from outside the IRA to pay the tax.* The difference is that with the highly appreciated property I am only paying taxes at capital gains rate—which is lower than the ordinary rate and sometimes it isn't all capital gain.

One pattern that sometimes emerges once you have retired is that your RMD, when combined with other sources of income, is more than you need for your living expenses. In that case, most people reading this book will pay tax on the RMD and put the balance into some type of after-tax investment. If that is the case, the after-tax investment could be profitably used to pay the taxes on a Roth IRA conversion.

Finally, you may choose to borrow the money to pay the taxes and hope your investment return on the money you used to pay the taxes on the Roth IRA conversion is more than the interest on the loan. This is classic arbitrage. I would be more excited about using arbitrage in this situation if you had the money to lose. John Bledsoe, author of the **Gospel of Roth,** said he would borrow the money in that situation.

For a minority, but clearly some IRA owners, we would also recommend considering the Roth Launcher strategy that is introduced in Chapter Ten. This would be in addition to what we recommended in this chapter. Please see Chapter Ten for the Roth Launcher strategy—an aggressive, paperwork heavy option that might enhance the benefits of a Roth IRA conversion.

Please note all this analysis is the same for employees who have 401(k) or 403(b) balances and have access to a Roth Designated Account. Please see "What's New" before Chapter 1.

—— $$$ ——

Key Lesson for this Chapter

Since the best time to make a Roth IRA conversion is when tax brackets are lowest, now is the time to evaluate your options and take a proactive approach. A series of small conversions may be your best option. With the sunset of the Bush era tax cuts and the 3.8% Health Care Reform surtax on the horizon, a Roth IRA conversion could be a financially wise decision.

Chapter Eight

How Much and When You Should Convert to a Roth IRA

"Common sense is not so common."

— Voltaire

Main Topics

- Know your numbers and/or seek professional advice—but make sure your advisor is on top of the Roth IRA conversion strategies
- Be very leery about using Roth IRA conversion software
- What to expect during a good Roth IRA conversion fact-finding process
- Factors to consider when converting to a Roth IRA
- A step-by-step guide for making a Roth IRA conversion
- A review of calculating tax rates
- A dynamic duo—using appropriate conversion levels along with the "Roth Launcher" strategy

Key Idea

One of the most important factors to consider when deciding how much to convert to a Roth IRA is the amount of income tax you would pay on different amounts that you are converting. This isn't necessarily an easy issue.

—— $$$ ——

First, let's eliminate, or at least understand, some of the *risks* of a few possible ways to determine how much to convert.

Please note all this analysis is the same for employees who have 401(k) or 403(b) balances and have access to a Roth Designated Account. Please see "What's New" before Chapter 1.

Roth IRA Conversion Software

There are many Roth IRA conversion calculators on the market, both free and available for purchase. Without wanting to implicate them all, I would be extremely cautious about relying on them. There are two basic problems with using Roth IRA conversion software. The first is that the software itself is less than perfect. The second, an unsophisticated consumer using most of the programs I have looked at, including ones offered by some of the largest financial companies, in my opinion could be worse off than if she or he had not used any software. Many of these programs give users a false sense of security that users have determined the appropriate amount to convert. From what I have seen of these programs, the amount is frequently far from optimal. If nothing else, some of the programs offered by some of the largest companies don't take into account what I consider the basics: understanding and measuring wealth in purchasing power rather than by total dollars. Determining an appropriate Roth conversion strategy is an analytical process that is not necessarily driven by a limited number of numerical inputs. Consideration of certain facts and circumstances not even considered by commercial software could change what we consider the appropriate conversion plan. Software can't always give you the right answer.

Frankly, I am spoiled. We have a wonderful CPA/Certified Specialist in Estate Planning, Steve Kohman who heads up our Roth IRA conversion planning department. Steve is a master at making these financial projections. I will attempt to describe what Steve does to offer you some guidance on finding your own advisor in this area and/or for doing it yourself. Please understand, however, that this chapter is not a substitute for seeing an expert in the area.

After a detailed fact finding process and often with input from me and Matt Schwartz, Steve starts making financial projections. He projects future income and tax situations, calculates the tax effects of conversions for current and future years, and develops an overall conversion plan best suited for their unique situation.

Key to this process is the detailed knowledge gathered about the client. This includes an assessment of not only the IRA owner, but also the children, grandchildren, siblings, parents, heirs, and any other beneficiaries. It is important to understanding the clients' needs, goals, and desires as well as potential risks they face in achieving them. Health issues, educational costs, inheritances, tax situations, and the financial security—including income, assets, and liabilities—of all relevant family members have to be taken into consideration. It takes a seasoned professional to assess all factors which may come into play, but the conversion plan that comes out of this process inspires confidence.

It is important to understand a client's goal. We could have two clients with identical finances, tax brackets, etc., but if they have different goals, our recommendations for each of them could be very different. We have many clients who are extremely interested in multiple generation wealth preservation. We have other clients who want to spend their last dollar and die. It is likely we would recommend higher conversions for the client interested in multiple generation wealth transfer, despite the fact that financial circumstances of the two clients are similar. Most clients fall somewhere between these two extremes.

Again, we are lucky because Steve has 20 years of experience and, as I do, he eats, breathes, and dreams about Roth IRA conversions. He reads, writes, studies, and helps me with articles and this book. For us, it is much more than a job or profession—it is a vocation, a way of life.

Obviously, there are other firms out there with genuine Roth conversion expertise. If you find a good professional with Roth IRA expertise, it will be well worth the fee to have him/her make calculations to determine your optimal Roth IRA conversion amount.

Making the calculation on your own certainly has risks. Working with an investment advisor who generalizes that, "Roth IRAs aren't good for older people" or "Roth IRAs are only for people who don't need to spend anything from their

IRA" is also risky. My strongest recommendation is to educate yourself and then look for good help. Reading this book is a good first step.

How to Calculate How Much Money You Should Convert to a Roth IRA Using a Comprehensive Analysis

So, with all those warnings, I will try to explain what I think is the best way to determine how much to convert to a Roth IRA.

I am going to assume that you have either read my basic discussion about tax brackets in Chapter Three, or that you have an excellent understanding of tax brackets. As I indicated in Chapter Three, making a Roth IRA conversion in an amount that would bring you to the top of your existing tax bracket may be an excellent start. I also indicated that there are occasions when it is appropriate to make a larger conversion at the expense of jumping into the next tax bracket, provided you have sufficient after-tax funds to pay the conversion taxes. What I didn't do, however, in Chapter Three is give you as much detail. That comes now.

Please keep in mind two very important factors regarding how much to convert to a Roth IRA:

1. The amount of income tax you will have to pay on the conversion. This tax cost, which can be expressed as a percentage of the converted amount, should be weighed against the ultimate taxes which would be paid on the traditional IRA or retirement plan withdrawals had a conversion not been done.

2. Purchasing power vs. total dollars.

What Assets Are You Allowed to Convert to an IRA?

Throughout the book, I often use the term "IRA and retirement plan" almost as if they are interchangeable. They are conceptually quite similar. Typically, though not always, retirement plans are transferred to IRAs at retirement or service termination. These transfers, typically called Rollovers, are tax-free transfers from one retirement vehicle, typically a 401(k), to another retirement plan vehicle, an IRA. For technical reasons, I prefer the term trustee-to-trustee transfer. I prefer that when this transfer takes place that the trustee of the 401(k) retirement plan make a direct transfer to the trustee or the custodian of the IRA with no withholding tax. For an in-depth discussion of whether you should transfer your 401(k) into an IRA at retirement and the entire rollover vs. trustee-to-trustee transfer, and the special caveats, please see *Retire Secure!* (Wiley, Feb., 2009).

If you are retired or service terminated from an employer, it is usually easy to get the appropriate forms from the employer and complete the trustee-to-trustee transfer to an IRA. (The biggest exception is for TIAA-CREF participants where there is usually a restriction on the transferability of your TIAA account.)

After the transfer to the IRA, you can do whatever you want in terms of making Roth IRA conversions or even setting up separate accounts and then making Roth IRA conversions.

But what if you are still working and the majority of your money is not in an IRA but in an employer-sponsored retirement plan, typically a 401(k) plan or a 403(b) plan for employees of non-profit organizations.

Let's say you want to make a significant Roth IRA conversion but most or all of your retirement assets are in your 401(k) plan at work. Can you take money from your retirement plan if you are still working?

That actually isn't a tax question. The IRS doesn't care. The answer will depend on the rules of your employer's retirement plan. The issue is whether your employer's plan will allow you to transfer money out of the retirement plan to another IRA or even just get access to your money. If you can, then you can do a Roth IRA conversion. If the plan will not let you have access to the money, then you will not be able to do a Roth IRA conversion of that money until you have access to it.

The current law is you can't do a 401(k) conversion to a Roth 401(k), though it has been proposed. We think and hope by the time your read this or shortly thereafter, you will be allowed to make a Roth IRA conversion from a 401(k) or 403(b) to a Roth 401(k) or a Roth 403(b). But remember, even if the law passes, your employer must offer a Roth 401(k) or a Roth 403(b).

More often than not, if you are under 59 and ½, most plans will not give you access to your money unless you retire or become service terminated. If you are over 59 and ½, most plans will give you access to the money you contributed and the growth, but not the employer portion of the retirement plan. If you are 70 and ½ or over, most plans will give you access.

If your employer doesn't offer a Roth 401(k) or a Roth 403(b) or if the proposed law is never passed, the likely eligibility for a Roth IRA conversion follows:

	YES	NO
IRA	X	
401(k), 403(b), or 401(a) Funds:		
Employer's Share		
Before 59 ½ Still Working		X
After 59 ½ Still Working		X
Retired or Service Terminated	X	
Employee's Share:		
Before 59 1/2 – Still Working		X
After 59 1/2 – Still Working	X	
Retired or Service Terminated	X	

NOTE: Employers can choose different options regarding withdrawal options from their plans. This chart, therefore, may not apply to your Plan.

NOTE: This chart will not be as relevant assuming the new law passes (See What's New, #1 before Chapter One). If your employer starts a new Roth designated account, you will be able to make a Roth IRA conversion even if you are working and your money is tied up in your employer's 401(k) or 403(b) plan.

When we make Roth IRA conversion recommendations to clients who are still working, we always determine ahead of time which dollars are eligible for IRA rollover (and hence Roth IRA conversion) and which are not. Sometimes that makes our Roth IRA conversion recommendations easy. For example, let's say we can tell by looking at the assets without doing any calculation that the conversion should be at least $100,000. If there is only a $20,000 IRA and the rest of the retirement assets are inside a retirement plan where our client has no access or ability to convert that money to a Roth IRA, then the recommendation is to do a $20,000 conversion. (Again, unless the new law applies and the employer offers the Roth designated account.)

Please note that the original manuscript included a highly technical section called *How Do You Make the Tax Cost Calculation*. Due to the limited number of readers who would take advantage of that section and because we had to cut somewhere to keep the book a manageable length, we cut that section. If you are interested in that section, please go to www.rothrevolution.com.

Story – Kevin & Debbie Smith: Married Couple in Mid-60s

Biography

Kevin and Debbie Smith just celebrated their 40th wedding anniversary. When they married, they had hardly any money. Their wedding took place at the town Community Center. Kevin found a job as an engineer for Westinghouse, a large company located in Pittsburgh. He started working right after they were married. Kevin's salary was sufficient to meet their needs, but after paying the mortgage, paying the expenses of raising their children, and providing college funding for their children, it was hard to save money. That is why after working 40 years, Kevin and Debbie had only $100,000 in savings. Kevin and Debbie, however, are relatively frugal and they regularly contributed the maximum into their 401(k) plan at work.

Kevin was one of the "grandfathered" employees at Westinghouse to keep his pension in addition to his 401(k) plan. Now, after retirement, money is actually much better than when he was working. Kevin is now 65, and Debbie is 63. Kevin and Debbie can actually afford to spend much more than they do. When I pointed that out, they said they had everything they wanted and were perfectly content to continue spending $70,000/year. They were happy living in their old house with an outdated kitchen and driving their two old cars.

The Smiths are financially conservative and feel uneasy about the future of the country. They have an uneasy feeling that taxes are headed up and though objectively they are in good shape for a secure retirement, they still have some concern for themselves and their children. Their primary goal is to provide for each other as long as they live. Their second goal is to provide the most purchasing power to their children and grandchildren at their death. Their children have jobs, but the parents are concerned about their children's financial security because of the uncertain job market and the fears they have for our economy.

Here are their assets:
    After-tax assets = $100,000
    IRAs and/or retirement plan assets – His = $1,100,000
    Allocation of investments – 75% fixed income; 25% equities
    Home and personal belongings = $300,000
    Other investments and assets = -0-

Income and tax return situation:
    Social Security now being received – His $2,200/mo. and hers
            $1,200/mo. (gross)
    His pension is $42,000/yr. growing with inflation
    Interest income, non-qualified dividends and short-term
            capital gains = $2,000
    Qualified dividend income & long-term capital gains = $2,000
    Standard deduction is used with real-estate tax allowance

Spending needs:
    Currently spending $70,000/yr. including taxes
    No mortgages or loans

$10,000 CONVERSION

Form **1040**	U.S. Individual Income Tax Return	**2009** (99)	IRS Use Only - Do not write or staple in this space.

For the year Jan. 1-Dec. 31, 2009, or other tax year beginning ____ , 2009, ending ____ , 20 ____   OMB No. 1545-0074

Label (See instructions on page 14.)
Use the IRS label. Otherwise, please print or type.

L A B E L   H E R E

Your first name and initial	Last name	Your social security number
KEVIN	SMITH (CASE STUDY)	123 45 6789
If a joint return, spouse's first name and initial	Last name	Spouse's social security number
DEBBIE	SMITH (CASE STUDY)	234 56 7890

Home address (number and street). If you have a P.O. box, see page 14.   Apt. no.

▲ **You must enter** your SSN(s) above. ▲

City, town or post office, state, and ZIP code. If you have a foreign address, see page 14.

PITTSBURGH, PA   15217

Checking a box below will not change your tax or refund.

Presidential Election Campaign ▶ Check here if you, or your spouse if filing jointly, want $3 to go to this fund (see page 14) ▶ ☐ You ☐ Spouse

Filing Status
Check only one box.

1 ☐ Single
2 ☒ Married filing jointly (even if only one had income)
3 ☐ Married filing separately. Enter spouse's SSN above and full name here. ▶
4 ☐ Head of household (with qualifying person). If the qualifying person is a child but not your dependent, enter this child's name here. ▶
5 ☐ Qualifying widow(er) with dependent child (see page 16)

Exemptions

6a ☒ Yourself. If someone can claim you as a dependent, **do not** check box 6a
b ☒ Spouse

c Dependents:		(2) Dependent's social security number	(3) Dependent's relationship to you	(4) ✓ if qualifying child for child tax credit (see page 17)
(1) First name	Last name			

Boxes checked on 6a and 6b   2
No. of children on 6c who:
● lived with you
● did not live with you due to divorce or separation (see page 18)
Dependents on 6c not entered above

If more than four dependents, see page 17 and check here ▶ ☐

Add numbers on lines above ▶ 2

d Total number of exemptions claimed

Income

Attach Form(s) W-2 here. Also attach Forms W-2G and 1099-R if tax was withheld.

If you did not get a W-2, see page 22.

Enclose, but do not attach, any payment. Also, please use Form 1040-V.

7	Wages, salaries, tips, etc. Attach Form(s) W-2	7	
8a	**Taxable interest.** Attach Schedule B if required	8a	2,000.
b	Tax-exempt interest. Do not include on line 8a	8b	
9a	Ordinary dividends. Attach Schedule B if required	9a	2,000.
b	Qualified dividends (see page 22)	9b	2,000.
10	Taxable refunds, credits, or offsets of state and local income taxes	10	
11	Alimony received	11	
12	Business income or (loss). Attach Schedule C or C-EZ	12	
13	Capital gain or (loss). Attach Schedule D if required. If not required, check here ▶ ☐	13	
14	Other gains or (losses). Attach Form 4797	14	
15a	IRA distributions 15a	15b	10,000.
16a	Pensions and annuities 16a	16b	42,000.
17	Rental real estate, royalties, partnerships, S corporations, trusts, etc. Attach Schedule E	17	
18	Farm income or (loss). Attach Schedule F	18	
19	Unemployment compensation in excess of $2,400 per recipient (see page 27)	19	
20a	Social security benefits 20a 40,800. b Taxable amount (see page 27)	20b	33,540.
21	Other income. List type and amount (see page 29)	21	
22	Add the amounts in the far right column for lines 7 through 21. This is your **total income** ▶	22	89,540.

Adjusted Gross Income

23	Educator expenses (see page 29)	23	
24	Certain business expenses of reservists, performing artists, and fee-basis government officials. Attach Form 2106 or 2106-EZ	24	
25	Health savings account deduction. Attach Form 8889	25	
26	Moving expenses. Attach Form 3903	26	
27	One-half of self-employment tax. Attach Schedule SE	27	
28	Self-employed SEP, SIMPLE, and qualified plans	28	
29	Self-employed health insurance deduction (see page 30)	29	
30	Penalty on early withdrawal of savings	30	
31a	Alimony paid b Recipient's SSN ▶	31a	
32	IRA deduction (see page 31)	32	
33	Student loan interest deduction (see page 34)	33	
34	Tuition and fees deduction. Attach Form 8917	34	
35	Domestic production activities deduction. Attach Form 8903	35	
36	Add lines 23 through 31a and 32 through 35	36	
37	Subtract line 36 from line 22. This is your **adjusted gross income** ▶	37	89,540.

910001 10-20-09

LHA **For Disclosure, Privacy Act, and Paperwork Reduction Act Notice, see page 97.**   Form **1040** (2009)

Form 1040 (2009)   **KEVIN & DEBBIE SMITH (CASE STUDY)**   123-45-6789   Page **2**

Tax and Credits	**38**	Amount from line 37 (adjusted gross income)	**38**	89,540.
Standard Deduction for -	**39a**	Check if: ☐ You were born before January 2, 1945, ☐ Blind. ☐ Spouse was born before January 2, 1945, ☐ Blind. } Total boxes checked ▶ 39a		
● People who check any box on line 39a, 39b, or 40b **or** who can be claimed as a dependent.	**b**	If your spouse itemizes on a separate return or you were a dual-status alien, see page 35 and check here ▶ 39b ☐		
	40a	**Itemized deductions** (from Schedule A) **or your standard deduction** (see left margin)	**40a**	12,400.
	b	If you are increasing your standard deduction by certain real estate taxes, new motor vehicle taxes, or a net disaster loss, attach Schedule L and check here (see page 35) ▶ 40b ☒		
	41	Subtract line 40a from line 38	**41**	77,140.
● All others:	**42**	**Exemptions.** If line 38 is $125,100 or less and you did not provide housing to a Midwestern displaced individual, multiply $3,650 by the number on line 6d. Otherwise, see page 37	**42**	7,300.
Single or Married filing separately, $5,700	**43**	**Taxable income.** Subtract line 42 from line 41. If line 42 is more than line 41, enter -0-	**43**	69,840.
Married filing jointly or Qualifying widow(er), $11,400	**44**	**Tax.** Check if any tax is from: **a** ☐ Form(s) 8814 **b** ☐ Form 4972	**44**	9,630.
	45	**Alternative minimum tax.** Attach Form 6251	**45**	
Head of household, $8,350	**46**	Add lines 44 and 45 ▶	**46**	9,630.
	47	Foreign tax credit. Attach Form 1116 if required	47	
	48	Credit for child and dependent care expenses. Attach Form 2441	48	
	49	Education credits from Form 8863, line 29	49	
	50	Retirement savings contributions credit. Attach Form 8880	50	
	51	Child tax credit (see page 42)	51	
	52	Credits from Form: **a** ☐ 8396 **b** ☐ 8839 **c** ☐ 5695	52	
	53	Other credits from Form: **a** ☐ 3800 **b** ☐ 8801 **c** ☐	53	
	54	Add lines 47 through 53. These are your **total credits**	**54**	
	55	Subtract line 54 from line 46. If line 54 is more than line 46, enter -0- ▶	**55**	9,630.
Other Taxes	**56**	Self-employment tax. Attach Schedule SE	**56**	
	57	Unreported social security and Medicare tax from Form: **a** ☐ 4137 **b** ☐ 8919	**57**	
	58	Additional tax on IRAs, other qualified retirement plans, etc. Attach Form 5329 if required	**58**	
	59	Additional taxes: **a** ☐ AEIC **b** ☐ Household employment taxes. Attach Schedule H	**59**	
	60	Add lines 55 through 59. This is your **total tax** ▶	**60**	9,630.
Payments	**61**	Federal income tax withheld from Forms W-2 and 1099	61	
	62	2009 estimated tax payments and amount applied from 2008 return	62	
	63	Making work pay and government retiree credits. Attach Schedule M	63	
If you have a qualifying child, attach Schedule EIC.	**64a**	**Earned income credit (EIC)**	64a	
	b	Nontaxable combat pay election	64b	
	65	Additional child tax credit. Attach Form 8812	65	
	66	Refundable education credit from Form 8863, line 16	66	
	67	First-time homebuyer credit. Attach Form 5405	67	
	68	Amount paid with request for extension to file (see page 72)	68	
	69	Excess social security and tier 1 RRTA tax withheld (see page 72)	69	
	70	Credits from Form: **a** ☐ 2439 **b** ☐ 4136 **c** ☐ 8801 **d** ☐ 8885	70	
	71	Add lines 61, 62, 63, 64a, and 65 through 70. These are your **total payments** ▶	**71**	
Refund	**72**	If line 71 is more than line 60, subtract line 60 from line 71. This is the amount you **overpaid**	**72**	
Direct deposit? See page 73 and fill in 73b, 73c, and 73d, or Form 8888.	**73a**	Amount of line 72 you want **refunded to you.** If Form 8888 is attached, check here ▶ ☐	73a	
	b	Routing number ▶ **c** Type: ☐ Checking ☐ Savings **d** Account number ▶		
	74	Amount of line 72 you want **applied to your 2010 estimated tax** ▶	74	
Amount You Owe	**75**	**Amount you owe.** Subtract line 71 from line 60. For details on how to pay, see page 74 ▶	**75**	9,630.
	76	Estimated tax penalty (see page 74)	76	
Third Party Designee		Do you want to allow another person to discuss this return with the IRS (see page 75)? ☐ **Yes. Complete the following.** ☐ **No** Designee's name ▶ Phone no. ▶ Personal identification number (PIN) ▶		
Sign Here Joint return? See page 15. Keep a copy for your records.		Under penalties of perjury, I declare that I have examined this return and accompanying schedules and statements, and to the best of my knowledge and belief, they are true, correct, and complete. Declaration of preparer (other than taxpayer) is based on all information of which preparer has any knowledge. Your signature Date Your occupation Daytime phone number Spouse's signature. If a joint return, **both** must sign. Date Spouse's occupation		
Paid Preparer's Use Only		Preparer's signature ▶ Date Check if self-employed ☐ Preparer's SSN or PTIN Firm's name (or yours if self-employed), address, and ZIP code ▶ EIN Phone no.		

910002 10-20-09

Form 1040 **U.S. Individual Income Tax Return** **2009** (99) IRS Use Only - Do not write or staple in this space.

NO CONVERSION

OMB No. 1545-0074

Label (See instructions on page 14.) Use the IRS label. Otherwise, please print or type.		

Your first name and initial: **KEVIN** Last name: **SMITH (CASE STUDY)** Your social security number: **123 45 6789**

If a joint return, spouse's first name and initial: **DEBBIE** Last name: **SMITH (CASE STUDY)** Spouse's social security number: **234 56 7890**

Home address (number and street). If you have a P.O. box, see page 14. Apt. no.

You **must** enter ▲ your SSN(s) above. ▲

City, town or post office, state, and ZIP code. If you have a foreign address, see page 14. **PITTSBURGH, PA   15217**

Checking a box below will not change your tax or refund.

Presidential Election Campaign ▶ Check here if you, or your spouse if filing jointly, want $3 to go to this fund (see page 14) ▶   ☐ You ☐ Spouse

Filing Status
Check only one box.

1 ☐ Single
2 ☒ Married filing jointly (even if only one had income)
3 ☐ Married filing separately. Enter spouse's SSN above and full name here. ▶
4 ☐ Head of household (with qualifying person). If the qualifying person is a child but not your dependent, enter this child's name here. ▶
5 ☐ Qualifying widow(er) with dependent child (see page 16)

Exemptions

6a ☒ Yourself. If someone can claim you as a dependent, **do not** check box 6a
b ☒ Spouse

Boxes checked on 6a and 6b: **2**

c Dependents:

(1) First name Last name	(2) Dependent's social security number	(3) Dependent's relationship to you	(4)✔ if qualifying child for child tax credit (see page 17)

If more than four dependents, see page 17 and check here ▶ ☐

No. of children on 6c who:
● lived with you ___
● did not live with you due to divorce or separation (see page 18) ___
Dependents on 6c not entered above ___
Add numbers on lines above ▶ **2**

d Total number of exemptions claimed

Income

Attach Form(s) W-2 here. Also attach Forms W-2G and 1099-R if tax was withheld.

If you did not get a W-2, see page 22.

Enclose, but do not attach, any payment. Also, please use Form 1040-V.

7	Wages, salaries, tips, etc. Attach Form(s) W-2	7	
8a	Taxable interest. Attach Schedule B if required	8a	2,000.
b	Tax-exempt interest. **Do not** include on line 8a	8b	
9a	Ordinary dividends. Attach Schedule B if required	9a	2,000.
b	Qualified dividends (see page 22)	9b	2,000.
10	Taxable refunds, credits, or offsets of state and local income taxes	10	
11	Alimony received	11	
12	Business income or (loss). Attach Schedule C or C-EZ	12	
13	Capital gain or (loss). Attach Schedule D if required. If not required, check here ▶ ☐	13	
14	Other gains or (losses). Attach Form 4797	14	
15a	IRA distributions 15a	b Taxable amount 15b	
16a	Pensions and annuities 16a	b Taxable amount 16b	42,000.
17	Rental real estate, royalties, partnerships, S corporations, trusts, etc. Attach Schedule E	17	
18	Farm income or (loss). Attach Schedule F	18	
19	Unemployment compensation in excess of $2,400 per recipient (see page 27)	19	
20a	Social security benefits 20a 40,800.	b Taxable amount (see page 27) 20b	25,040.
21	Other income. List type and amount (see page 29)	21	
22	Add the amounts in the far right column for lines 7 through 21. This is your **total income** ▶	22	71,040.

Adjusted Gross Income

23	Educator expenses (see page 29)	23	
24	Certain business expenses of reservists, performing artists, and fee-basis government officials. Attach Form 2106 or 2106-EZ	24	
25	Health savings account deduction. Attach Form 8889	25	
26	Moving expenses. Attach Form 3903	26	
27	One-half of self-employment tax. Attach Schedule SE	27	
28	Self-employed SEP, SIMPLE, and qualified plans	28	
29	Self-employed health insurance deduction (see page 30)	29	
30	Penalty on early withdrawal of savings	30	
31a	Alimony paid b Recipient's SSN ▶	31a	
32	IRA deduction (see page 31)	32	
33	Student loan interest deduction (see page 34)	33	
34	Tuition and fees deduction. Attach Form 8917	34	
35	Domestic production activities deduction. Attach Form 8903	35	
36	Add lines 23 through 31a and 32 through 35	36	
37	Subtract line 36 from line 22. This is your **adjusted gross income** ▶	37	71,040.

910001 10-20-09

LHA For Disclosure, Privacy Act, and Paperwork Reduction Act Notice, see page 97.

Form **1040** (2009)

Form 1040 (2009)   KEVIN & DEBBIE SMITH (CASE STUDY)   123-45-6789   Page **2**

Tax and	38	Amount from line 37 (adjusted gross income)	38	71,040.

Tax and Credits

Standard Deduction for -
• People who check any box on line 39a, 39b, or 40b **or** who can be claimed as a dependent.

39a	Check if: ☐ **You** were born before January 2, 1945, ☐ Blind. ☐ **Spouse** was born before January 2, 1945, ☐ Blind. } **Total boxes checked** ► 39a
b	If your spouse itemizes on a separate return or you were a dual-status alien, see page 35 and check here ► 39b ☐
40a	**Itemized deductions** (from Schedule A) **or your standard deduction** (see left margin) 40a	12,400.
b	If you are increasing your standard deduction by certain real estate taxes, new motor vehicle taxes, or a net disaster loss, attach Schedule L and check here (see page 35) ► 40b ☒
41	Subtract line 40a from line 38 41	58,640.

• All others:

Single or Married filing separately, $5,700

Married filing jointly or Qualifying widow(er), $11,400

Head of household, $8,350

42	**Exemptions.** If line 38 is $125,100 or less and you did not provide housing to a Midwestern displaced individual, multiply $3,650 by the number on line 6d. Otherwise, see page 37 42	7,300.
43	**Taxable income.** Subtract line 42 from line 41. If line 42 is more than line 41, enter -0- 43	51,340.
44	**Tax.** Check if any tax is from: a ☐ Form(s) 8814 b ☐ Form 4972 44	6,564.
45	**Alternative minimum tax.** Attach Form 6251 45	
46	Add lines 44 and 45 ► 46	6,564.
47	Foreign tax credit. Attach Form 1116 if required 47	
48	Credit for child and dependent care expenses. Attach Form 2441 48	
49	Education credits from Form 8863, line 29 49	
50	Retirement savings contributions credit. Attach Form 8880 50	
51	Child tax credit (see page 42) 51	
52	Credits from Form: a ☐ 8396 b ☐ 8839 c ☐ 5695 52	
53	Other credits from Form: a ☐ 3800 b ☐ 8801 c ☐ 53	
54	Add lines 47 through 53. These are your **total credits** 54	
55	Subtract line 54 from line 46. If line 54 is more than line 46, enter -0- ► 55	6,564.

Other Taxes

56	Self-employment tax. Attach Schedule SE 56	
57	Unreported social security and Medicare tax from Form: a ☐ 4137 b ☐ 8919 57	
58	Additional tax on IRAs, other qualified retirement plans, etc. Attach Form 5329 if required 58	
59	Additional taxes: a ☐ AEIC payments b ☐ Household employment taxes. Attach Schedule H 59	
60	Add lines 55 through 59. This is your **total tax** ► 60	6,564.

Payments

If you have a qualifying child, attach Schedule EIC.

61	Federal income tax withheld from Forms W-2 and 1099 61	
62	2009 estimated tax payments and amount applied from 2008 return 62	
63	Making work pay and government retiree credits. Attach Schedule M 63	
64a	**Earned income credit (EIC)** 64a	
b	Nontaxable combat pay election 64b	
65	Additional child tax credit. Attach Form 8812 65	
66	Refundable education credit from Form 8863, line 16 66	
67	First-time homebuyer credit. Attach Form 5405 67	
68	Amount paid with request for extension to file (see page 72) 68	
69	Excess social security and tier 1 RRTA tax withheld (see page 72) 69	
70	Credits from Form: a ☐ 2439 b ☐ 4136 c ☐ 8801 d ☐ 8885 70	
71	Add lines 61, 62, 63, 64a, and 65 through 70. These are your **total payments** ► 71	

Refund

Direct deposit? See page 73 and fill in 73b, 73c, and 73d, or Form 8888.

72	If line 71 is more than line 60, subtract line 60 from line 71. This is the amount you **overpaid** 72	
73a	Amount of line 72 you want **refunded to you.** If Form 8888 is attached, check here ► ☐ 73a	
b	Routing number ► c Type: ☐ Checking ☐ Savings d Account number ►	
74	Amount of line 72 you want **applied to your 2010 estimated tax** ► 74	

Amount You Owe

75	**Amount you owe.** Subtract line 71 from line 60. For details on how to pay, see page 74 ► 75	6,564.
76	Estimated tax penalty (see page 74) 76	

Third Party Designee

Do you want to allow another person to discuss this return with the IRS (see page 75)? ☐ **Yes.** Complete the following. ☐ **No**

Designee's name ►   Phone no. ►   Personal identification number (PIN) ►

Sign Here

Joint return? See page 15. Keep a copy for your records.

Under penalties of perjury, I declare that I have examined this return and accompanying schedules and statements, and to the best of my knowledge and belief, they are true, correct, and complete. Declaration of preparer (other than taxpayer) is based on all information of which preparer has any knowledge.

Your signature	Date	Your occupation	Daytime phone number
Spouse's signature. If a joint return, **both** must sign.	Date	Spouse's occupation	

Paid Preparer's Use Only

Preparer's signature	Date	Check if self-employed ☐	Preparer's SSN or PTIN
Firm's name (or yours if self-employed), address, and ZIP code ►		EIN	
		Phone no.	

910002
10-20-09

Analysis, Discussion and Recommendation

The Smiths should consider delaying their Social Security and making a Roth IRA conversion before they reach age 70. Please see Chapter Twelve.

The long-term outlook for their tax situation is similar to today's tax situation except that their income will include RMDs from the IRA. Their income currently is indexed for inflation, so they will not end up in a lower tax bracket over time. Without conversions, their RMD income will be $50,000 – $70,000 when they start in 2014. They will be in the 25% or higher tax bracket in the future, with or without RMD income. With the 2011 tax increase, the 28% tax bracket is more likely.

Our basic Roth conversion illustrations show it is good to convert to a Roth if you pay 28% tax on the conversion and end up in the 25% tax bracket, as long as you have enough money in the after-tax environment to pay the taxes on the conversion. Based on this and these calculations, it makes reasonable sense to convert $140,000 now and face up to paying an additional $38,266 of tax (27.33%) on the conversion.

In 2011 they could do another $140,000 of conversions and pay another approximately $38,000 of tax on the conversion. There are still five years to convert prior to RMD income and even after that, there could still be conversions done in the 28% tax bracket. Because they spend about what their income is and they have only about $100,000 of after-tax funds, they may be limited to doing only another one to two conversions after 2010. The Roth Launcher strategy would likely add options for them. (See Chapter Ten).

Converting $140,000 in 2010 results in about 1/4 of the traditional IRA converted. If they converted much more than that, they might run out of after-tax money. Additional conversions would not be nearly as valuable. Borrowing the tax money to do more conversions and paying it back from remaining traditional RMD income after age 70 may be a good idea in some cases. Another reason to convert more is that their children are doing well and appear to be in the 25%+ tax bracket for the long term.

Kevin & Debbie Smith
2010 IRA Conversion Planning

RECOMMENDATION: For year 2010 convert $140,000 to top of 28% bracket

Assumptions for 2010 - Nothing unusual

Estimated tax situation for 2009 (using 2008 rates):

Roth Conversion Amount	Total Federal AMT & Income Tax	FYI AMT Included	Overall Tax on the Conversion	Overall Conversion Tax %	Taxable Income	Incremental Taxable Income	Incremental Income Tax	Incremental Conversion	!! FOCUS HERE!! Incremental Conversion Tax %	Bracket - Notes
0	6,564	0	0		51,340					Some of SS not taxable
5,000	7,951	0	1,387	27.74%	60,590	9,250	1,387	5,000	27.74%	SS becoming increasingly taxable, still in 15% TB, QDs still not taxed
10,000	9,630	0	3,066	30.66%	70,640	10,050	1,679	5,000	33.58%	SS almost fully taxable, just out of the 15% TB and into the 25% TB, QDs now taxed at 15%
20,000	12,716	0	6,152	30.76%	80,980	10,340	3,086	10,000	30.86%	SS now fully, 25% TB, QDs now taxed at 15% taxed
70,000	24,920	0	18,356	26.22%	130,980	50,000	12,204	50,000	24.41%	Near top of 25% tax bracket
140,000	44,278	0	37,714	26.94%	200,980	70,000	19,358	70,000	27.65%	Near top of 28% tax bracket
296,000	97,712	1,644	91,148	30.79%	360,114	159,134	53,434	156,000	34.25%	Near top of 33% bracket - some phaseouts and AMT
550,000	184,657	0	178,093	32.38%	613,414	253,300	86,945	254,000	34.23%	Maximum 35% bracket
1,100,000	377,157	0	370,593	33.69%	1,163,414	550,000	192,500	550,000	35.00%	Maximum 35% bracket

Gifting Recommendations

I also offered additional advice to the Smiths on the issue of gifting. They should be thinking about making gifts. Debbie was most receptive to that idea. I suspect Kevin thought I should keep my mouth shut, but he really knew I was giving appropriate conservative advice. Using a safe withdrawal rate (the amount of money they could safely withdraw from their portfolio expressed as a percentage of their portfolio) of 4%, (another subject for another day) they could afford to be withdrawing $44,000/yr. from their portfolio ($1,100,000 times 4%). Since they aren't using any of that money for their spending, they should consider a gifting program.

I like three types of gifts for grandparents.

1. Gifts to children for current needs

2. Second-to-die life insurance for children for long-term wealth preservation and tax efficiency

3. Education funds (Section 529 plans) for grandchildren (which they could get back if they needed it)

A total gift package of $15,000 per year split evenly between the three types of gifts mentioned would still give them a cushion of $25,000/yr. They decided to buy a small second-to-die life insurance policy that costs $5,000/year; they bought $5,000/year of Section 529 plans; and they gave their kids $5,000/year to do whatever the kids wanted to do with the money. This is actually a conservative recommendation. If times ever became hard, they could stop gifting to their children and stop making education gifts for their grandchildren.

Estate-Planning Documents

They also had traditional A/B wills—which really wasn't appropriate. The traditional documents would have restricted the surviving spouse, as well as reducing options for their children. We recommended Lange's Cascading Beneficiary Plan™ to provide flexibility for the surviving spouse and the children. Please see Chapter Seventeen.

In the Final Analysis...

The Smiths did follow our Roth IRA conversion recommendation, but didn't do the Roth Launcher discussed in Chapter Ten. They ended up compromising and making a 10% shift of their portfolio to stocks. They also implemented a gifting program of $7,500/year.

Over all, I think it was a good result for the Smiths. They will be more secure with the Roth conversions and their children and grandchildren will be hundreds of thousands—perhaps millions—of dollars better off because of the Smiths' Roth conversions. The gifts will allow the children to enjoy some of the money while they are still young and need it more. The small second-to-die life insurance policy will guarantee a good rate of return investment that will be free of income taxes and estate taxes. The change in the wills and beneficiary forms will provide many more options for the surviving spouse and the children.

—— $$$ ——

Key Lesson for this Chapter

The key to knowing when and how much to convert is based ultimately on tax brackets and goals. A thorough analysis would include information about you and your family.

Chapter Nine

Converting Non-deductible IRAs and After-Tax Dollars in Retirement Plans without Having to Pay Any Taxes

"There may be liberty and justice for all, but there are tax breaks only for some."
— Martin A. Sullivan

Main Topics

- The five groups of people who can convert to a Roth IRA tax-free
- What to do when after-tax dollars are inside your IRA
- A loophole for "getting around" the aggregation rules
- Why you may need to establish your own 401(k) plan

Please note this chapter is important for you only if:

1. *You have after-tax dollars in your retirement plan or if you have non-deductible IRAs.*

2. *If you have earned income and your total income is more than $177,000 for married filing joint returns and $120,000 for single in which case, you should consider non-deductible IRAs.*

If the answer to #1 and #2 are no, you can skip this chapter.

If you don't know if you have after-tax dollars in your retirement plan, you probably don't. To qualify, you must have had income so high that you were not allowed to deduct your entire contribution to your retirement plan or had been on the highest earnings level. If you think you might, try to find out.

Key Idea

The Tax Code requires you to aggregate all of your IRA money to determine how much of it is taxed if you do a Roth IRA conversion. So, if you have a $1,000,000 IRA within which is $50,000 in after-tax money (how this gets there will be explained), you can't convert the $50,000 and ignore the $950,000. There is, however, a way around the rule.

—— $$$ ——

First, this chapter is one of the harder ones in the book. It describes a somewhat complex action plan for Roth IRA conversions. Though it isn't easy, the rewards for those who can do it, and will do it, could be worth 10,000 times the cost of this book—or more.

> It is possible under certain conditions to make a Roth IRA conversion without having to pay the tax.

It is possible under certain conditions to make a Roth IRA conversion without having to pay the tax. You can do this if you meet certain requirements and have after-tax dollars inside your retirement plan or if you have its close cousin, non-deductible IRAs or your income is too high to contribute to a Roth IRA. In practice, taking an asset that is growing tax-deferred and turning it into an asset that is growing tax-free—without paying any tax on the transaction—almost seems too good to be true. But, given the right conditions, you can do it.

Please note that conceptually after-tax dollars in a retirement plan is similar to a non-deductible IRA. With a regular retirement plan or a traditional IRA, you received a deduction on the contribution made to the retirement plan or the IRA. The money grows tax-deferred and upon withdrawal, you have to pay tax on the entire distribution. With a non-deductible IRA or after-tax dollars inside a retirement plan, you contribute to a retirement plan or an IRA but you do not receive a deduction. The money grows income-tax deferred. When you or your heirs withdraw the money, a portion of it is tax free, the return of your capital. A portion of the distribution is taxable, which represents the growth on the money between your contribution and your withdrawal.

With a Roth IRA, you don't get a deduction, but the money grows tax free. A Roth IRA is always preferable to a non-deductible IRA. If you can convert your non-deductible IRA or after-tax dollars in your retirement plan to a Roth IRA without having to pay the tax, that has to be a splendid accomplishment.

Usually when you make a Roth IRA conversion, you are paying tax up front in order to achieve income tax free growth on IRA and retirement plan assets in the future. Even though making a Roth IRA conversion and paying the tax is often the indicated and recommended course of action, it isn't nearly as much fun as making a Roth IRA conversion and not having to pay the tax.

Working individuals who make too much to qualify for a Roth IRA may contribute to a non-deductible IRA. Before Roth IRAs existed, many taxpayers contributed to their IRAs but their income was too high for them to claim a deduction. The result is many of you reading this book will have non-deductible IRAs. These non-deductible IRA owners and individuals who have accumulated after-tax assets in their employer-sponsored retirement accounts may qualify for an unparalleled opportunity to convert the growth on those assets *from tax-deferred to tax-free.*

Five groups of people can benefit from the conversion strategy set forth in this chapter. Please note you may fit in one or more of the five categories listed below:

- Wage earners who make too much money to qualify for a Roth IRA contribution.

- Active employees with after-tax assets in qualified retirement plans, such as 401(k)s and 403(b)s.

- Active employees with after-tax dollars in their IRA.

- Retired employees who can take a lump-sum distribution from a qualified plan or tax-sheltered annuity that includes after-tax dollars.

- Retired employees with after-tax dollars in their IRAs (but who can create some earned income).

Please note: the following analysis does not address the material in the sequence listed above. All five of the situations are covered, but they are arranged in a progression that allows the reader to build on the concepts as they evolve.

Converting Non-deductible IRAs to Roth IRAs

The first concept to understand is: if you have a straightforward non-deductible IRA, you can make a Roth IRA conversion of that non-deductible IRA without having to pay the tax. Let's say you contributed $5,000 to a non-deductible IRA (now you are allowed to contribute $6,000 if you are 50 or over) and there was no growth and that was the only IRA you had. You could make a Roth IRA conversion of that $5,000 without having to pay the tax. Why would you want to do that? You would be converting an investment that is growing tax-deferred to an investment that is growing tax free. Good idea. The non-deductible $5,000, if you did not make a Roth IRA conversion, would still be tax free when you withdraw it. If we add growth back into the picture, however, all growth on the $5,000 would be taxable. If there were no growth on the $5,000 and you converted the non-deductible IRA to a Roth IRA, any future growth would be tax free.

A much more common situation for your non-deductible IRA, however, is that it is mixed with your traditional or regular IRA. Please keep in mind the growth on a non-deductible IRA is taxable and for our purposes is considered a deductible or traditional IRA. If you have both non-deductible IRAs and deductible or traditional IRAs, you have to worry about the pro-ration rules. But we will show you how in some situations, you can get around the pro-ration rules.

But, first let's talk about the pro-ration rule if you have a non-deductible IRA and a deductible IRA (which could be in the same account). For example, let's say you made a $5,000 contribution to a non-deductible IRA and in ten years that IRA is worth $8,000. Conceptually you have a non-deductible IRA of $5,000 and a traditional IRA of $3,000. If you wanted to withdraw that $8,000, the $5,000 would be deemed a return of capital and the $3,000 would be considered taxable.

If you wanted to make a Roth IRA conversion of the $8,000, you would have to pay taxes on the $3,000 growth but the $5,000 portion could be converted to a Roth IRA without tax.

What we will be working on in this chapter is how to isolate the $5,000, make a Roth IRA conversion, and leave the $3,000 in the tax-deferred environment.

In addition to having after-tax dollars inside your IRA (or non-deductible IRA), it is also possible to have after-tax dollars inside your retirement plan.

After-Tax Dollars Inside Your Retirement Plan

It is not unusual for me to meet a new client who has $1,000,000 in his retirement plan and of that $1,000,000; $50,000 is after-tax or non-deductible. There were two main ways this happened.

Money was contributed to certain plans and the IRS did not allow a tax deduction for the contribution—but did allow tax-deferred growth.

Your retirement plan allowed you to contribute additional money to your retirement plan beyond the amount the IRS would allow you to deduct. Today, the IRS is far more generous and will allow contributions to a 401(k) plan of $16,500 or $22,000 if you are 50 years old or older. In year 2002, the maximum contribution that was deductible was $11,000/year.

Despite the $11,000/year deductible limitation, employees were often able to contribute up to 15% of their salary into their retirement plan or 401(k). Assume an employee made $100,000 a year. A contribution of 15% of this salary equals $15,000 and exceeds the $11,000 limit on tax-deferred contributions to 40l(k) plan by $4,000. The employee wishing to shelter the most money allowed would contribute $11,000 on a pre-tax basis (which would not be included in his W-2 for federal income tax purposes), and $4,000 after-tax, which would be included in his W-2 income. Though the employee did not get a tax deduction for the $4,000, the money did grow tax deferred. The principal though, the $4,000, is considered after-tax dollars in a retirement plan.

After-Tax Dollars Inside Your IRA

There are two ways that you may have after-tax dollars in your IRA. The first is that you made contributions to a non-deductible IRA. The second is that you made contributions of after-tax dollars in your retirement plan and at some point rolled that retirement plan into your IRA.

The after-tax dollars in the 401(k) or in the IRA is considered to have basis—money you contributed to a retirement plan that did not receive a tax deduction. (Most IRA owners—even those with after-tax dollars in their account—have a much greater portion of their funds in the deductible portion.) If we go back to the example at the beginning of the chapter of the $5,000 in a non-deductible IRA, we would say the value of the IRA was equal to the basis. If all your IRAs had a basis equal to the fair market value of the IRA (which would mean you essentially had no growth) you would be allowed to make a Roth IRA conversion from that non-deductible IRA without having to pay the tax.

The real advantage of this Roth IRA conversion is that the Roth IRA will grow ***income tax free,*** not ***income tax deferred,*** as it would if you did nothing. In addition, there are the additional benefits that come with a Roth IRA, i.e., no required minimum distributions at 70½ and the extended advantage of continued tax-free growth on an inherited Roth IRA. The chart below shows the advantage in total spending power which results from making a $50,000 Roth IRA conversion of a non-deductible IRA with $50,000 basis and assuming there is no income tax on the transaction.

Figure 12

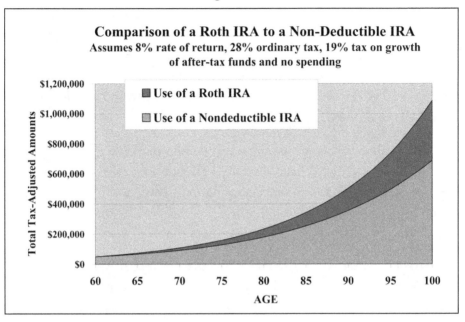

Basically, in the unlikely event that all you have in an IRA is a non-deductible IRA of $50,000 and you make a Roth IRA conversion of $50,000 of a non-deductible IRA, you will be better off by $400,000 in 40 years. Even if you are not around in 40 years, your children and/or grandchildren will be, and they will enjoy tax-free—as opposed to tax-deferred—growth. Unless there are extenuating circumstances, all those who qualify and have $50,000 or more in their retirement plan, should make the conversion. Because there are some complications and administrative burdens with the conversion, it would not likely be worth the time and trouble if there were only a small amount, say $5,000 of after-tax dollars inside the retirement plan.

How to Qualify to Make a Tax-Free Roth IRA Conversion If You Have Both After-Tax and Pre-Tax in Your IRA

Now we address the next issue of how to make a Roth IRA conversion of after-tax dollars inside a retirement plan and/or an IRA. Let's assume now that you have the much more likely scenario where some of the money in your IRA is non-deductible but some of the money in your IRA is traditional.

First, let's start with what you are not allowed to do that I bet you want to do. Let's assume you have some non-deductible IRA money that you could convert to a Roth IRA for free—but you also have some traditional IRA money that you would have to pay tax on if you converted that money. I bet what you would like to do is to convert only the after-tax portion of your IRA to a Roth IRA, not paying the tax; and then be left with a Roth IRA and a traditional IRA and go your merry way.

The problem is that you are not allowed to do that. You must combine all your IRAs (including SEP and Simple IRAs) and take them all into account when making a Roth IRA conversion because you are subject to the pro-ration rules.

Let's say you have a $50,000 IRA and of that $50,000, $40,000 is traditional and $10,000 is after-tax or basis. You could make a Roth IRA conversion of the entire $50,000 and have to add only $40,000 to your income. That would be better than paying tax on $50,000, but it still isn't ideal. You could convert $25,000 to a Roth IRA and pay tax on $20,000. You would have to pay tax on $20,000 because you would have to pro-rate your entire IRA and find that 80% of it is pre-tax. If you convert $25,000 then you multiply that amount by 80%. Thus, you have to pay taxes on $20,000.

Again, not bad, but not ideal. Let's say you have one non-deductible IRA of $10,000 and another deductible IRA of $40,000. Could you make a Roth IRA conversion of the $10,000 without paying tax and leave the $40,000 deductible IRA alone? No. Good try. The aggregation rules say you must aggregate all your IRAs, using year-end IRA values, including conversion and rollover amounts, for the purpose of how much tax you have to pay on the traditional portion that is being converted to a Roth IRA.

No matter how many IRA accounts you may have, the Tax Code considers all your IRA money to be in "one pot." Any already taxed money in the IRA environment is your basis, regardless of which specific IRA account contains the after-tax money. For every dollar removed from the IRA environment, the ratio of your total after-tax IRA basis to your total tax-deferred IRAs (year-end values plus the conversion amounts) determines the proportion of the distribution that is taxed.

So, can we get around the aggregation rules? Fortunately, there is a way.

I hesitate to reveal this loophole for fear that someone from the IRS may be reading this and attempt to get Congress to close it. (I think essentially the transaction I describe in this chapter is a loophole the IRS never intended). Other IRA experts including Natalie Choate, Bob Keebler and Gary Picker—and I am sure others—have all written on this topic and the IRS still hasn't closed the loophole. Let's hope they never do. At a minimum, let's hope you take advantage of the loophole and if they close it later on, you will be "grandfathered" because you took advantage of it while it was still allowed. In other words, if they change the law for future conversions, the current law will apply to your conversion if you make it before they change the law.

There are two scenarios if you have $10,000 of non-deductible IRA or basis and $40,000 traditional. The first is if you are still working.

For Readers Who Are Still Working and Also Have a Non-deductible IRA

Let's start making our assumptions:

1.   You are still working.

2.   You have a 401(k) plan at work.

3.   Your 401(k) plan will accept an IRA rollover (that is to say can roll your IRA into your 401(k) plan).

But let's also assume that:

4.   Your 401(k) plan states it will not accept after-tax dollars in your IRA for the rollover. It will accept only the traditional or pre-tax dollars in your IRA.

These are all relatively common provisions.

So, let's go back to our example where you have a $50,000 IRA with $40,000 pre-tax and $10,000 after-tax. You take the $40,000 deductible portion of your IRA and roll it into 401(k) plan at work, because that is all the 401(k) will accept. (Though there are some differences, the 401(k) has more or less the same rules as the IRA in terms of long-term, tax-deferred growth.) The $10,000 balance represents the after-tax dollars in your IRA. Now you go to make a Roth IRA conversion of your IRA. Since that is the only money in your IRA, you don't have to worry about the pro-ration rules. In addition, since that is the only IRA, you don't have to worry about the aggregation rules. You make the $10,000 Roth conversion and pay no taxes because your $10,000 IRA has a $10,000 basis. Now, it would seem fair if the IRS made you consider both your IRA and your 401(k) for the purposes of the pro-ration rules and the aggregation rules. But they don't, and that's what gives us this splendid opportunity. We just made a $10,000 Roth IRA conversion of after-tax dollars in our IRA and didn't have to pay any tax even though we started with an IRA that had both *pre- and after-tax dollars*. Is this a great country or what?

To be fair, I have to mention the potential disadvantage of this plan. If you prefer to make your own investments, or you have a money manager who you think can outperform the 401(k), you are giving up control. After the transaction, that $40,000 will be held in your 401(k) plan at work. Presumably, your 401(k) plan will offer you a number of options, but you will not have the entire universe of possibilities that you would if the money were in an IRA.

At some point after the conversion, however, you could consider rolling money from your 401(k) back into an IRA.

What If You Are Retired?

What if you are already retired from your main job and have rolled your 401(k) to an IRA? Let's say you have a $1,000,000 IRA and $950,000 is pre-tax and $50,000 is after-tax. First, let's look at your choices. You could roll the $1,000,000 into a Roth IRA and add $950,000 to your income. That could be good in some situations, but probably not ideal for most situations. You could roll $500,000 into a Roth IRA and using the pro-ration rules, pay taxes on $475,000. Also, not ideal. You are not allowed to take the $50,000 and roll it into a separate IRA and make a Roth IRA conversion of that money and ignore the other $950,000 because that would be a violation of the aggregation rules.

Is there a loophole for you? Maybe.

What you need to do is to establish your own 401(k) plan. If you had your own 401(k) plan, then you could execute the same strategy the employee with a 401(k) did as shown in the previous section. He was able to roll the pre-tax dollars into his 401(k) at work and isolate the after-tax dollars in his IRA, avoid the pro-ration and aggregation rules and make the Roth IRA conversion for free. In this example, however, I said that I assumed that you were retired from your main job.

What I am suggesting is that even though you may be retired from your main job, you could still use the same strategy if you set up your own one-person 401(k). The difference with this example and the one using the company 401(k) plan is that instead of using the 401(k) plan at work, you are using a 401(k) plan that you set up for yourself. Many self-employed people who want to make contributions to a retirement plan set up a SEP or Simplified Employee Pension plan. A one-person 401(k) is close to a SEP but has some additional advantages. For our purposes here, a SEP will not work (because it is considered an IRA under the aggregation rules), and you would need to set up your own one-person 401(k) plan.

The biggest problem you are likely to face in setting up your own one-person 401(k) is that you need to have earned income. If you are completely retired and will never have earned income again, this entire plan won't work. Let's assume, however, that there is some way for you to legitimately have some earned income. Perhaps you could do some consulting for your former employer on a contract basis, not as a W-2 employee. Perhaps you could help out at the golf course. Perhaps you could do some work for a family business. Perhaps you could start your own little business. I have clients who have children with businesses and they consult with or do actual work for their children's businesses. It is important, however, for our purposes that you are paid as an independent contractor. You will then report your income on your tax return, most likely with a Schedule C on U.S. Form 1040—not with a W-2. You don't need much earned income. Even with $10,000 (after deductions) you can establish your own one-person 401(k) plan. Of course, it is true that you could make an additional retirement plan contribution to the one-person 401(k) plan. You could even have a one-person 401(k) plan with a Roth component known as a Roth 401(k) plan. What I am more interested in, however, is that you choose a one-person 401(k) plan that specifically allows a rollover of pre-tax or traditional IRA dollars but will not accept a rollover of after-tax dollars from the IRA. That isn't too difficult to find in practice.

Now you roll over the $950,000 of your pre-tax or traditional IRA into your one-person 401(k) plan. You are left with the $50,000 after-tax dollars inside the IRA. You then make a Roth IRA conversion of that $50,000 and since that $50,000 has basis and you aren't subject to either the pro-ration rules or the aggregation rules, you are not required to pay any taxes.

The chart earlier showed the advantage of converting a $50,000 after-tax or non-deductible IRA to a Roth IRA without having to pay the tax. To repeat, the benefit over a 40-year-period is $400,000.

I have done some variation of the previous strategy many times over the years. Many people are enjoying tax-free income and they and their families will be hundreds of thousands of dollars better off.

Please note if you are a financial advisor, this is a splendid strategy that can add tremendous value for your clients. Over the years presenting some variation of this idea to thousands of advisors, I get more questions about this issue than any other issue. This is a good thing because it means that the advisor asking the question is attempting to implement this plan, which typically doesn't result in any immediate business for the advisor. In fact, in the first example, if you are managing the $50,000, you may be reluctant to take money you were managing and have it rolled into a 401(k) that you are not managing. In the second example, presumably you are the advisor who would be managing the one-person 401(k) plan so it would be a push in terms of your fee. The reason you do it, however, is because *it is the right thing for your client*. I firmly believe if you consistently do the right thing for your client, your business will grow because your clients and prospects will develop trust in you, will give you more work, and will refer you to their friends and colleagues. It has worked that way for me.

Roth IRA Conversions of After-Tax Dollars in Your Retirement Plan if You Are Still Working

Prior to the issuance of IRS Notice 2009-68, it was commonly assumed under the applicable sections of the Internal Revenue Code that you could rollover the pre-tax dollars in your retirement plan to an IRA. Then rollover the after-tax dollars in your retirement plan directly to a Roth IRA. IRS Notice 2009-68 challenges this assumption. It states that if a qualified plan account holder elects to rollover only a portion of the account in a direct rollover, then the rollover contains a pro-rata share of pre-tax contributions and after-tax contributions.

For example suppose you have a $1M qualified plan [like a 401(k)] account with $50,000 of after-tax contributions and want to rollover $950,000 to a traditional IRA and $50,000 to a Roth IRA. Under Notice 2009-68, the $950,000 rollover is considered to have $902,500 of pre-tax dollars and $47,500 of after-tax dollars. Many tax advisors have requested that the IRS reconsider this Notice and clarify their position on this important issue to be consistent with the previously commonly assumed consequences of the above-described conversion. Until then, you are acting at your peril if you are assuming that you can get a $50,000 tax-free Roth IRA conversion under these circumstances.

If you can, however, do a rollover of the entire qualified plan account and have no other IRAs, there is another way to get the $50,000 tax-free Roth IRA conversion. If you are transferring to a new company that will accept a rollover of IRAs, you can rollover the entire qualified plan account into an IRA, then rollover the pre-tax dollars into the new company's plan and the after-tax dollars into a Roth IRA. Alternatively, if you are self-employed and have a retirement plan for your self-employment income, you could do a direct rollover of the entire qualified plan account to an IRA and then rollover the pre-tax dollars into your self-employment plan and the after-tax dollars into a Roth IRA.

Active Employees Making Ongoing IRA and Retirement Plan Contributions

In *Retire Secure!* (Wiley, Feb., 2009), I examine the best ways to accumulate money for your retirement if you are still working. The conclusions, subject to some exceptions, can be summarized as follows:

1. Contribute any amount to your retirement plan that your employer is willing to match or even partially match.

2. Maximize both your Roth 401(k) and Roth IRA possibilities.

3. If you have maxed out your Roth possibilities, maximize your traditional retirement plan possibilities. Usually, this mean if you don't have access to a Roth 401(k), max out your Roth IRA and then max out your traditional 401(k).

4. If you make too much money to contribute to a Roth IRA (i.e., you are married and your income is above $177,000), then I generally recommend a non-deductible IRA for you and your spouse of $5,000 each—or if you and/or your wife are 50 or older, then $6,000 each.

Let's assume you are following this advice and your income is too high to make a Roth IRA contribution and that you have no other IRAs. So, you make two contributions of $6,000, one for you, and one for your spouse to a non-deductible IRA. Then, you make a Roth IRA conversion of the two non-deductible IRAs. Since you have no other IRAs, you don't have the aggregation or pro-ration rules to worry about. What you have effectively done is to make two $6,000 contributions to a Roth IRA though you would normally be precluded from making a Roth IRA contribution because your income is too high.

If you do have other IRAs and you do have to worry about the aggregation rules and pro-ration rules, then you have to assess whether it is worth it to go through the contortions listed above. Alternately, you could just make non-deductible IRAs and not bother with a Roth IRA conversion or at least not bother with the contortions listed above.

The Reporting and Accounting of After-Tax Dollars Inside Your IRA and Retirement Plan

Unless you prove otherwise, the IRS considers all withdrawals from retirement plans or IRAs as taxable. How do you prove some of the IRA and/or 401(k) are after-tax? You document. Keep good track of the paper trail establishing the non-deductible contributions to your IRA. The way you report this information to the IRS on an annual basis is to file a Form 8608 on U.S. Form 1040. We recommend as soon as $1 is contributed to a non-deductible IRA, or that you make an IRA rollover from an account that has after tax dollars in it, that you file this form every year for the rest of your life as long as you have non-deductible IRAs.

If you are an employee, presumably the 401(k) plan administrator is responsible for keeping track of your pre- and after-tax contributions to your retirement plan. It is absolutely critical that you get this information from your employer when you retire and maintain that documentation. If you are still working, I would ask for that information now.

Please be aware of a tremendously common and costly mistake that retirees make. They don't bother keeping track of the after-tax dollars in their retirement plan. Sometimes, they go to a financial advisor after they retire. Many financial advisors don't even know about this issue. I think financial advisors should pro-actively aid their client and ask if there are any after-tax dollars in the 401(k) plan. If the employee doesn't know, then an inquiry should be made to the benefits department or the 401(k) plan administrator. I prefer a statement showing what, if any, of the retirement plan is after tax. If there are after-tax dollars, it is critical that those dollars be accounted for. If the money is rolled into an IRA, even without all the contortions described in this chapter, the reader should be filing a Form 8608 every year from here on in and show what portion is traditional and what portion is after tax.

I can't tell you how frustrated I feel when I meet a client who had an advisor recommend an IRA rollover, but he or she never mentioned checking for after-tax dollars in the account. Many times, those after-tax dollars just get lost in the shuffle. It is critical that at retirement someone check to see if there are any after-tax dollars in the plan and if so, that the appropriate action, preferably a Roth IRA conversion, take place.

It is also critical for you and/or your advisor to check for NUA (Net Unrealized Appreciation) in a retirement plan before rolling a retirement plan to an IRA. NUA is essentially company stock that is afforded a favorable tax treatment. To oversimplify, in certain situations company stock in a retirement plan, if properly treated, could eventually be taxed at capital gains rates rather than ordinary tax rates which, in some cases, could reduce the tax on the IRA distribution by as much as 20%.

Please note most of this analysis is the same for employees who have 401(k) or 403(b) balances and have access to a Roth designated account. Please see "What's New" before Chapter One.

—— $$$ ——

Key Lesson for this Chapter

It is possible to make a Roth IRA conversion, under certain circumstances, without paying taxes if you have non-deductible IRAs or after-tax dollars in your retirement plan.

An Aggressive Strategy— The Roth Launcher—Recharacterizing or Undoing a Roth IRA Conversion

"A wise man changes his mind, a fool never."

— Spanish Proverb

Main Topics

- An overview of the recharacterization strategy

- Reducing investment risk with recharaterizations

- Factors to consider when recharacterizing a Roth IRA conversion.

- A loophole that can be extremely profitable for you

- Important dates to remember for recharacterizing a Roth IRA

- The "November Shuffle"—an advanced strategy

- The "Roth Launcher" strategy

Key Idea

You can opportunistically take advantage of the recharacterization rules. It's possible to do a series of conversions and recharacterize or "undo" the investments that don't perform well. You can also pro-actively separate IRA accounts, convert them, and recharacterize ones that don't perform well.

—— $$$ ——

Before we start this next subject, please understand it is the most technical chapter in the book. It is presenting an aggressive strategy that most IRA owners will not want to implement in its entirety. For those of you, however, who are willing to plod through this chapter and suffer through the inevitable extra paperwork aggravation, there are splendid riches as your reward.

The problem with betting on a horse race is if you bet on a horse and it loses, you can't go back to the bookie and change your bet to the horse that won. Neither is it a good strategy to bet on all horses because your losses would still outweigh your winnings. Wouldn't it be wonderful if you could bet on all the horses, collect the winnings from the horse that won and ask for a refund on all the bets you made on the horses that didn't win? The Roth Launcher strategy in this chapter is somewhat like that.

The Problem This Strategy Solves

One of the things that can go wrong with a Roth IRA conversion is if you make a big conversion and the value of the underlying investment goes way down soon after you make the conversion. For example, let's say you have ten IRAs of $100,000 each. Each IRA is invested quite differently for diversification purposes. You decide to convert a $100,000 IRA into a Roth IRA in February, 2011. You select one of the $100,000 IRAs that happens to be invested in large companies for the conversion. Assume for discussion sake the conversion costs you $30,000 in taxes. Then, in September, 2012, your $100,000 investment in that Roth IRA goes down in value to $50,000. Had you known that would happen you would never have paid $30,000 in taxes to convert to a $100,000 Roth IRA. It is doubly frustrating because a different $100,000 IRA—the one invested in international funds—doubled to $200,000. It would have been much better if you had selected that IRA and converted it instead of the one you converted. For the same tax cost of $30,000, you would have a $200,000 Roth IRA instead of a $50,000 Roth IRA. But you are stuck. You can't take it back, right? You already filled out the paperwork to make the Roth IRA conversion, submitted the paperwork, paid the tax, and have been receiving regular statements evidencing your loss in your Roth IRA that is valued at $50,000 in September, 2012. Well, should you just take your lumps and move on or is there something you can still do?

Actually, in the case of a Roth IRA conversion you can undo, or technically "recharacterize" a Roth IRA conversion. If you recharacterize a Roth IRA conversion, it puts you in the same position as if you had never made the conversion in the first place. You must recharacterize the Roth IRA conversion by the deadline which is October 15 (with an IRS election or a valid extension of your federal tax return) of the year following the year you made the conversion. You will be in the same position as if you never made the conversion in the first place. In this example, if you complete the paperwork to recharacterize the conversion, your Roth IRA that used to be $100,000, that is $50,000 in October, 2012, reverts to being a regular IRA. You would also file an amended tax return (or if you had not yet filed your tax return because it was on extension, file your tax return) and ask for a refund of the $30,000 you paid in taxes on the conversion.

This chapter explores some of the detailed rules regarding recharacterizations and shows an aggressive strategy that proactively exploits the recharacterization law. This strategy is not for the meek. Also, there is much that could go wrong with it. If all goes as planned, however, and you are willing to accept that additional paperwork that goes with it, it could add tremendous value to you and your family. Most readers will not implement this strategy in its entirety. There is, however, a middle ground that will appeal to many readers.

Hedge Your Bets

By implementing the aggressive strategy, you may be able to "hedge your bets" to take the full advantage of a Roth IRA conversion or a series of Roth IRA conversions.

> Essentially, you bet on all the horses in the horse race, keep the winner, and ask for a refund for all the losing tickets that you bought.

Simultaneously, the strategy can also reduce the risk of a downturn in the market after making a Roth IRA conversion. Essentially, you bet on all the horses in the horse race, keep the winner, and ask for a refund for all the losing tickets that you bought.

The essence of this strategy in our example is that you convert all ten separate IRAs of $100,000 in 2011. Before October 15, 2012 you keep the Roth IRA that grew to $200,000 and you recharacterize or undo the rest of the conversions.

Ultimately, you will still have to pay tax on one $100,000 conversion, $30,000 in our example, but you will be able to keep your $200,000 Roth IRA instead of being stuck with the account that diminished to $50,000.

I prefer to elaborate on this by going in a logical progression starting with the rules governing recharacterizations. Then we will provide several examples of situations that will allow you to take advantage of these rules.

Do You Really Have to Segregate Your Roth IRA Accounts?—Yes!

First, I have to tell you what you may want to do in this area is not allowed. I suspect a number of you would prefer having one IRA consisting of a variety of investments and converting to one Roth IRA. There may be nothing wrong with converting different assets from one IRA. If you only converted to one Roth IRA account, however, once converted, when a particular asset in that one Roth IRA goes up or down, you might want to convert or recharacterize that one asset and leave the others alone. If you were allowed to do that, you may be able to get some of the benefits of this section without all the paperwork. Sorry, you can't do that. For this strategy to work, you must segregate your Roth IRAs which you converted and you should only count on "recharacterizing" or "keeping as the Roth" each particular account.

An Example of the Wrong Way to Do It

Let's say you make a conversion from one or more IRAs of multiple assets, but keep everything you converted in just one Roth IRA account. Then, let's say that some of the assets in the account go up and some go down. If you had not gone to the trouble of separating the Roth IRA accounts into different accounts, you won't be allowed to keep the assets that went up as Roth IRAs and recharacterize the assets that went down. You would be required to allocate the total loss or gain in the Roth IRA to each asset pro-ratably.

For example, let's say in January, 2011, you have $1,000,000 in one IRA account. The account consists of two investments worth $500,000 each. Financial projections indicate the appropriate amount to convert to a Roth IRA is $500,000. In January, 2011, you convert the entire $1,000,000 IRA into a

Roth IRA consisting of two equal investments of $500,000 each but all inside one IRA account. Let's assume a flat 40% tax rate. Let's assume you file an extension in April 2012 and pay $200,000 ($500,000 times 40%) with your extension. (Hang on, I know you converted $1,000,000 and paid tax only on $500,000). Let's assume you don't segregate and in October, 1, 2012, one of the investments inside the Roth account goes up by $200,000 and the other one goes down by $200,000. So now you have a $1,000,000 Roth IRA. You could keep the $1,000,000 as a Roth IRA, but then you would have to pay taxes on the additional $500,000 or $200,000 ($500,000 times 40%) plus penalty and interest. You could recharacterize the Roth IRA and get your tax extension payment money back. But that would put you in the same position as if you had never converted anything. Recharacterizing everything doesn't really help you because you would be recharacterizing the winner as well as the loser.

You can't cherry pick and say I want to recharacterize the investment that went down and keep the one that went up as a Roth because they are all in one account. You could recharacterize $500,000 but you would have to pro-rate the investments. You would be left with a $500,000 Roth IRA and a $500,000 traditional IRA. After pro-rating the investments, you would then still only have a Roth IRA of $500,000 for a tax cost of $200,000 ($500,000 times 40%).

If, on the other hand, let's assume you divide the $1,000,000 IRA to two separate $500,000 IRAs in January 2011 and convert both IRAs to Roth IRAs. You file an extension for your taxes on April 15, 2012, and include an estimated extension payment of $200,000 ($500,000 times 40%) just as you did in the prior example. By October 1, 2012, one of the Roth IRA accounts has declined to $300,000 and the other one has grown to $700,000. Then, before the deadline expires (October 15, 2012), you recharacterize the loser. You keep the winner as a Roth. You would have a Roth IRA of $700,000 and a regular IRA of $300,000. By engineering the transaction through the segregated accounts, you end up with a $700,000 Roth IRA and a $300,000 regular IRA. Compare that to not segregating and for the same tax cost of $200,000, you would have only a $500,000 Roth IRA instead of a $700,000 Roth IRA. You effectively saved $80,000 by segregating. ($200,000 ties 40%) Not bad for a little extra paperwork. Separating into even more accounts, invested differently, increases the chances that this strategy will save you money.

Rules Governing Recharacterizations

The Internal Revenue Service permits IRA owners to recharacterize Roth IRA conversions back to traditional IRAs. The deadline for recharacterizing a conversion is the *extended due date* of your tax return for the year you made the Roth IRA conversion. This would normally be April 15 following the year of the conversion, or October 15, if you have filed for and obtained an extension. Let's assume you made a conversion in 2011 and filed your tax return in April 2012 and paid taxes on the conversion. If you decide to recharacterize by October 2012, you must file an amended tax return to get back the taxes that you paid on the conversion. So, in our example, if you make a Roth IRA conversion in January 2011, you generally have until October 15, 2012 to recharacterize that conversion.

There are also rules limiting the frequency of conversions, recharacterizations, and reconversions. You may not make a Roth conversion, recharacterize or "unconvert" it and reconvert the same IRA money in the same year. Even if you straddle different calendar years, you must still wait 30 days before reconverting a Roth IRA that you had previously converted and "unconverted." Taken together these rules can be summarized: if you make a Roth IRA conversion of a particular account and you recharacterize that Roth IRA conversion, you must wait for the longer of:

- the beginning of the calendar year following the year you converted to a Roth IRA, or
- 30 days after you recharacterized the Roth IRA

Before you can convert the money you just recharacterized.

Procedure for Re-characterizing a Converted Roth IRA Back to a Traditional IRA

I have actually presented this technique hundreds of times to different audiences. Steve Kohman and I wrote an article and published it years ago in *The Journal of Retirement Planning* and not much has changed since then. I often am asked questions on the mechanics of recharacterizing. Though I won't go into the nitty-gritty of how to fill out the form, here are the basic requirements to get a valid recharacterization:

- You are required to notify your financial advisor or your IRA custodian that you want to "unconvert" or recharacterize a particular Roth IRA into a traditional IRA.

- If you are doing it yourself, you have to fill out the appropriate form. There is no universal form. For example, if you are a Vanguard investor, Vanguard will have their own form for recharacterizing a Roth IRA back to a traditional IRA. If you invested with Charles Schwab, there would be a special Charles Schwab form. Presumably, the forms would be fairly similar.

If the person making the conversion dies before completing the recharacterization, the executor, administrator, or other person responsible for filing the decedent's final tax return can complete the recharacterization by providing the following information:

- the type and amount of the conversion to the Roth IRA to be recharacterized;

- the date on which the conversion was made and the tax year for which it was made;

- a direction to the trustee to transfer, in a trustee-to-trustee transfer, the amount of the conversion and any net income allocable to it; and

- any additional information needed to make the transfer, including the names of the trustees involved.

You must also report the recharacterization on the tax return for the tax year in which you made the original Roth conversion or if that return has already been filed, you must file an amended tax return (US Form 1040X).

Note that once the recharacterization has taken place, it is irrevocable. Although you can reconvert the same money if you wait the requisite time period (see above), you cannot "undo" a recharacterization that has been completed. Therefore, you must use caution when deciding that a recharacterization is the best strategy for you.

Multiple Roth Conversions and Recharacterizations

The rules allow more than one Roth conversion to be made in a single year as long as the money used does not come from a recharacterization. For example, if you want to convert $1,000,000, you could do it in a single transaction. For reasons that will be clear later, we would recommend that, in the spirit of this chapter, you would first set up ten separate Roth IRA accounts and do ten separate Roth IRA conversions from the IRA into each Roth IRA separately. The rules allowing recharacterization of conversions apply to each individual Roth IRA separately. So if you did ten separate conversions, you could then choose to recharacterize one or more of those ten separate conversions.

Is this a pain in the neck as far as additional paperwork is concerned? Absolutely. Is the additional paperwork worth it if your total IRA is $10,000? Probably not. You will have to determine in your own situation whether you think it will be worth the aggravation of doing all the additional paperwork to achieve the goals of this chapter.

If multiple conversions are made, they could be done into one receiving Roth IRA account. Or—as we recommend—into new and separate Roth IRA accounts. Assuming the same beneficiaries are used on all the accounts, multiple accounts would have the same effect in terms of making the conversion whether you used a single Roth IRA account or multiple Roth IRA accounts. The differences come from the result of any recharacterizations.

The Amount Recharacterized Differs from the Conversion Amount

The recharacterization transfer amount includes any investment income or loss generated in the Roth account after the conversion. In the case of a single Roth account used for ten separate $100,000 conversions made at the same time, the recharacterization amount will be the same no matter which conversion is recharacterized. The income allocated to the conversion is based on the performance of the entire account—and not individual securities within the account. If, however, ten separate Roth IRA accounts are used for the conversion and invested differently, the recharacterization amounts based on the different investment returns for each account will vary.

Case Study: Roth IRA Conversion Made in Year One

Suppose you have one $1,000,000 IRA and convert it to ten Roth IRAs of $100,000 each. Each Roth IRA is invested in one of five different asset classes: two are invested in large cap stocks, two in small cap stocks, etc. Any conversions or subsequent re-characterization or "unconversions" will be made from a separate Roth IRA account. Let's assume you, possibly with the help of an advisor, determine that the appropriate amount to convert based on your current and future tax brackets would be $100,000 for 2011, which we will call year one. What are your options?

Option 1: You could make a $100,000 conversion now and invest in any one of the asset classes and hope for an increase in the value of the investment that you choose to convert. (This option was discussed in the introduction to this chapter).

Result: This is a crap shoot. If you convert $100,000, and your investment increases to $200,000 by October 15 of year two, you will have a $200,000 Roth IRA for the tax on $100,000 conversion. This is a great deal!

But if your investment declines, it is not a great deal. If you convert an investment that is valued at $100,000 on the conversion date and it drops to $50,000 by the following October, you will be stuck paying income tax on $100,000 and owning a $50,000 Roth IRA.

Therefore, if the investment goes down, you should recharacterize the Roth IRA to avoid the tax on a $100,000 conversion. If you recharacterize or "unconvert" your Roth, you will be in the same position to where you would have been if you had never made the conversion.

Assuming the traditional IRA would also have declined in value had it been left alone, you will have a $50,000 IRA (and your experimental foray into the Roth environment will have had no tax consequences). Although it is discouraging that your investment went down, it isn't as bad as if you had had to pay income tax on a $100,000 conversion and been left with a $50,000 IRA. This strategy, of picking and choosing among the accounts to convert, ends up being a winner if you pick the right asset class to convert.

Option 2: You could take $20,000 each from five IRAs and convert the new $100,000 IRA to a Roth IRA.

Result: This strategy is an attempt to hedge. This strategy will produce no windfall from overall investment returns, but it is a safer bet because it uses diversification to spread your money around. You may still "unconvert" some or all of the account if it breaks even or loses money, although this will reduce the total conversion amount; and possibly not fulfill your original objective of a $100,000 conversion.

Option 3: Don't make any Roth IRA conversions.

Result: A "do-nothing" strategy misses any opportunity to enjoy the tax-free growth offered by Roth IRA conversions.

Option 4: Do the Roth Launcher. Segregate the $1,000,000 traditional IRA to ten IRAs and convert all ten to Roth IRAs. Now you would have 10 separate Roth IRAs. You could then prepare to "unconvert" or re-characterize the investments that do the worst from the time of conversion to October 15, of year two, assuming a valid extension or election is obtained.

Result: In September of the following year of the conversion (year two or in this case 2012) with perfect hindsight, you "unconvert" nine accounts that were originally $100,000 each. You recharacterize the $900,000 of your original investments that did not perform as well as the $100,000 that you chose to retain as a Roth IRA. Lucky you can now reap a tremendous windfall of tax-free growth in any one of the asset classes that went up the most.

You will still have to pay income tax on the $100,000 income for tax year one (for the asset class you chose to retain as a Roth). The value, however, of the Roth will have increased. Then, you could re-balance both your traditional IRA portfolio and your Roth IRA portfolio. The result is that you now have a larger, well-diversified portfolio, including a Roth IRA and a traditional IRA with reduced tax costs.

If your portfolio comprises individual securities, the same principle would apply, if separate accounts are used to convert them. You could retain as Roth

IRAs the securities that did well and recharacterize the ones that did not—as long as they are converted into separate accounts.

If the future works out differently, you would respond differently. If all the asset classes in separate accounts went down, you could consider re-characterizing all of them—and then consider a future conversion based on lower values.

Pitfalls of the Roth Launcher (Option 4)

Of course many people may feel uncomfortable with the Roth Launcher approach. It may seem like too much of a gamble. There could be "follow through" failures. For example, you might forget to "unconvert," and that could present a financial disaster. Or you might die and your executor, administrator, or other person responsible for filing the final tax return, may not be aware of the plan to "unconvert."

Another practical problem with the conversion and recharacterization strategy is that it can be a paperwork nightmare. You would have 10 accounts instead of one. To do it right, you would have to keep track of all the ten accounts and get the paperwork straight on all ten accounts. Form 1099s could be fouled up. You could receive additional attention from our friends at the IRS even if you and the investing company do everything right. Eventually, that will be worked out with either a letter or phone call, but it is extra work and you should be warned about it before you do it.

Your broker or financial advisor might botch it. They will also likely consider you a pain for creating extra work for them by opening new accounts. This strategy, however, will still appeal to taxpayers who want the most "Bang for their Buck" on Roth conversions, and I have seen it work successfully in the past. For those who are willing to do the legwork to properly implement this strategy, the potential for reward is considerable.

Time Line for Converting to a Roth IRA and Then Recharacterizing Back to a Traditional IRA

What follows is a potential time line for the conversion and recharacterization process.

Year One

Make a conversion before year end. Please note that many brokerage houses need at least a week and sometimes longer to process the paperwork. Therefore, I would consider the practical deadline to be about December 15 of year one to make the conversion.

As a practical matter, however, for the maximum "look-back" period, you would want to convert at the beginning of the year as opposed to the end of the year. Therefore, if all other factors are the same, you may want to consider making your conversions in the early part of the year.

Year Two

April 15: Pay your taxes and file your extension for your year one tax return, if you want more time to decide on your year one conversion. As noted above, you can file your return if you are ready and still take advantage of the six-month additional period to make the recharacterization. But you must be prepared to execute the transfer and file an amended return by October 15. Note that if you make ten $100,000 conversions with the intention of keeping the one that does the best, it would be appropriate to add $100,000 to your income and project your year 1 estimated taxes you are paying with your year one extension on April 15, year two based on a $100,000 Roth IRA conversion. Then you should send in an extension tax payment for year one that includes the tax on an additional $100,000 of income. In our example, you would pay an extra $40,000 ($100,000 times 40%) with your extension for year one in April of year two.

What could occur by waiting till later to file the return is you might find even more than one $100,000 does extremely well and you then may want to have converted both and decide not to recharacterize two accounts. Thus you would owe tax on $200,000 of conversions. If this is a potential situation you may have, consider paying more tax (for example pay $800,000 with your extension ($200,000 times 40%). If you end up keeping only a $100,000 conversion, you will ask for $40,000 back when you file your return. ($100,000 times 40%). If you keep $200,000 of the conversions, you will avoid late payment penalties and interest.

September 15: Technically, the deadline is October 15 of year two to recharacterize year one conversions. October 15 is the final deadline to "unconvert" undesirable year one conversions and file by the close of the "automatic" extension period. In reality, because of potential problems and delays, I would want all the paperwork on the recharacterizations started by September 15 even though technically the deadline is October 15.

October 1: Check on the status of the recharacterizations that you made on September 15. If the recharacterizations are not completed by the first of October of year two, you should go in panic mode, call the broker, and make sure the recharacterization occurs before the October 15 deadline.

October 15: This is the real deadline for recharacterizing year-one conversions. If October 15 falls on a Saturday or a Sunday, you have until the following Monday. It is also the deadline for filing your tax return for year one if you have not already done so.

October 16: If you made ten $100,000 conversions and meant to recharacterize nine of them and forgot to recharacterize, you have big tax problems. Don't sue me. In addition, to the regular disclaimer for this book, I warned you this was a risky strategy.

Also on this date or earlier if the recharacterizations were done earlier than the October 15th deadline, you may consolidate your multiple Roth IRA accounts back into one Roth IRA account. You do not need to keep separate accounts forever, although they can be useful for future years' Roth conversions. So you may consolidate the Roth conversions you keep in a master Roth account that will not have any potential for recharacterizations and keep the empty separate ones for future conversions or close them out.

November 16: This is the first opportunity for you to reconvert your recharacterized traditional IRA. (You could do this earlier if the recharacterization was done earlier than the October 15th deadline).

December 15: This is the last chance for initiating additional Roth conversions for year two, assuming 16 days are needed to accomplish them.

This time line does not project beyond year two, but barring other tax-law changes, the same logic would continue to apply for future years.

The November Shuffle -The Really Advanced Convert and Recharacterize Strategy

If you like what you read, you may consider an even more advanced and complicated strategy. In the example above, you could consider not converting all of your $1,000,000 in IRAs in year one but rather converting most but not all of it to separate Roth accounts. You leave some of the money in the traditional IRA account or accounts. Then, in November of year one you take another look at the IRAs that you did convert. Let's assume that you have some winners and some losers. Recharacterize the losers to a separate IRA. Then, you could make a conversion of the remaining IRA accounts you never converted.

The point of this advanced strategy is to take advantage of a declining investment market where all your investments from the original conversions go down in value. You can get around the restrictions of the rule on making conversions and recharacterizing and converting again the same money in the same year.

If you didn't have that rule to worry about, the spirit of the horse-betting strategy would have you convert all the separate accounts. Since you do have the restrictions of the "convert, recharacterize, and convert again in the same year" rule, you could not recharacterize your losers before year end and convert them again in that year—which would give you even more options to keep or recharacterize depending on performance.

This strategy is a rule to safeguard against investment declines after conversion and it works around that restricting rule.

Let's do an example.

You start with either one IRA worth $1 million or ten equal IRAs of $100,000 each. You convert $700,000 consisting of seven $100,000 accounts to a Roth IRA conversion in the early part of year one. You then re-examine in November of year one. As an aside, I am picking November year one instead of December year one because I don't want to do this transferring back and forth in December when it is difficult to transact any official business.

Let's say in November of year one of the seven accounts that was converted, three are under water. You recharacterize those three into the separate IRA accounts or a separate IRA account. Now, because of the rule limiting your ability to convert, recharacterize and reconvert in the same calendar year or 30 days, you can't do anything else with those account(s) until year two.

In November of year one, you convert the unconverted amounts to three new separate Roth IRA accounts that were never converted because you held off originally.

As a result, you will have seven Roth IRAs. Four are above the value you converted which was early year one and three are at the same value that you just converted in November, year one. Then, in January of year two, you reconvert the three IRAs that were originally converted, went down in value, and recharacterized in November, year one.

At this point, you could just do nothing and look at everything again in September, year two. (Again, I say September instead of October 15 because I don't want mechanical mistakes due to a time deadline). Alternatively, if this strategy isn't complicated enough for you and you have nothing to do with your time, you could take another look before you file your first extension.

Depending on the performance of these different accounts, you could consider recharacterizing more accounts that have gone down in value.

In September of year two, you have some more decisions. Let's assume you originally decided you really wanted to keep a conversion of $100,000, but engaged in those horse-betting strategies to get the most for your tax on the $100,000 conversion. You could just keep the top investment, recharacterize the rest, and go home. Alternately you could "get cute" and keep the accounts that you converted (or reconverted) in year two because the deadline for recharacterizing those conversions is not until October 15, year three.

In either case, you could just plan to keep the $100,000 conversion that did the best—which could be $150,000 because of the gain since the day you made the conversion. That way you would have a $150,000 conversion for the tax cost of $100,000. Let's assume that the extra $100,000 income was taxed at 28% and you paid $28,000 in taxes on the conversion. You could look at it as a 28% tax on the conversion. Another way to look at it is that your real tax on the Roth IRA conversion is really 18.66% because you paid $28,000 on what is now a $150,000 conversion. Taking this logic a step further, you may decide to keep more of your Roth IRAs because looking at the conversion in this light, you are willing to pay a lower tax percentage on the conversion because you aren't paying tax on the increase from the day you converted to September, year two.

At this point, you have four converted accounts that are above water…and maybe a headache.

The Mechanics of Filing Your Tax Return with this Horse Bet Strategy

Let's say you always intended to keep and pay taxes on a $100,000 conversion. Let's also say you are one of those people who always file their tax returns by April 15 of year two for year one, and you never file tax extensions. You could still do the "horse bet" strategy. The problem is that if you make a $1,000,000 or even $700,000 conversion in year one, you would appear to have a large chunk of taxes due in April, year two if no recharacterizations are done. You may be inclined to pay the taxes. Then, before October 15, year two, you finish all your recharacterizations. At which point you would file an amended tax return, U.S. Form 1040X, and ask for a refund. You will probably get it, but there are two problems with this strategy:

- You made an interest-free loan to the IRS
- Who is kidding whom? If you ask the IRS to write you a check for several hundred thousand dollars, I think you will increase the odds of attracting unwanted attention.

If you file the return on April 15 and don't pay the tax, because you anticipate doing recharacterizations, then I think you will have a hard time responding to an IRS inquiry about this if your recharacterizations are not yet completed. I do not think this is likely since the Form 1099-R showing the recharacterizations is not filed until after year two anyway. But potentially there could be a problem—which is also not fun.

What is our recommendation? On April 15, file a tax extension, US Form 4868. And with the extension, make an extension payment for how much you think you will really owe. Even if you converted $700,000 or $1,000,000, you could add $100,000 to the income you would have had with *no* conversions. If that amount would be taxed at the 28% bracket, you could send in an extension payment of $28,000 assuming all your other taxes are paid and/or estimates have been made.

Then, in October year 2, if you keep only $100,000 of the conversion and recharacterize the rest, you would file your return and presumably owe nothing. If you decide to keep more than $100,000 of the amount originally converted, then you would owe taxes, penalty, and interest. For example let's assume you decide to keep another $100,000 conversion that has grown to $200,000. Then you will have to make a payment in October of year two for the additional taxes on the extra $100,000 income, in addition to penalty and interest. My guess is that in most cases if you have that big of a gain that the additional value of the conversion far exceeds the cost in taxes, penalty and interest. As mentioned before, however, it is better if you feel that may be a possibility, to pay potential additional tax with the extension. You can get your money refunded after your return is filed if you paid too much additional tax.

Combining Strategies into One Great Roth Launcher Process

We believe the ultimate Roth IRA conversion strategy combines the material in the *How Much to Convert* chapter, Chapter Eight, along with this aggressive approach. The combination of this technique of multiple conversions and recharacterizations and the material in Chapter Ten is the full blown Roth Launcher Process.

Warning! Warning! Warning! and Disclaimer

This strategy is risky. Though neither I—nor any experts I know—see any problem from the legal side, we are at best exploiting a loophole. I believe the entire reason the IRS allows us to recharacterize a conversion is a throwback to the years when you were not allowed to make a Roth IRA conversion unless your income was less than $100,000. Let's say it was November of year one and you thought your income was going to be less than $100,000. You made the conversion and then in year two, your Forms 1099s or K-1 or capital gains statements came in and it turns out that your income was over $100,000. The IRS would let you undo your conversion.

Also, the IRS issued guidance that stated that a recharacterization can be done for any reason, not just when your income is over the $100,000 limit. This was decided after the dot com stock bubble burst and many people owed more tax on the conversion than what they had left in their Roth accounts. It is also necessary to cover unrelated situations where people make Roth contributions when they were not allowed to and allows people to subsequently move a non-deductible IRA contribution that they made into a Roth IRA. The recharacterization rules cover all Roth and IRA contributions as well as conversions.

From what I can tell, that is the purpose of the recharacterization rules. I don't think it was the IRS' intent to let us do the Roth Launcher strategy I have suggested. Therefore, the IRS might become angry and make changes in the future. Presumably, the changes would be prospective—that is, affecting transactions in the future and not ones that have already been made. Presumably, transactions that have already been made would be "grandfathered." But maybe I am wrong. Maybe they will try to nail people who have essentially done what I propose. It would not be the first time I was wrong. I have much support from all of the IRA experts I know, but please consider yourself officially warned.

What I think is a bigger risk is the potential of a mechanical mistake or just added aggravation that made the entire transaction more of a pain than it was worth. I received a really nasty letter from a client who went to one of my workshops and made a plain $100,000 conversion even though he had $1,000,000 in this IRA. The value of the converted amount went down and he had much trouble even completing a presumably simple recharacterization. He warned me that I should warn others they might have the same problems. He (and I suspect he incorrectly completed the paperwork), faced a series of letters, phone calls, wasted time, and aggravation. If you add the complications of multiple accounts, the chances of a mechanical mistake and aggravation go up geometrically. The advice in this chapter should be undertaken only with full understanding of the risks and preferably under the direction of a qualified advisor; and even then, I would be extremely careful.

The Epiphany of the Aggressive Strategy with Steve's "Roth Launcher" Process

Steve Kohman is the CPA and Certified Specialist in Estate Planning in our office who is largely responsible for doing Roth conversion analyses and making recommendations for our clients. Steve views this aggressive strategy as an extremely exciting possibility for many clients. He calls his entire process of developing a Roth conversion plan and incorporating the potential benefits of this aggressive strategy discussed above as the "Roth Launcher" conversion strategy.

Steve knows that developing and implementing an optimal Roth conversion plan can launch you and your family's financial future onto higher ground. In addition, the aggressive strategy discussed above will launch your Roth IRA to a higher value in the first year after a conversion. The magnitude of the higher value of the separate investment results will magnify the potential benefits your family can reap.

Steve realizes that simply comparing the conversion tax with the future tax on RMDs if a conversion is not done is not sufficient to make a Roth conversion decision. As noted in Chapter Eight, *How Much and When You Should Convert to a Roth IRA* there are many other additional subjective and objective factors to consider in determining a conversion plan, but it often comes down to a consideration of the conversion tax. If the conversion tax was lower, in many cases, a larger conversion would be done.

The traditional advice is that if the conversion tax percentage is too much higher than the future incremental tax rates, a conversion should not be done. The results of this approach without the aggressive strategy is that many people are missing the opportunity to convert more to Roth IRAs than they had previously thought because the taxes on the conversion Roth IRA were limiting the size of their conversions. The aggressive strategy can essentially lower the conversion taxes and allow higher conversions. It can be an epiphany for you to realize that you can change the tax rate on the Roth IRA from the conversion using the aggressive strategy with the Roth Launcher!

Steve offers this example:

You have to pay 35% tax on additional conversions now but will be in the 28% tax bracket later; thus, you don't know whether it is worth it. Consider the situation where your overall portfolio goes nowhere, but you use the Roth Launcher process creating multiple Roth IRA accounts and you manage to get a 30% rate of return on one of the Roth conversions. You keep that one, say from a $100,000 conversion, while you lose on all the others and you recharacterize or undo them. Overall, you see no growth in the accounts as a whole.

Where are you after a year? If you had a well diversified single account Roth IRA, you would have only $100,000 in the Roth. With the Roth Launcher, you have a Roth worth $130,000 – that's where. And you paid only $35,000 in taxes to get it. That is 26.9% tax on the value after a year.

That is less than the future 28% tax you will face on traditional IRA withdrawals. It was worth it. EPIPHANY! You have really launched your Roth into higher values not obtainable in a well diversified portfolio that earned nothing.

The epiphany is to realize that with this logic, accepting a higher conversion tax augments your potential for significant Roth conversion benefits. If straightforward financial projections as indicated in previous chapters would indicate a $100,000 conversion, you may end up keeping more than $100,000 as a Roth with a reduced tax cost per amount converted. The idea of converting different assets, presumably with negative correlations, and keeping the winners—thus lowering your Roth IRA conversion tax percentage—is terrific.

The Middle Road

I have talked about this strategy to people and have presented this strategy hundreds of times to both consumers and financial professionals. Few people actually do it and I understand that. Some do. It does seem risky and I suspect even without the risks, it seems like too much paperwork for most readers and advisors.

You could, however, embrace the spirit of this chapter but take the middle road. For example, let's assume you really want to make a $100,000 Roth IRA conversion. You could make two $100,000 conversions in two different accounts, and then keep the one that does better and recharacterize the one that doesn't do as well.

Another middle road approach is if you are on the border of whether to make a conversion or not, make it and then determine in September of year two whether you want to keep it or not.

In reality, there are multiple middle-road approaches. Frankly, there are no official guidelines on this issue. In one example above, I showed the benefits of this strategy even if you separate the Roth IRA into two accounts as opposed to just leaving it in one account.

This section will not be the same for employees who have 401(k) or 403(b) balances and have access to a Roth designated account.

I have rarely seen clients do the "all in" approach or even the November Shuffle. Even people with millions of dollars in conversions don't want the aggravation of all the paperwork. The money managers I work with balk at all the paperwork. If they are working with me, they will do it, but only if they are managing at least $1,000,000.

At the time of writing this book, I am looking into making this service available for people with less than $1,000,000. I am also looking at integrating this service into other services our office provides.

—— $$$ ——

Key Lesson for this Chapter

Roth IRA conversions and recharacterizations afford taxpayers *many* options. The benefits of a recharacterization can range from "undoing" a conversion that went bad to pro-actively and opportunistically converting more IRAs to Roths, with the idea that you will recharacterize many—if not most—of them.

Chapter Eleven

The Potential Pitfalls of a Roth IRA Conversion

"The road to success is always under construction."

— Lily Tomlin

Main Topics

- The three biggest mistakes IRA owners make
- The investment risk
- Potential changes in the tax law
- The risk of income taxes being eliminated
- The risk of lower tax rates in the future
- Charities as beneficiaries

Key Idea

There are certainly potential downsides to Roth IRA conversions. Before making a conversion, you should evaluate them to determine whether you are comfortable with the risks.

—— **$$$** ——

People often say I am a big Roth IRA conversion fan. I prefer to think of myself as a tax-sensitive trusted advisor trying to optimize a client's assets using whatever tools are available. It just so happens that Roth IRA conversions are an excellent tool for many, if not most, of my clients, readers and listeners.

There are times, however, when Roth IRA conversions are clearly inappropriate. In addition, there is certainly an element of risk that you acknowledge and accept before you make a Roth IRA conversion. This chapter will highlight some of the downsides and risks of making a Roth IRA conversion.

Don't Get Me Wrong and Let This Chapter Dissuade You

The biggest mistake that most IRA owners make is they fail to make at least a partial conversion of their traditional IRA. The second mistake is not making a big enough Roth IRA conversion. The third mistake is not developing a long-term Roth IRA conversion plan. I attribute most of these mistakes to lack of information—or worse yet, relying on less than optimal advice.

That said; let's look at the risks and downside of making a Roth IRA conversion.

Investment Risk

The biggest risk of a Roth IRA conversion is the investment goes down in value over the long run. Earlier, we talked about recharacterizing a Roth IRA conversion that goes down in value. But, that strategy is only helpful if the investment goes down by October 15 of the year following the conversion. If the investment goes down after that date and stays down for a long time, you could be worse off, not better off.

Here is one scenario. You make a large Roth IRA conversion or for that matter a series of smaller conversions. Then, there is a terrorist event or some other factor that creates a big and sustained loss in the market. You need the invested money for living expenses, so you spend the Roth IRA before the market recovers. In that scenario, you are clearly worse off than if you had never made a Roth IRA conversion.

Roth IRAs are best considered long-term investments. For example, it is somewhat risky for a 70-year-old single IRA owner with limited funds and no children to make a large Roth IRA conversion. If the market goes down and takes ten or 15 years to recover, chances are he will be worse off with the conversion. For a younger, wealthier IRA owner, with kids and grandkids, who is not likely to need the Roth IRA, it is less risky. Assuming that eventually the market will recover, his family is likely to benefit from the Roth IRA conversion. That said, good financial planning should follow the medical ethic: First, do no harm.

Potential Changes in the Tax Law

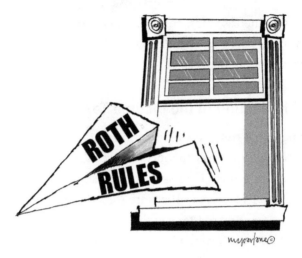

Changing the Rules

As I discussed in Chapter Three, future changes in the tax laws could hurt you. With respect to levying income taxes on Roth IRAs, I concluded that Congress could certainly make a change, but the change would most likely apply to future conversions; and your conversion, assuming you made it before the law change, would be protected from future income-tax changes. I believe you would be "grandfathered" because it is part of the Internal Revenue Code that you would be grandfathered. But I could be wrong.

In addition, Congress could devise some type of excise tax. It would not be an income tax as we know it, but some other type of tax. At different points in history, Congress has implemented an excess accumulation tax and an excess distribution tax. Neither were income taxes. They have also both been repealed. They had the impact, however, of levying a tax on IRA and retirement-plan owners who had listened to the prevailing wisdom and contributed the maximum to their IRA and/or retirement plans. I can't promise a future Congress won't do something similar. Of course, that risk is extremely difficult to measure. Personally, I think the risk of future income-tax increases is far more likely than

> Personally, I think the risk of future income-tax increases is far more likely than tax changes that would hurt a Roth IRA conversion.

tax changes that would hurt a Roth IRA conversion. Therefore, even though there is certainly a risk of disadvantageous tax changes, that risk is overshadowed by the more likely prospect of tax increases. If there are tax increases, the Roth IRA conversions would be even more valuable. I can't promise, however, that Congress will not devise some type of excise tax.

Risk of the Elimination of the Income Tax

The other potential risk is the elimination of the income tax. If the United States were to decide to abolish the income tax in favor of a sales tax—or use tax or value-added tax—there is a risk that the taxes you paid on the Roth IRA conversion will not be recovered. There are some fairly credible commentators who recommend a value-added tax for the United States. Personally, I think if that type of tax is instituted, which I do see as a possibility, it will more likely to be in addition to, not a replacement for, the income tax.

Risk of Lower Tax Rates In the Future

Presumably, if you follow the concepts and guidelines in Chapter Eight, on how much and when to convert, your risk of over-converting will be reduced. If you are working and you will be in a lower tax bracket in retirement, you want to guard against over-converting. And there is one common mistake both consumers and advisors make in assessing the tax-bracket trap.

Let's assume you have a large IRA and when you or your advisors are making projections, you are taking into consideration the future required minimum distributions of that IRA. The RMDs will certainly figure into your calculation of how much and when to convert. One problem that is easy to overlook is if you make a large Roth IRA conversion, you will reduce or eliminate your RMDs. That future reduction in your RMDs could result in your being in a lower tax bracket. You being in a lower tax bracket in the future could mean you over-converted. For example, if you make a Roth IRA conversion so that your marginal tax on the conversion is 25% and you end up in the 15%

bracket because you will have no—or reduced—RMDs, you have certainly hurt yourself—not helped yourself—at least in the short run.

One possibility that doesn't even deserve its own separate subhead is that of over-all general tax reduction. Theoretically, we could have reduced taxes for the country—in which case a Roth IRA conversion could be harmful.

Finally, the risk of a flat tax doesn't bother me yet. First, I don't think it is too likely. Secondly, I think even if it happened, it would be at a high enough tax bracket that it won't likely hurt you or your family in the long run.

Charitable Beneficiaries

If you want to leave all your money to charity, a large Roth IRA conversion is not prudent. The charity doesn't care about purchasing power. They care about total dollars. And yet, most charitable individuals still leave some money to non-charitable heirs. If that is the case, making a partial Roth conversion, and leaving that money to the heirs and leaving the unconverted traditional amount to the charity, will typically solve that problem. Please see Chapter Fifteen for combining Roth IRA conversions and charitable intent.

The Risk (or Certainty) of Additional Complication and Paperwork

It is extremely rare that I get any negative feedback from any client, reader, or listener. I did, however, recently receive a letter with a complaint. I made a recommendation that a client make a $100,000 Roth IRA conversion. He did it in 2008. After the market went down in 2009, we contacted him and suggested he recharacterize his Roth IRA. He was neither an investment client, nor a will client and he processed all the paperwork on his own with Vanguard. There was a problem with the paperwork in terms of recharacterizing the Roth IRA. It took him a number of phone calls and several letters to get it straight. He was angry with me because I didn't warn him that there is additional paperwork and a chance of a mishap with a Roth IRA conversions and recharacterization. So, consider yourself warned.

It is likely that if you make a Roth IRA conversion, the IRS will receive a copy of the Form 1099 that the investment house will send to you; and the IRS will be expecting to see your conversion on your tax return. That part isn't usually the problem. The problem is if you recharacterize, the IRS may or may not get the paperwork straight on that transaction. Therefore, it is possible if you make a conversion or multiple conversions and recharacterization you could get a letter from the IRS. It will take some time to straighten the problem. As a practical matter, we have had clients make conversions and recharacterizations and the IRS sent erroneous notices indicating a tax liability. There is an excellent change you will have the same problem. If you are converting and recharacterizing $5,000, is it worth the aggravation? Probably not. If you are converting and/or recharacterzing $100,000 or more, is it worth the aggravation? I think so. For numbers in between, I will leave that to your discretion.

Story – Vincent & Edith Butler: Sometimes a Roth IRA Conversion Doesn't Pay

Biography

Vince and Edith Butler are good people living in Chambersburg, Pennsylvania. Vince is now 78 and Edith is 74. They both enjoy excellent health. Both of their parents lived into their nineties and Vince and Edith figure that they probably will too. Edith volunteers at different church functions. Vince plays cards with the guys at the Volunteer Fire Department. He usually wins too, but a big day might be winnings of $10. They are the kind of people you just like as soon as you meet them.

They have two daughters and four grandchildren. Both their daughters are doing well financially and aren't looking to inherit anything. Compared to some of the other people mentioned in the book, they don't have a lot of money. They, however, consider themselves blessed. All their children live nearby. They babysit frequently and genuinely love their grandchildren. At the end of the day, however, they are happy to say, "That was great! Here are your kids back!"

They live within their means but feel that money is tight. Right now, most of their money is in CDs and cash. They are afraid of the stock market. They read about Roth IRA conversions and found my material on the internet. They purchased my book, *Retire Secure!* (Wiley, Feb., 2009), and took advantage of my free consultation. They wondered if Roth IRA conversions would be good for them and their family. They drove over two hours to see me.

Here are their assets:
> After-tax assets = $50,000
> IRAs and/or retirement plan assets – $450,000
> Home and personal belongings = $200,000
> Other investments and assets = $-0-

Income and tax return situation:
> Social Security now being received – his $16,000/yr., hers
> $11,000/yr. (gross)
> Pension income $12,000/yr. not growing with inflation
> Interest income, non-qualified dividends and short-term
>   capital gains = $1,000
> Qualified dividend income & long-term capital gains = $2,000
> RMD income is currently $22,167
> Standard deduction is used with real-estate tax allowance

Spending needs:
> Currently spending $60,000/yr.
> No mortgages or loans
> Like to make occasional gifts to children or grandchildren as needed

Analysis, Discussion and Recommendation

The Butler's situation is common. Clients who received Social Security income mistakenly think they are in a low tax bracket for a Roth IRA and that a Roth conversion could be done at a low tax cost. Frequently, the main concern is assuring that their money will last the rest of their lives. They probably will need to use their IRA during their own lifetimes as opposed to treating it as an inheritance for their children.

Please refer to the "2010 IRA Conversion Planning spreadsheet" which shows tax calculations on different levels of conversion income in 2010. As you can see in 2010, without any Roth IRA conversions, their income tax is $3,071 on income including the $22,167 of RMDs from the IRA. At most, they would have paid 13.85% tax on that RMD income.

This is a very low income tax rate, and it is not expected to change much in the future. They are low income retirees and benefit greatly from the low taxability of Social Security. Between the pension, Social Security and RMDs, they have the means to pay their bills. This is good and they have a general skepticism about Roth conversions where the additional taxes would eat into their nest egg. That would not be comfortable for them.

If they were to do a Roth conversion of a small amount, say $10,000, they would pay 27.75% tax on it. A $20,000 conversion is taxed overall at 23.48% and even the best choice of a $30,000 conversion is taxed at 22.33% tax. This is too high for my liking. I would not recommend a conversion for the Butlers based on these tax rate issues alone. We have done a calculation showing there is a 28-year break-even point for paying such a high rate of tax on the conversion when RMDs would have been taxed at such a low rate.

The children, the beneficiaries, earn about $90,000. They have sizable itemized deductions and personal exemptions for their family and are still in the 15% tax bracket.

If the children inherit 1/4 of the IRA, their own RMDs would be small enough to keep them in the 15% tax bracket, so there would not be a great advantage to getting a Roth instead of the IRA and after-tax funds. But in reality, there may not be much IRA left to inherit as Vincent and Edith may have to use it themselves.

I would not recommend a Roth conversion for this situation.

Though the Butlers came to see me about Roth IRA conversions, as you might expect, I had other advice for them. I was afraid with the long-life expectancies and their extremely conservative investing that they were going to be crushed with inflation and their purchasing power would be severely limited in their older age.

I recommended taking 25% of their portfolio and investing it in the stock market. That suggestion went nowhere. I also recommending taking roughly 25% of their portfolio and purchasing an immediate annuity. This is considerably different than a tax-deferred or commercial annuity. This is a simple product. You give the insurance company money and they provide a guaranteed income stream for the rest of both of Vince's and Edith's lives. I recommended they take an inflation-adjusted-immediate annuity. That means their initial monthly payments would be smaller than an immediate annuity without an inflation adjustment, but the annuity will increase with the cost of living as time goes by. I more fully analyze immediate annuities in *Retire Secure!* (Wiley, Feb., 2009). It may seem like belt and suspenders, but we ended up buying three $33,000 immediate annuities from three different companies. The downside of three different companies is that they receive three monthly checks. The upside is if one of the companies goes belly up and the state insurance fund doesn't cover them (which it should), then they will at least get income from the two other companies.

Vincent & Edith Butler
2010 IRA Conversion Planning

RECOMMENDATION: For year 2009 convert $140,000 to top of 28% bracket

Assumptions for 2009 - Nothing unusual

Estimated tax situation for 2009 (using 2008 rates):

Roth Conversion Amount	Total Federal AMT & Income Tax	FY1 AMT Included	Overall Tax on the Conversion	Overall Conversion Tax %	Taxable Income	Incremental Taxable Income	Incremental Income Tax	Incremental Conversion	!! FOCUS HERE!! Incremental Conversion Tax %	Bracket - Notes
0	3,071	0	0		27,834					Over half of SS not taxable
10,000	5,846	0	2,775	27.75%	46,334	18,500	2,775	10,000	27.75%	SS becoming taxable, in the 15% TB
20,000	7,766	0	4,695	23.48%	59,117	12,783	1,920	10,000	19.20%	SS now fully taxable but in the 15% TB
30,000	9,769	0	6,698	22.33%	69,117	10,000	2,003	10,000	20.03%	Moving from 15% to the 25% TB
40,000	12,269	0	9,198	23.00%	79,117	10,000	2,500	10,000	25.00%	In the 25% tax bracket
50,000	14,769	0	11,698	23.40%	89,117	10,000	2,500	10,000	25.00%	In the 25% tax bracket

—— **$$$** ——

Key Lesson for this Chapter

Like all crucial decisions, a Roth IRA conversion comes with a few risks you must consider before making your final choice. Don't ignore these risks, but don't let them sour you either. Roth IRA conversions, by and large, are excellent tools for providing you and your family tax-free growth for generations.

Chapter Twelve

The Synergistic Strategies of Roth IRA Conversions and Delaying or Even Returning Your Social Security

"When prosperity comes, do not use all of it."

— Confucius

Main Topics

- The benefits of delaying Social Security
- Should you consider giving back your Social Security
- The synergy between delaying or giving back your Social Security with Roth IRA conversions

Key Idea

Weigh your options when it comes to taking Social Security. If you don't need the money, you may be better off delaying Social Security and making a series of Roth IRA conversions. Some should consider returning their Social Security, getting a tax deduction and making a Roth IRA conversion in the same year.

—— **$$$** ——

The first part of this chapter will examine synergy between delaying your Social Security and making a Roth IRA conversion. The second part of the chapter will examine the issue of returning your Social Security and making a Roth IRA conversion in the year you give back your Social Security.

Delaying Social Security and Roth IRA Conversions

Here is the scenario: you are collecting Social Security and in your tax bracket it is not subject to income taxes. If you make a Roth IRA conversion, the additional income on your conversion would cause your Social Security to be taxable, and you would jump from the 15% tax bracket to the 28% bracket or higher. Please see Chapter Seven for an example of when and how this taxation of Social Security benefits kicks in.

One way to get around the tax jump is to defer taking your Social Security. If you elect to wait to take your Social Security, you are potentially cutting your taxes not only on your Social Security benefits, but also could put yourself in a lower tax bracket for a Roth IRA conversion, making the conversion even more profitable. Generally speaking, individuals who don't really need the money immediately are well served by making a series of Roth IRA conversions and holding off on collecting Social Security for the primary wage earner.

> Generally speaking, individuals who don't really need the money immediately are well served by making a series of Roth IRA conversions and holding off on collecting Social Security for the primary wage earner.

I can see some of your eyes popping out of your head right now. "What? Give up Social Security just to reduce taxes on a Roth IRA conversion? Never!" But wait, you are not giving it up forever. In fact by delaying taking Social Security until 66 or even age 70, you might end up setting yourself up for a richer financial future.

Larry Kotlikoff,[5] an economics professor at Boston University has done an excellent analysis on the optimal time to take Social Security. Larry's suggestion of delaying taking your Social Security benefits came without even considering the benefits of a lower tax on Roth IRA conversions. Larry thinks that holding off on your Social Security until age 70 is usually a good deal for you. Most of us know that if we hold off collecting Social Security, we will get a bigger Social

---

5 Larry has much to offer on the issue of deferring or giving back your Social Security as well as on other financial issues. He has written some extensive financial software. He has a free version that can be found at www.esplanner.com. He also has a more extensive program that you can purchase.

Security check when we do start collecting. Larry would maintain that in many cases it is worth delaying your Social Security, particularly for the spouse who has the higher Social Security earnings.[6]

Larry claims that holding off on Social Security is the most cost-effective method of purchasing "longevity insurance." The idea is you attempt to provide for the risk of surviving a long time and running out of money.

I have done some analysis on this issue as to the optimal time to take Social Security. The way I analyzed it was that I assumed you didn't need the money to meet your monthly expenses. I also assumed if you started taking Social Security earlier, you could invest the proceeds. Then, I would take an interest factor, 3% after inflation. I would then grow the income from Social Security at this 3% real rate and graph the result.

Then, I would compare that graph to a graph where you don't take Social Security early. I also analyzed if you should take it at age 66 or wait until you are age 70 to take Social Security. Obviously, if you are taking Social Security based on your earnings history—and not your spouse's earning history—you will get a much bigger check if you hold off taking your Social Security until you are age 70. During the early years, you will have less money than the person who started taking smaller payments, but started taking them earlier.

Eventually if you lived long enough, your balance in the account where you waited to take Social Security would exceed the amount that you would have if you had taken it earlier. At some point, in your early 80s—depending on your assumptions—you would "break even." If you live beyond that point, you will enjoy a higher income for the rest of your life. Of course the risk is if you died earlier than that breakeven point, you would lose—and in retrospect it would have been a mistake to hold off taking your Social Security.

Larry Kotlikoff, however, says that isn't really the best way to think about it. He calls that "thinking like an actuary." (I have been accused of worse).

Larry declares, "Don't think like an actuary on this issue. Think like an economist." Larry would say, if you think about it like an economist, you would

---

6 I recommend listening to my radio show when Larry Kotlikoff was talking about the optimal timing for taking Social Security. That show can be found at www.retiresecure.com.

think that the idea is to include "longevity insurance" into your calculations. That is, if you die earlier and even if you don't break even, it won't make any difference to you because you will be dead.

Larry continues: what you really want to do is to make sure you have enough money to live comfortably for the rest of your life—where the rest of your life could be a very long time. If you hold off on Social Security and you end up living far beyond the projected break even point, you will not only be better off, but you will also not run out of money. Larry claims to have analyzed this issue to death and frankly, I believe him. So after analyzing all the nuances of Social Security and taking all the factors into account, Larry claims that holding off on Social Security is the most cost-effective method of purchasing "longevity insurance." The idea is you attempt to provide for the risk of surviving a long time and running out of money.

In the second edition of *Retire Secure!* (Wiley, Feb., 2009), I actually analyzed "longevity insurance." There is an insurance product called a longevity annuity similar to an immediate annuity: you make a large payment up front, which is like a regular immediate annuity. The difference with a longevity annuity is that you must wait a certain number of years in the future before you get any payments. It is not a popular product, but one that I think is a good solution for people who are afraid of outliving their money.

Larry's analysis leads him to believe an economical method of insuring against the risk of longevity is actually deferring when you start collecting your Social Security.

Larry has much to offer on the issue of deferring or giving back your Social Security as well as on other financial issues. He has written some extensive financial software. He has a free version that can be found at www.esplanner. com. He also has a more extensive program that you can purchase.

Larry's analysis fits in very nicely with my goal of not wanting you to pay income tax on your Social Security income if you make a Roth IRA conversion. This is probably particularly appropriate for people who are in the 15% bracket who might trigger a significant tax on Social Security if they make a Roth IRA conversion. One combination strategy is to hold off on your Social Security and make a series of Roth IRA conversions every year until you reach 70. Then later, when you reach age 70 you have a RMD and Social Security which will put you in a higher tax bracket. You will have, however, already converted at least a portion of your IRA to a Roth while you were in a lower tax bracket.

Preliminary indications, however, indicate that readers who don't really need the money immediately are well served by making a series of Roth IRA conversions and holding off on collecting Social Security for the primary wage earner.

If you are married, there is one other reason to wait until age 70 to start collecting your Social Security retirement benefits. As Larry discusses at www.esplanner.com (click *Learn More,* click *Case Studies* and then click *When Should I Take Social Security?*), after both spouses have reached their full retirement ages, the Social Security system permits one spouse (not both) to collect spousal benefits without forcing the other spouse to start collecting his or her retirement benefits. Let's say that the wife and the husband are both age 66 and have reached their full retirement ages. Let's also assume that the husband was the higher earner. Then he can apply for retirement benefits, but immediately suspend the collection of these benefits. Indeed, he can suspend collection until age 70. By suspending collection, his benefit, when he ultimately receives it, will continue to grow due to Social Security's delayed retirement credit. But by applying for his retirement benefit (even though he also suspends its collection), he permits his wife to apply for a spousal benefit based on his earnings record. Meanwhile, she can continue to defer collecting her own retirement benefit until age 70. Thus the wife collects spousal benefits with no real penalty associated with doing so. In effect, she collects spousal benefits for several years for free. As Larry explains, the Social Security Administration prevents both spouses from doing this unless they are ex-spouses and legally divorced. Then both can collect free spousal benefits.

Returning Your Social Security Benefits

Larry even goes a step further. He often recommends that people who have already collected Social Security give it back and apply for higher benefits! You would then, in effect, be treated as if you never started collecting Social Security. That means your benefit will be higher for the rest of your life. You would have received the use of the money and when you pay it back, you don't have to give back the interest. Even better, the repayment of past benefits is tax deductible.

Presumably, the best age to do this is right before you turn 70. If you are much older, you might not have enough life expectancy for your increased payments to make up for the fact you gave up your Social Security. If you are much younger, you don't have as much Social Security to give back.

Frankly, most readers and clients would not even seriously consider giving their Social Security back. I could show them all the numbers in the world, and they still would not give their Social Security back, even if by doing so would pay the taxes on a Roth IRA conversion. I have had people look at me as if I suggested they take their money, turn it into cash and burn it in a big bonfire.

The obvious objection is if you are willing to pay back Social Security, how do you know for sure Social Security won't go broke or at least be crippled? Maybe you won't get your money back even if you live a long time. That is a good objection. I will leave that objection to the economists who understand these issues better than I do. Larry Kotlikoff is such a man. He discusses that issue on my radio show, and you can listen to the show at www.retiresecure.com. Other economists may disagree.

> *"An economist's guess is liable to be as good as anybody else's."*
>
> — Will Rogers

In any case, the point of including this discussion in this book is twofold.

1. Make you aware of the strategy. My recommendation is that, at a minimum, it is worth exploring even if you don't like the sound of it.

2. The second reason for including this discussion in a book focused on Roth IRA conversions is to examine the huge synergistic benefits of combining the Social Security giveback with a Roth IRA conversion.

Let's assume you have examined the issue of giving back your Social Security, and you are entertaining the idea. If you decide to repay your Social Security benefits, you do get a significant tax benefit.

One of your tax choices, the most relevant for our purposes, is deducting (a miscellaneous itemized deduction on Schedule A not subject to 2% of your AGI) the repayment. Another choice is recalculating your prior taxes and claiming a tax credit on the Social Security benefits that you are repaying. IRS Publication 915 explains the specific mechanics on the two choices that you have. If you go this way, it would be helpful if either you or preferably an appropriate advisor, were to do an analysis of which way is best for your situation. If you are a Roth IRA conversion candidate, it is probably an easy call: take the deduction.

Let's assume you and/or your advisor have now determined that it makes economic sense to repay your benefits and delay the collecting of them until you reach age 70. You can implement a Roth conversion strategy in the year that you repay the Social Security benefits. You decide to repay the $117,647 of benefits that you collected the past four years. Of this total repayment, you had included $100,000 (or 85% of the total benefits received in your gross income) over the past four years. Your current year adjusted gross income is $100,000 and you deduct the $100,000 on Schedule A. There is a good chance that you are probably wasting a large portion of that deduction as well as other deductions and the tax benefits are minimal.

If you do a $100,000 Roth conversion to offset the $100,000 deduction, you have effectively done a conversion at very little tax cost. You would lose a little of this $100,000 deduction due to the reduction of your overall itemized deductions when you increase your adjusted gross income by the $100,000 conversion to $200,000. You could also choose to do a conversion consistent with the tax-bracket strategy I am also advocating in this book.

—— $$$ ——

Key Lesson for this Chapter

Although some may balk at the idea, delaying or even giving back Social Security in conjunction with a Roth IRA conversion, it may make good financial sense. Although delaying or giving back your Social Security is controversial, it also may be a good idea. The synergy, however, between delaying or repaying your social security and making a Roth IRA conversion can be extremely beneficial. At a minimum, it is worth considering.

Chapter Thirteen

Specific Advice to Taxpayers in Different Tax Brackets

"In theory there is no difference between theory and practice. In practice there is."

— Yogi Berra

Main Topics

- Specific recommendations for taxpayers in:
- 0% tax bracket
- 10% tax bracket
- 15% tax bracket
- 25% tax bracket
- 33% tax bracket
- Top tax bracket

Key Idea

Over the years we have found repeated patterns of useful strategies for clients and IRA owners in different brackets. We present these useful strategies in the hope you can examine your tax bracket and see if some of our common recommended strategies are appropriate for you.

—— $$$ ——

Please note all this analysis is the same for employees who have 401(k) or 403(b) balances and have access to a Roth Designated Account. Please see "What's New" before Chapter One.

Zero Percent Tax Bracket Readers

You might think that anybody in the zero percent bracket would not bother reading this book. You are probably right. There are, however, IRA owners in the zero percent bracket that could reap huge benefits for themselves and/or their families by making a Roth IRA conversion.

One fairly common zero percent bracket IRA owner who should consider a Roth IRA conversion is someone who has for one reason or another, extraordinarily high deductible expenses and ends up wasting those deductions. I would like to change that.

For example, let's assume you or even someone you know—or even your parents—has extraordinarily high medical expenses. This often occurs later in life when an IRA owner needs long-term care either at a facility or even in their own residence. Today I saw a client with minimal taxable income who is entering a retirement home and will receive a medical deduction of $150,000. It would be criminal if we didn't do a Roth IRA conversion so he and his family could enjoy tax-free growth at what will essentially be at no tax cost.

Many, if not most, legitimate expenses for medical care are properly deductible and many times out-of-pocket medical costs are $60,000/year or more. Let's assume that including exemptions, deductions, etc. that deductible expenses exceed income by $25,000. If you did nothing about a Roth IRA conversion, taxable income would be minus $25,000. Even if we did a $25,000 conversion, it would offset the excess of expenses over income and bring taxable income and tax to zero. In effect, we are getting a $25,000 Roth IRA conversion for free.

In the case where the IRA owner is getting a large, one-time deduction, a large, one-time Roth IRA conversion would be indicated and we would be doing a fine thing for the family.

If during the year you, or your friend, or a client, has these extraordinarily high deductions, it should trigger the thought that that person should be making a significant Roth IRA conversion. It is possible that somebody could make a $150,000 or even higher Roth IRA conversion and still not be subject to any taxes because the conversion will just go to offset the deductible expenses.

It is terribly frustrating to me when I see IRA owners who have gone to low-cost tax preparers (or worse, high-cost tax preparers) who did not pick up on the idea that their client had an opportunity to make a Roth IRA conversion without having to pay any taxes.

In a separate chapter we address the issue of a year with large deductible business losses. (Please see Chapter Eight). It is basically the same concept, which is to make a Roth IRA conversion so you won't waste deductions or losses.

The Ten Percent Bracket Readers

Ten percent bracket taxpayers might have an opportunity to make a Roth IRA conversion in an amount that will take them to the top of—but not to exceed the ten percent bracket. If they were to do a conversion that would take them over the ten percent bracket into the 15 % bracket, then you have a five percent or a 50 % increase in the taxability of that additional income. For most ten percent taxpayers that will be a heavy burden. But if this is an extraordinarily low year, and future years look better, it might very well be a good strategy to make a Roth IRA conversion past the point of the 10% bracket.

We dealt with one relatively wealthy couple who was in the ten percent bracket because the wife who was terminally ill had extraordinary medical bills. The husband, who was the one who came to see me was a retired engineer and didn't want to make a Roth IRA conversion of any amount that would push him above the 10% bracket. In his case, though, since his wife had a relatively short life expectancy, it would be likely that in the near future, he would be single and not have much medical expense. We projected he would be in the 25 percent bracket. Therefore, making Roth IRA conversions that went beyond the top of the ten percent bracket made sense. The point about making a Roth IRA conversion when you are married and expect to be single (and hence be in a higher tax bracket) often holds true in the year of the first spouse's death when the surviving spouse can still benefit from the married tax tables.

The Fifteen Percent Bracket Readers

One of the interesting facets of clients in the 15 percent bracket is that there is often an opportunity for a profitable Roth IRA conversion, but also an opportunity for an expensive Roth IRA conversion mistake. In practice, one of the issues that we commonly run across is the taxability of Social Security. Accordingly we have included an entire section on the taxability of Social Security as it relates to Roth IRA conversions. Please see Chapter Seven.

The other problem or challenge for people in the 15 percent bracket is that their dividends and or capital gains are often taxed at a lower rate and when you add income for a Roth IRA conversion, the income tax rate on the dividends and capital gains increases significantly.

> Making Roth IRA conversions for IRA owners who are in the 15% bracket is an area where we often find a little knowledge is a dangerous thing.

Making Roth IRA conversions for IRA owners who are in the 15% bracket is an area where we often find *a little knowledge is a dangerous thing*. A common mistake for taxpayers in the 15 percent bracket is to ignore the higher marginal tax rates on Social Security, the qualified dividend preferred tax rate and the capital gains tax rate. What happens is even though their actual taxable income still falls within 15 % percent marginal tax rate, their true marginal tax rate on the conversion is significantly higher.

For 2010, the maximum tax rate on qualified dividends and long-term capital gain transactions is 15%. Even if you are in the highest marginal tax bracket (35%), you pay a maximum of 15% on these types of income. Taxpayers in the 15% marginal tax bracket, however, pay 0% tax rate on their qualified dividends and long-term capital gains. The important point is, that if your conversion makes your taxable income greater than the 15% tax table amount, the qualified income is taxed at 15% rather than being tax-free. This will cause the conversion tax you pay to be much greater than your marginal tax rate.

The above-mentioned tax rate reductions are set to expire in 2010. In 2011, the maximum long-term capital gains tax rate goes back up to 20% from 15%. A lower 10% tax rate is used by taxpayers who are in the 15% tax bracket. In 2011, dividend income will be taxed as ordinary income at your highest marginal tax rate. Although these changes are set to occur there is a high probability that new legislation will be passed to impose the higher rates on high income households ($200,000 for individuals: $250,000 for families). The lower, more favorable capital gains and dividend tax rates could remain intact for lower-and middle-income households.

Another problem for 15 percent taxpayers is if they make a conversion that even without considering the "tax tricks" (please see Chapter Seven), the conversion could push them into the next tax bracket which is the 25 percent tax bracket. That's quite a jump from 15 percent to the 25 percent tax bracket. When you make that big of a leap in tax brackets, the break even point or time it takes to get your tax money back in terms of purchasing power is not day one (Please see Chapter One for a breakeven of day one). Rather the break even period could be ten years or longer. We usually discourage 15 percent tax bracket IRA owners to make a Roth IRA conversion that would take them above the 15 percent tax bracket. Conversely, if there is a reason their tax bracket would go up in the future, such as hitting your RMD age, or becoming widowed and having to pay tax at single tax rates, doing conversions above the 15% tax bracket may be appropriate.

Interestingly enough, we actually have quite a few clients who are in the 15% tax bracket but still have investments worth over $1,000,000. They are typically retirees who no longer have income from their wages or businesses. They are, however, younger than age 70, so their RMDs have not kicked in. They are prime examples of clients whose long-term tax rate will go up, even forgetting tax increases due to new laws. For many of these clients, it will make sense to make Roth IRA conversions at least up to the top of the 15% bracket and sometimes up the top of the 28% tax bracket.

The Twenty-Five and Twenty-Eight Percent Tax Bracket Readers

I mentioned earlier that it is often a good strategy to make a Roth IRA conversion that would take your income to the top of your existing tax bracket, in this case, the 25% tax bracket. Doing a series of those Roth IRA conversions over a number of years would be an excellent strategy. I also mentioned that even though you would not be breaking even on day one making a conversion that would push your income to the top of the 28% tax bracket, is still feasible. So, assume you don't have any income-tax-bracket tricks (please see Chapter One and your taxable income before a Roth conversion is $100,000 in 2010. You could convert $37,300 and still be in the 25% bracket. If on the other hand, you converted $109,250, the first $37,300 would be in the 25% bracket and the next $71,950 would be taxed at the 28% bracket. It is a fairly typical to recommend a series of conversions that would take you to the top of the 28% bracket, even recognizing that we aren't breaking even on day one. (Please see Chapter One for a discussion of breaking even on day one).

Another factor relevant for 25% taxpayers is that starting in 2011, their income will be taxed at the 28% bracket. (At least that is the law as of now which may change). So making a Roth IRA conversion to the top of the 28% bracket, in effect, is actually breaking even if not on day one, at least in year one—more motivation to make a Roth IRA conversion to the top of the 28% bracket.

I would hesitate, however, to take the 25% bracket taxpayer who is likely to be in the 25% or even the 28% bracket for a long time and then do a conversion to the top of the 33% tax bracket. That would be a fairly large jump in not only tax but tax bracket. You should only do that conversion if you understand the long break-even period. Depending on your age, making a conversion for a 25% taxpayer that bumps them up to the 33% bracket might be more of an estate-planning strategy than something that is going to help you during your lifetime. It would be even a better strategy if you had at least one wealthy child to whom you were planning to leave the Roth IRA.

Please note that Steve Kohman, CPA, CSEP says, "One of the ways you can get around this strategy is to use the Roth Launcher strategy as described in Chapter Ten."

The Thirty-Three Percent Tax Bracket Readers

If you are in the 33% bracket and your income will not go down in the near future, life starts getting interesting. You should probably be taking a look at a very significant Roth IRA conversion.

If you are in the 33% bracket in 2010 and your income is the same in 2011 and future years, your taxes are going up.

Please see the chart below. The chart summarizes tax rates between 2010 and 2013 (2010 being the last year of the Bush Era tax cuts and 2013 being the year when the 3.8% Health Care Reform Surtax takes effect).

Taxable Income – Married Filing Jointly	2010	2011	Top Rate with Surtax 2013*
$0 – 16,750	10%	15%	15%
$16,750 – 68,000	15%	15%	15%
$68,000 – 137,300	25%	28%	28%
$137,300 – 209,250	28%	31%	31%
$209,250 – 373,650	33%	36%	39.8%
Over $373,650	35%	39.6%	43.4%

The starting point for the amount that you should consider for a Roth IRA conversion is now going to be less dependent on tax brackets and more dependent on your current cash flow. If you have sufficient money outside of the IRA or retirement plan, and your cash flow is still good, then making very significant Roth IRA conversions and perhaps using the strategy of multiple conversions and doing a look back—though it seems aggressive—(the Roth Launcher), might actually be a reasonable starting point for what you should be thinking about.

The Roth IRA conversions work best for taxpayers in the highest tax bracket—much better than it does for readers with middle income and lower income brackets. You break even (measured in purchasing power) on day one, or perhaps year one. Remember, we are using our purchasing power paradigm established in Chapter One.

If lower-and middle-income taxpayers make too large of a Roth IRA conversion, they would not just pay more tax but pay tax at a higher tax rate than their tax rate after the conversion. In your case, if you are always going to be in a high tax bracket of 33% or higher, then it is going to be even more beneficial for you than it would be for lower or middle income taxpayers.

Perhaps one of the tougher issues that you might face is that you might not remain in that tax bracket forever—your job or business might not continue indefinitely. In that case, it might not be as advisable to make a significant Roth IRA conversion.

Please assume you're earning $250,000 and you're in the 33% tax bracket. You have only two more years before you retire. After retirement, you will have a number of years where you will not yet be age 70 and you will have no required minimum distribution and no income from your job or business. In that case, you could actually end up dropping down to perhaps the 15% tax bracket.

If you had paid income tax at the 33% tax bracket to save taxes at the 15% tax bracket, that would certainly not be good. It would make more sense in that situation to wait until your income bracket is low and then make either a large Roth IRA conversion at that point or perhaps, a series of Roth IRA conversions.

If you are in your fifties and you have ten or more years of projected high income and then at retirement you have lower income, it is a much tougher issue. Then it would make sense to do financial projections, taking all of your income and your individual circumstances into account. One of the problems with making projections for someone in their fifties is that there are so many variables: interest rates, job stability, income, etc.

People in the Top Tax Brackets Who are Likely to Remain There

I would say the starting point for people in the highest tax brackets who will remain in the highest tax brackets and whose family will always be in the high tax brackets is to make a Roth IRA conversion of the entire IRA. This assumes, of course you have the money to pay the tax on the conversion. Perhaps you should consider the multiple IRA approach and converting everything and keeping the winners as described in Chapter Ten with the Roth Launcher strategy. The Roth IRA conversion will likely benefit you and your family more than it will any of the other readers.

The other advantage for the people, who are in the 35% bracket and are considering Roth IRA conversions of perhaps a million dollars or more, is that the estate-tax advantage of reducing your estate adds tremendous value to the conversion.

For example, we did a series of projections for a sophisticated client who was in the top tax bracket and will likely always be in the top tax bracket. He is also headed for federal estate taxes. Both he and his wife were reluctant to make significant gifts and since they were not insurable, life insurance wasn't an option. In this case, even before he came to me, he had concluded that the right thing to do was to make a Roth IRA conversion of the entire IRA, which was at least in one case more than two million dollars. We basically confirmed his gut instinct and the main suggestion that we made was that he break it up into multiple accounts and use the Roth Launcher strategy discussed in Chapter Ten.

We did find an interesting quirk when we make financial projections for people in the 35% tax brackets. If you are always going to be in the top bracket, it tends to be a relatively easy call to make a conversion of the entire IRA. In most situations we conclude converting the entire IRA or using the Roth Launcher strategy and converting it all is the best solution. Then issues like gifting, life insurance, some of the more popular methods of leverage gifting such as Grantor Retained Annuity Trust, Grantor Retained Income Trust, Family Limited Partnerships, Leveraged LLCs, etc. become more relevant.

It should also be noted that people in the top tax brackets and particularly people with significant wealth, perhaps ten million dollars or more, should consider not making Section 529 Plans contributions.

In many cases if you are going to be alive while your grandchildren are actually attending college, they will likely be better off if you make a tuition payment directly to either a private school or a college because it is not considered a gift. Then, you could still give $13,000 (or if you are married, $26,000) to your grandchild. If, instead, you make significant contributions to a 529 Plan, that is deemed a gift. Then when that money is used for college, you would not be able to make an additional gift.

Please note all this analysis is the same for employees who have 401(k) or 403(b) balances and have access to a Roth designated account. Please see "What's New" before Chapter One.

—— $$$ ——

Key Lesson for this Chapter

We have identified common patterns for taxpayers in every tax bracket. You should at least look to see what pattern and potential advice we have for readers in your tax bracket.

Chapter Fourteen

Times When You Should Spend Your Roth IRA

"I have enough money to last me the rest of my life, unless I buy something."

— Jackie Mason

Main Topics

- When spending Roth IRA dollars first makes sense
- Spending a large amount in a single year
- Spending smaller amounts over several years

Key Idea

In select cases, it can make sense to spend your Roth IRA dollars before your traditional IRA dollars. The reason is that sometimes spending Roth dollars will keep you from paying a high tax rate on the withdrawal of your traditional IRA.

—— $$$ ——

This is another fairly tough chapter that could be skipped. If you have a lot of money outside of your IRAs and Roth IRAs, you would be an especially good candidate to skip this chapter. If most of your wealth is in traditional IRAs and Roth IRAs and your spending needs exceed your required minimum distribution, this chapter is on point for you.

In Chapter Seventeen I talk about our recommended spending order for your different "pots" of money. In general, I recommended spending after-tax dollars first, then IRA dollars, and finally, Roth IRA dollars. I did, however, qualify the advice with *subject to exceptions*. This chapter highlights those important exceptions.

There might come a time when you have exhausted your after-tax dollars. Let's assume you find yourself with nothing but traditional IRAs and Roth IRAs. In that case, it will likely be prudent to spend at least some of your Roth IRA dollars. We examine two situations where it makes sense to spend your Roth IRA dollars before your IRA dollars.

Roth IRA Useful for Large Single Year Spending Needs

A new client, Bill, came to us for advice on how to finance a unit in a retirement community that he would like to join. This particular retirement community will not accept mortgages. You have to pay cash. The purchase price is $375,000.

Consider Bill's situation:

Traditional IRA	$1,600,000
Roth IRA	300,000
After-Tax Assets	5,000
TOTAL	$1,905,000

Bill is 75 years old and normally has spending needs of $60,000/year (indexed for 3% inflation) over and above his pension and Social Security. Now he wants to spend an extra $375,000 for the unit in the retirement community. He is normally in the 25% tax bracket but if he takes additional money from his traditional IRA, he will pay 35% tax. Another option is to spend the RMD ($69,869 in the first year) from the traditional IRA and take the rest as needed from his Roth IRA. We assume an 8% rate of investment return and only 18% tax on after-tax investment income. Comparing these two options, we find that at the end of the year, he has the following assets remaining:

	Spending From Traditional IRA	Spending From Roth IRA
Traditional IRA	$1,150,966	$1,658,131
Roth IRA	324,000	1,330
After-Tax Assets	5,400	5,400
TOTAL	$1,480,366	$1,664,861

And we should compare the remaining balances not just at the end of the first year, but perhaps at the age of 90 or 100. Using these assumptions at age 90, the remaining balances differ greatly in composition as follows:

Spending From Spending From

	Traditional IRA	Roth IRA
Traditional IRA	$1,081,414	$2,122,574
Roth IRA	1,027,783	4,218
After-Tax Assets	5,000	408,080
TOTAL	$2,114,197	$2,534,872

In comparing these two options, we must use an appropriate tax rate to reduce the measurement of the pre-tax traditional IRA (the "liquidation rate"). A 25% liquidation rate is probably appropriate because this approximates his future tax rate on normal withdrawals.

Our calculations find there is an advantage by spending the Roth IRA first as follows:

Age 75	Age 90	Age 100
$57,703	$160,385	$179,009

The conclusion is that there are circumstances where there is a long-term advantage for the IRA owner to spend his Roth IRA before his IRA. In this particular example, Bill needed a large distribution to pay for the retirement community.

Roth IRA Useful for Smaller Multi-Year Spending Needs

We made financial projections for Burt and Helen, a couple who had a much different situation than did Bill. We also concluded that they should start spending at least a portion of their Roth IRA. Just as conversions are better when the taxes you pay on the conversion are lower, spending the Roth is better when the taxes saved are the greatest.

The following presents how Burt and Helen benefit from spending a small amount of their Roth IRA to save taxes in a single year. Burt and Helen are 75 years old. They have $700,000 in an IRA and $300,000 in a Roth IRA. They don't have any other savings. They spend $90,862 per year.

Burt and Helen have $40,000 in total Social Security income, a $12,000 pension, and they usually spend $50,000 from the IRA to meet their spending needs. While making financial projections, we noticed they would benefit from spending their Roth IRA before their traditional IRA. Since they have $700,000 in their IRA, their RMD is only $30,568. The 2010 taxes are projected to be as follows by taking withdrawals only from the traditional IRA and assuming that they will take the standard deduction:

Pension income	$12,000
Taxable Social Security income – 85%	34,000
Traditional IRA withdrawal	50,000
Adjusted gross income	$96,000
Taxable income	$75,100
Income Tax	$11,138

The calculation of the amount available for spending is as follows:

Pension income	$12,000
Total Social Security income	40,000
Traditional IRA withdrawal	50,000
Income tax	(11,138)
Spending	$90,862

You cannot reduce your IRA withdrawals to the RMD amount unless you spend money from your Roth IRA. By doing so, however, the taxes are decreased significantly as follows:

Pension income	$12,000
Taxable Social Security income – 54.5%	21,783
Traditional IRA withdrawal	30,568
Adjusted gross income	$64,351
Taxable income	$43,451
Income tax	$ 5,681

Spending needs are met as follows:

Pension income	$12,000
Total Social Security income	40,000
Traditional IRA withdrawal	30,568
Roth IRA withdrawal	13,975
Income tax	(5,681)
Spending	$90,862

By reducing the taxable IRA withdrawal to the RMD amount and meeting spending requirements by taking $13,975 from the Roth IRA, the taxes are reduced by $5,457. The main tax break in this example is that Social Security benefits become less taxable without the RMD income from the IRA. Using this strategy, the tax savings are 39% of his Roth IRA withdrawal.

The 39% tax savings is far above their normal income tax bracket of 25%. This is a great way for them to use their Roth IRA during their lifetime in 2010 and future years. If this couple paid 25% tax to get money into the Roth IRA and saved 39% taxes by taking money out of the Roth IRA, they are way ahead of the game—even without consideration of the tax-free growth in the account. Spending Roth IRAs before traditional IRAs might also be profitable to preserve tax credits or deductions. In addition, sometimes it is useful to reduce your Alternative Minimum Tax (AMT). AMT increases as income goes marginally higher. In these kinds of situations, spending from the Roth instead of the traditional IRA can produce favorable tax saving results as well. The specifics of each year's tax situation should be considered in making these decisions.

—— **$$$** ——

Key Lesson for this Chapter

While it is our general preference for you to spend other money first, there are times, usually to keep you from withdrawing money from your traditional IRA at too high a tax rate, when it makes sense to spend your Roth IRA before your traditional IRA.

Chapter Fifteen

Roth IRA Conversions and Charitable Beneficiaries

"I resolved to stop accumulating and begin the infinitely more serious and difficult task of wise distribution."

— Andrew Carnegie

Main Topics

- Combining charitable gifts and Roth IRA conversion strategies
- Using life insurance to fund large charitable gifts
- Charitable Replacement Trusts

Key Idea

If you are leaving all your money to a charity at your death, a large Roth IRA conversion is probably not advisable. But, if you leaving some but not all of your money to charity, then a Roth IRA conversion could still be extremely beneficial.

—— **$$$** ——

One legitimate objection to making a Roth IRA conversion is that Roth IRAs are not good assets to leave to charity. That doesn't mean, however, just because you have charitable intent, you should not do a Roth IRA conversion.

Charities don't pay income taxes and they don't care if they receive money in the form of an inherited Roth IRA, traditional IRA, after-tax dollars, life insurance, etc. They just want the most money. So, there are "no income tax consequences" of leaving money to charity. Also, money left to charity will be estate-inheritance-and income tax-free. This is much different than if your heir or heirs are people. People should be using purchasing power, not total dollars (please see Chapter One) as their unit of value, and furthermore estate, inheritance, and income taxes will come into play.

Perhaps a few examples would help.

Bill has $1,000,000 in an IRA and $300,000 outside the IRA. Please assume an income tax rate of 30%. Bill, the IRA owner, made a Roth IRA conversion of the entire $1,000,000 IRA and used the remaining after-tax dollars to pay the tax on the Roth IRA conversion. He left his entire estate to charity and then died. The charity received $1,000,000. The IRS received the $300,000 taxes on the conversion.

If he hadn't made a Roth IRA conversion and he left his entire estate to charity, the charity would receive $1.3 million because there would be no taxes on the IRA because charities don't have to pay taxes on money left to them. The IRA money would have the same value to the charity as the face amount of the IRA. The IRS would have received nothing. The Roth IRA conversion in this case would be a mistake.

In my experience though, even if you are charitable, you are not likely to want to leave your entire estate to charity. For our next example, assume the same amount of money but let's assume that you want to leave at least some money to charity but leave most of your money to members of your family. Would a Roth IRA conversion still be a good idea for you?

Probably yes, but an accurate response is, "it depends." Let's assume you have an IRA of $1M and you want to leave $100,000 to the charity of your choice. In that case, as long as you don't make a Roth IRA conversion of more than $900,000, you will not be hurting the charity. In that situation, I would say to make the appropriate financial projections and convert the indicated amount, but no more than $900,000. Leave $100,000 of the IRA to the charity and everything else to your family. This would result in income tax savings to your family compared to leaving the charity $100,000 from your will instead of your IRA beneficiary form. They would have received the same amount of money, but by leaving the $100,000 to the charity through the beneficiary designation of the IRA instead of the will, you saved your family taxes on $100,000.

Non-Proportional Beneficiary Designations Adds Value for Heirs and Charities

If you have IRA dollars, Roth dollars and after-tax dollars available, you should normally fill charitable intentions with IRA dollars. Mechanically, this means that you have to change the beneficiary designation of the IRA—not leave a bequest in my will or revocable trust. I rarely see attorneys do this in practice. Usually, I see money going to a charity as a bequest in a will. What makes more sense is if the charity were named as part beneficiary of an IRA or retirement plan.

Let's start with our general rule that $1 of after-tax dollars are worth a dollar to an heir, a Roth IRA dollar is worth $1.40 to an heir due to the potential for extended tax-free growth (please see our article, *The Value of a Roth in an Estate*, on our website at http://www.rothira-advisor.com/rothvalue.htm) and an IRA dollar is worth less than a $1 to an heir due to pending income taxes on those savings. By leaving different types of dollars to different types of entities, we are maximizing our estate for all the beneficiaries. In effect, by cutting the pie up differently, we are making a bigger pie for our heirs.

A Common Mistake

Let's assume you have a simple situation where you have $500,000 in an IRA and $500,000 outside the IRA in after-tax dollars. Let's also assume you want to leave half your estate to your favorite charity and the other half to your children. Most readers in that situation would have wills and beneficiary designations of 50% to children and 50% to charity. I am suggesting to name the charity as the beneficiary for your IRA and to leave the after-tax dollars to your children.

Most of my clients want to leave the majority of their money to members of their family and a smaller percentage to charity. If that

> I am suggesting to name the charity as the beneficiary for your IRA and to leave the after-tax dollars to your children.

is the case with you, I would probably recommend you carve out a portion of an IRA, or for simplicity's sake, name the charity of your choice as the beneficiary for a separate IRA. This is far more tax effective than naming a charity in your will to receive a certain amount of money.

Legacy Impact of Combining Charitable Gifts with Roth IRA Conversions

This brings up the possibility of giving the charity $100,000 now using after-tax dollars, claiming the income tax deduction and then making the Roth IRA conversion of the entire million. The charitable donation will reduce the tax on the conversion. If you have an interest in giving some money away during your lifetime, this opens up tremendous opportunities.

Please consider the following table which shows the different ways a charity could be provided for. Here we are assuming the 35% income tax bracket and a taxable estate using a $3.5m exemption equivalent amount. We are also assuming a $100,000 bequest. Though the numbers would obviously be much lower for a smaller bequest or gift to charity, the same concepts would apply.

Providing for Charity and Roth IRAs for Heirs

	Other Bequest Without a Conversion	IRA Bequest Without a Conversion	Other Bequest With a Roth Conversion	IRA Bequest With a Roth Conversion	Lifetime Gift With a Roth Conversion
IRA Assets	$1,000,000	$1,000,000		$ 100,000	
Roth IRA			$1,000,000	900,000	$ 1,000,000
After-Tax Savings & Investments	3,000,000	3,000,000	2,650,000	2,685,000	2,585,000
Other Assets - Real Estate etc.	2,000,000	2,000,000	2,000,000	2,000,000	2,000,000
Total Estate	6,000,000	6,000,000	5,650,000	5,685,000	5,585,000
Bequest to Charity	(100,000)	(100,000)	(100,000)	(100,000)	0
Taxable Estate	5,900,000	5,900,000	5,550,000	5,585,000	5,585,000
Federal & State Inheritance Taxes	(1,226,025)	(1,226,025)	(1,059,863)	(1,076,479)	(1,076,479)
Income Tax Allowance	(350,000)	(315,000)	0	0	0
Net to Heirs	$4,323,975	$4,358,975	$4,490,137	$4,508,521	$4,508,521
Net to Charity	$100,000	$100,000	$100,000	$100,000	$100,000
Advantage over Other Bequest		**$ 35,000**	**$ 166,162**	**$ 184,546**	**$ 184,546**
Net to Heirs:					
IRA Assets	1,000,000	900,000	-	0	1,000,000
Roth IRA	-	-	1,000,000	900,000	1,508,521
After-Tax Savings & Investments	1,673,975	1,773,975	1,490,137	1,608,521	2,000,000
Other Assets - Real Estate etc.	2,000,000	2,000,000	2,000,000	2,000,000	
Net to Heirs	4,673,975	4,673,975	4,490,137	4,508,521	4,508,521
Alternately Valued Net to Heirs:					
IRA Assets - 65% Value	650,000	585,000	0	0	0
Roth IRA - 140% value	0	0	1,400,000	1,260,000	1,400,000
After-Tax Savings & Investments	1,673,975	1,773,975	1,490,137	1,608,521	1,508,521
Other Assets - Real Estate etc.	2,000,000	2,000,000	2,000,000	2,000,000	2,000,000
Net to Heirs	$4,323,975	$4,358,975	$4,890,137	$4,868,521	$4,908,521
Advantage over Other Bequest		**$ 35,000**	**$ 566,162**	**$ 544,546**	**$ 584,546**

In all these possibilities, we are assuming a $100,000 gift to charity, either while you are alive or after you are dead. In the first column on the left, we have the common allowance for charity in the will which provides after-tax funds for the charity – and here we assume no Roth conversion is done. The second column shows the $35,000 advantage of using the IRA for the charitable bequest rather than after-tax savings.

The third column shows the result if a $1,000,000 Roth conversion is done and the bequest is made from after-tax savings. This shows an advantage of $166,162 due to the lower estate and inheritance taxes. Also if we assume that the inherited Roth IRA is valued at 140% due to its future tax-free earnings potential, as we did in the previous example, then the advantage for the heirs is a much larger $566,162.

The fourth column shows the result if a $900,000 Roth conversion is done and the $100,000 bequest is made from the remaining IRA. This shows a larger advantage of $184,546 (due to $149,546 of lower estate and inheritance taxes combined with the $35,000 of income tax savings). If, however, we assume that the inherited Roth IRA is valued at 140% due to its future tax-free earnings' potential, then the advantage for the heirs is a smaller $544,546 due to the smaller Roth amount inherited.

The last column shows the result if the $1,000,000 conversion is done with the $100,000 tax deductible gift to charity from after-tax funds occurring before death in the year of the conversion. While initially it seems like the advantage is the same as in the fourth column where the charity received $100,000 from the traditional IRA, if we assume that the inherited Roth IRA is valued at 140% due to its future tax-free earnings potential, then the advantage for the heirs is the largest amount of all at $584,546 since the heirs received the full $1,000,000 Roth IRA.

Life Insurance with Charitable Bequests and Roth Conversions

Many times we have done tax calculations in Roth IRA conversion plans and used the deduction from charitable gifts to reduce the income so a Roth IRA conversion could be made and taxed at lower rates. One of our favorite charitable strategies combines current charitable giving, Roth IRA conversions, and life insurance.

In one situation, we had a client who wanted to make a multi-million dollar gift to a favorite charity. They could not afford to make the gift during their life time, but since they had a large pension, they could afford the premium on a $2M life insurance policy. They went to their favorite charity and had it purchase the life insurance policy on their life. They then committed to pay to the charity the amount of the premiums. Since they were giving money directly to the charity, they were able to deduct the amount of money that was used to pay the premiums. In this case, the charity was the owner and beneficiary of the policy.

The policy was structured so the premiums would be paid and deductions incurred to optimize their Roth IRA conversion strategy. By offsetting charitable deductions with Roth IRA conversions, they were able to get a tremendous bang for their charitable buck.

It turns out after preparing financial projections and tax calculations that their family ended up with more purchasing power than if they had not bought the insurance, not made the Roth IRA conversion, and just died. The heirs would have had to pay estate tax, inheritance tax, and income tax on the IRA. The family was also better off than if they had just left their IRA to charity and not made a Roth IRA conversion.

Now to be fair, the family would have been better off by purchasing the life insurance, making a Roth IRA conversion and leaving nothing to the charity. One legitimate way to look at the combination of Roth IRAs and charity, however, is that the money you are leaving to charity is in effect at least to some extent replaced by the value added to your family by making the Roth IRA conversion.

Of course there are excellent charitable strategies with life insurance that do not include Roth IRA conversions. The old charitable replacement trust idea still works. In that strategy, you fund a charitable remainder trust with highly appreciated assets. You and your spouse typically retain the income from that trust. After you and your spouse die, the remainder of your trust goes to charity. The income you receive is used to purchase life insurance, usually in the form of an irrevocable trust. The proceeds of the policy "when the policy matures" go to your heirs income-tax free and estate-tax free to replace the amount of money that went to the charity.

You could combine the charitable remainder trust strategy above and a Roth IRA conversion. In this case, you would use the charitable deduction of your initial gift to the trust to offset the taxes to convert to a Roth IRA. Your heirs would then have two sources of income-tax free money. The proceeds of the life insurance would not be subject to estate and inheritance taxes. It would also not be subject to income taxes.

The inherited Roth IRA would be subject to estate and inheritance taxes. As we examined in Chapter One, however, there would still be a reduction of estate and inheritance taxes on the Roth IRA conversion. Perhaps more importantly, the proceeds of the inherited Roth IRA—assuming the heirs chose to slowly take distributions of the inherited Roth IRA—will continue to grow income-tax free over the life of the beneficiaries.

Story – Sarah Wilson: Charitably Inclined Reader

Biography

The great tragedy of Sarah's life is that she lost her only daughter to cancer ten years ago. Five years later, her husband died, leaving her a widow with no surviving children or grandchildren. Sarah is now 74. She has one nephew. Sarah is a giving woman, both of her time and her money, to a variety of charitable causes. Her primary cause is the Cancer Research Center. She prays that one day science will make great advances in order that no one has to go through what her daughter experienced.

Sarah is not your stereotypical little old lady. Before deciding on the Cancer Research Center as her primary charity and her primary beneficiary, she found that the Cancer Research Center received an A rating from the American Institute of Philanthropy. She also met with the development officer at the Cancer Research Center on numerous occasions to see where her money would go and what it would be used for. She established a Memorial Fund for her daughter.

Before she met with me, she had attended my workshop and actually read *Retire Secure!* (Wiley, Feb., 2009) Her copy of *Retire Secure!* (Wiley, Feb., 2009) was filled with yellow highlights throughout the charitable chapter.

Her basic goals were to provide for her own retirement and make sure that she would be comfortable for the rest of her life. She also wanted give some money to the Cancer Research Center while she was alive. She wanted the bulk of her money to go to the Cancer Research Center upon her death. She did want to provide some money for her nephew. She wanted to absolutely minimize her taxes and get the biggest bang for her charitable buck.

Here are her assets:
> After-tax assets = $400,000
> IRAs and/or retirement plan assets – $800,000
> Home and personal belongings = $300,000

Income and tax return situation:
> Social Security now being received – $2,200/mo.
> Her pension is $60,000/yr. growing with inflation
> Interest income, non-qualified dividends and short-term
>> capital gains = $8,000
> Qualified dividend income & long-term capital gains = $8,000
> Itemizes deductions – real estate taxes of $6,000, charitable
> contributions of $2,000 plus any large charitable gifts are made

Spending needs:
> Currently spending $70,000/yr., including taxes
> Planning to make charitable gifts – about $300,000 during her
>> lifetime and a $1,000,000 bequest at her death
> Remainder of her assets she wants to go to a nephew

Analysis, Discussion and Recommendation

A recent change in the law allows one to donate up to $100,000 from an IRA to charity; the donation can be used to satisfy the RMD requirement. For our purposes, however, suppose that Sarah already received her RMD. Therefore, she decides to donate $300,000 of after-tax funds to charity in 2010.

This is nice, but the deduction for charitable donation will not all be used up in 2010 due to the 50% AGI limitation. Without doing any Roth conversion, there will be a $252,780 carryover that will take four years to use. If Sarah does a Roth conversion, the charitable donation can be used up much more quickly and low-cost Roth conversions can be done—essentially cutting the tax on the conversion in half due to coordinating the conversion with the donation.

Please see the "2010 IRA Conversion Planning" spreadsheet for tax calculations on different levels of conversion income – both with and without the $300,000 charitable donation in 2009. Sarah is currently in the 28% tax bracket even without her RMD income if there are not large charitable donations. Even with a charitable donation she is in the 25% tax bracket. There is a risk that Sarah might die before these carryovers are fully used up and they would be wasted. Sarah can make Roth conversions and use up her large charitable donation carryover to reduce this risk.

Assuming Sarah had a worthwhile nephew who could benefit from the long-term tax benefits of a Roth, Sarah could convert $270,000 to a Roth and pay $42,403 in taxes. This will leave her with some after-tax money, but much of her $400,000 will be used up with the gift and taxes on the conversion. The $530,000 remainder of the traditional IRA can be used to fund a bequest for the charity since it does not pay any income tax.

This is a good plan but even better would be for Sarah to get a $1,000,000 life insurance policy for the benefit of the charity. Much of Sarah's future wealth will come from her pension which stops at her death. If she lives, she can use pension proceeds to fund the premiums and if she dies early, the charity gets the $1,000,000. If she survives to an old age, the charity will have to wait longer to get the $1,000,000 but her pension will be received for all those years.

If the insurance plan is chosen, then more of Sarah's Roth IRA can be used to benefit the nephew with lower cost Roth conversions at 28% tax cost over a period of years. When set up properly with the charity owning the life insurance policy, the annual premiums Sarah makes will be in the form of tax-deductible charitable donations to the charity. It is a win-win-win-win situation. The nephew gets more Roth IRA, Sarah gets a warm heart for her charitable intent, the first charity gets $300,000 and the other charity eventually gets $1,000,000 rather than just $530,000. The IRS of course is the loser as the charitable donations, when fully used up, save a great deal in income taxes.

Some additional financial projections may be appropriate after the cost of the life insurance is determined. If it presents a cash-flow problem for Sarah in the long term, it may be appropriate to purchase a smaller life insurance policy for the charity and name the charity as beneficiary of the traditional IRA and not convert as much to a Roth IRA.

Sarah Wilson
2010 Roth IRA Conversion Planning

<u>Assumptions for 2010 - Nothing unusual, no large charitable donation</u>

RECOMMENDATION: For 2010 convert $83,000 to top of 28% bracket - only if Sarah wants nephew to inherit that much

Estimated tax situation for 2010 (using 2008 rates):

Roth Conversion Amount	Total Federal AMT & Income Tax	FYI AMT Included	Overall Tax on the Conversion	Overall Conversion Tax %	Taxable Income	Incremental Taxable Income	Incremental Income Tax	Incremental Conversion	!! FOCUS HERE!! Incremental Conversion Tax %	Bracket - Notes
0	17,013	0	0		85,872					In the 28% bracket
83,000	40,228	0	23,215	27.97%	168,892	83,020	23,215	83,000	27.97%	Near top of the 28% bracket
276,000	104,535	0	87,522	31.71%	364,316	195,424	64,307	193,000	33.32%	Near top of the 33% bracket
500,000	183,079	0	166,066	33.21%	588,807	224,491	78,544	224,000	35.06%	In the 35% tax bracket

<u>Assumptions for 2010 - Charitable Donations of $300,000</u>

RECOMMENDATION: For year 2010 convert $270,000 (to use up some of charitable donation) only if Sarah wants nephew to inherit that much and use life insurance for charity

Estimated tax situation for 2010 (using 2008 rates):

Roth Conversion Amount	Total Federal AMT & Income Tax	FYI - AMT Included	Overall Tax on the Conversion	Overall Conversion Tax %	Taxable Income	Carryover of Charitable Contributions	Incremental Taxable Income	Incremental Income Tax	Incremental Conversion	!! FOCUS HERE!! Incremental Conversion Tax %	Bracket - Notes
0	5,115	0	0		38,652	252,780					In the 25% bracket. Large carryover of donation
95,000	17,150	0	12,035	12.67%	86,409	205,280	47,757	12,035	95,000	12.67%	Near top of the 25% bracket. Large carryover of donation
270,000	42,403	0	37,288	13.81%	176,036	117,780	89,627	25,253	175,000	14.43%	Near top of the 28% bracket. Large carryover of donation
506,000	82,194	0	77,079	15.23%	296,616	0	120,580	39,791	236,000	16.86%	In the 33% tax bracket, used up all donation
606,000	116,162	0	111,047	18.32%	397,616	0	101,000	33,968	100,000	33.97%	In the 33-35% tax bracket no more donation to use

The Most Cost Effective Method of Providing for Charity for Senior IRA Owners

If you are age 70 and ½ or older and have an IRA and want to make a contribution to a charity, you can get a huge bang for your charitable buck. You must, however, do things differently than you have in the past.

The choice of funds you use to make charitable contributions could have a significant impact on your tax bill. Congress has provided a limited opportunity for individuals age 70½ and older to give up to $100,000 per year directly from their IRAs to the charity of their choice.

Make whatever charitable contributions you are going to make anyway directly from your RMD of your IRA. If you have an IRA with a RMD, it is a "no brainer" to make your charitable contribution directly from your IRA for as much as you want to give, but not more than the RMD.

If you want to make a charitable contribution for amounts in excess of the minimum distribution of your IRA, we recommend that you use appreciated after-tax assets to make that contribution.

Because IRA contributions of $100,000 or less made directly from your IRA to your favorite charity (or charities) do not count as income, you can reduce your AGI as well as benefiting charity by making a direct transfer from your IRA to a charity.

You Can Deduct a Greater Amount of Large Charitable Gifts by Using your IRA to Help Fund the Gifts

The adjusted gross income (AGI) income limitations related to charitable gifts (cash gifts can be deducted up to 50% of your AGI and non-cash gifts can be deducted up to 30% of your AGI), you may not always be able deduct the full amount of your charitable contribution in the year of the charitable gift. To get a tax benefit for the entire gift, you may have to carry over your charitable deductions to future years (there is a maximum carryover period of five years). If you otherwise would not be able to deduct the full amount of your charitable gifts this year or next year because of the 50% AGI limitation for cash gifts and 30% AGI limitation for non-cash gifts, you should strongly consider funding as much of their charitable gifts as possible with your IRA. To the extent that the gift is funded with your IRA, it will have no impact on your AGI limitation because IRA contributions to charity are not counted as income. In addition to enabling you to fully benefit from your charitable gifts this year and next year, donating part of the IRA to charity may enable you to deduct your charitable gifts that were carried forward from previous years that would have otherwise been non-deductible due to the AGI limitation. So, if you are age 70½ or older and are planning a large charitable gift, you should definitely consider using your IRA to fund the gift.

Consider Supersizing Your IRA Charitable Gift by Using it to Fund a Life Insurance Policy for Your Charity

Combining life insurance with your charitable gift is a wonderful way to maximize the leverage of your gift. A 75-year-old husband and wife who can each give $100K from their IRAs could potentially fund a second-to-die life insurance policy owned by the charity with a $1M death benefit depending on their health. Maximizing your gift may give you greater control to direct the disposition of the proceeds for the benefit of your charity of choice.

If You Have After-Tax Dollars in Your IRA, Making IRA Gifts Now Will Make Roth IRA Conversions More Attractive in the Future

If you have an IRA that includes after-tax contributions (amounts that have already been subject to income tax), please read this paragraph carefully. Because the new law states that an IRA contribution to charity will be treated as only being contributed from the taxable dollars in your IRA, you can give part of the taxable portion of your IRA to charity now so that you can pay less income tax to convert the IRA to a Roth IRA in a future year. This could be a tremendous opportunity for you to make a Roth IRA conversion at a significantly reduced cost, depending on the total size of the IRA and the size of your IRA after-tax contributions.

Reducing Your AGI through Using your IRA to Make Charitable Gifts Can Have Many Additional Tax Benefits for You

To the extent that you have not taken your RMD from your IRA, you can direct your RMD to charity through making a charitable gift. Directing your RMD to charity will reduce your AGI which may reduce your taxes on your Social Security income and minimize the impact of phase outs on miscellaneous itemized deductions, medical expense deductions and itemized deductions if you are a higher income taxpayer. In addition, the reduction in AGI may permit you to deduct rental losses, to increase your exemption deduction and may even make you eligible for a Roth IRA contribution if you have earned income. As an additional point, if you are a non-itemizer who has not taken your RMD from your IRA, contributing your IRA to charity is the only way that you can reduce your AGI because you are still not eligible to deduct charitable gifts unless you are an itemizer.

This strategy would be particularly beneficial for readers who are older than age 70 and don't need their RMDs to maintain their life style.

—— $$$ ——

Key Lesson for this Chapter

Roth IRA dollars are not the best assets to leave to charity. Charities are concerned with receiving the most in total dollars, not dollars for purchasing power. Unless you are leaving all your money to charity, don't let your charitable intent dissuade you from making a Roth IRA conversion.

Chapter Sixteen

Roth IRAs, Roth 401(k)s and Roth 403(b)s in the Accumulation Years

"The time to save is now. When a dog gets a bone, he doesn't go out and make a down payment on a bigger bone. He buries the one he's got."

— Will Rogers

Main Topics

- Optimal order for accumulating money while still working

- Traditional IRAs vs. Roth IRAs

- Roth 401(k)s and Roth 403(b)s

- Roth 401(k) vs. traditional 401(k)

Key Idea

When working, first contribute what the employer matches. Then maximize your Roth options, then your traditional options and last non-deductible IRAs if you aren't eligible for Roth IRAs.

—— **$$$** ——

Please note all employees who are still working also have to consider not only Roth IRA, Roth 401(k) contributions, but also whether you should make a Roth conversion from your 401(k) to a designated Roth Account. Please see "What's New" before Chapter 1.

This chapter will present a reality check about saving for retirement if you are still working. We will then provide a description of Roth IRAs, Roth 401(k)s and Roth 403(b)s. Then we will present the short version of what I consider to be the best way to accumulate money for your retirement if you are still working. I will also provide a few related thoughts about priorities regarding retirement savings that would normally be beyond the scope of this type of book—but I couldn't help myself.

You Are On Your Own Because Big Brother Can't Spare a Dime

Today's workers face worrisome problems that didn't exist for many workers 20 or 30 years ago. In the old days if you had a job with a good company, there was a good chance you would be able to keep that job for 30 years or until you wanted to retire. You could often count on eventually retiring with a guaranteed pension that would provide income for you and your spouse for your lives.

In addition, you felt good about the likelihood of collecting full benefits for Social Security. The combination of the pension and the Social Security would often meet or exceed regular spending needs. By the time you were retired, the house was usually paid for and the children's college education expenses were also out of the way. Workers could enjoy a secure retirement without doing a tremendous amount of planning.

There are obviously still millions of taxpayers who have pension plans. That number—at least in terms of percentages—is drastically dropping and it is no longer the norm for workers or even retirees. In addition, millions of people who expected good pensions have been disappointed as more and more companies are freezing and/or eliminating their traditional pension plans and replacing them with 401(k) plans.

In addition to the tremendous decline of traditional pensions, today's workers can't count on keeping a job for 30 years or longer. It is much more likely you have had more than one job than did workers of 20 or 30 years ago. Depending on your age and profession, you could have several more jobs before you retire.

Even Social Security benefits seems less certain than before, especially for workers now in their fifties or younger.

In other words, you're on your own to provide for your own retirement. Big Brother Corporation isn't going to look after you anymore. Big Brother Government isn't either.

One thing the government has done to help your cause is give you new tools to help yourself. The relatively new Roth 401(k) and Roth 403(b) may be available to you. You also are allowed to make much larger contributions to both traditional 401(k)s and 403(b)s as well as the new Roth 401(k) and Roth 403(b) and still receive favorable tax treatment. I assume you are contributing everything that an employer is willing to match, even if your employer is matching only a portion of your contribution. If not, please read Chapter One, *Retire Secure!* (Wiley, Feb., 2009). Then, assuming you are contributing what an employer is willing to match, let's start with the plain Roth IRA.

Basic Roth IRA Information

When you make a contribution to a Roth IRA, you do not get a tax deduction. On the other hand, the money will then grow income-tax free for the rest of your life, your spouse's life if you pre-decease your spouse and will continue to grow tax-free for the lives of your children and grandchildren. As a bonus, there is no required minimum distribution when you reach age 70 and a half. In addition, if you die and leave the inherited Roth IRA to your spouse, he or she may continue the tax-free growth without the requirement of taking a RMD. Your children or grandchildren or any non-spousal heir will have to take a RMD based on their life expectancy. Please see Chapter Two.

Roth IRA Eligibility Rules

You must have earned income to contribute to any IRA, including a Roth IRA. If your income is too high, you are ineligible to make a full Roth IRA contribution. If your income is below that threshold, but still high enough, you will be able to make a partial Roth IRA contribution. If you are eligible for the full contribution, you may contribute $5,000/year or $6,000/year if you are age 50 or older. If you meet income limitations, you can also contribute $5,000/year for your spouse or $6,000 if your spouse is age 50 or over.

In order to be eligible to contribute the maximum to your Roth IRA when you have a non-working spouse, your total earned income must exceed the combination of the two Roth IRAs. For example if you and your non-working spouse are over age 50 and you have earned income of $10,000, you can make a $6,000 Roth IRA contribution and a $4,000 Roth IRA contribution for your wife.

Here are the income limitations:

2010 Eligibility Rules for Roth IRAs

	Full Contribution	Reduced Contribution	No Contribution
Single & Head of Household	Up to $105,000	$105,001 – 119,999	$120,000+
Married Filing Jointly	Up to$167,000	$167,001 – $176,999	$177,000+

Phase-out income ranges for future years will be adjusted for inflation.

Traditional IRAs

All taxpayers with earned income are allowed to contribute to a traditional IRA without regard to income level. If neither you nor your spouse participate in an employee-sponsored retirement plan, you can deduct the full amount of the traditional IRA contributions. If you or your spouse are covered by a retirement plan at work, there are adjusted gross income (AGI) limits for allowing full deductions, partial deductions, and limits above which no deductions are permitted.

With a traditional IRA, assuming you meet the more stringent contribution requirements, you can get a tax deduction for your contribution. The IRA will grow tax deferred, not tax free. That means you will not have to pay income taxes on the IRA until you make a distribution. When you, or perhaps after you are gone, and your wife or children or grandchildren make an IRA or inherited IRA withdrawal, that withdrawal is taxable.

Roth IRA vs. Traditional IRA

A Roth versus a non-deductible IRA is a no-brainer: Always go for the Roth. To determine whether a Roth IRA would be better than a traditional deductible IRA, you must take the following into account:

- The value of the tax-free growth of the Roth versus the tax-deferred growth of the traditional IRA, including the future tax effects of withdrawals

- The tax deduction you lost by contributing to a Roth IRA rather than to a fully deductible IRA

- The savings from the tax deduction from choosing a deductible, traditional IRA

In most circumstances, the Roth IRA is significantly more favorable than a regular IRA. The below Figure shows the value to the owner of contributing to a Roth IRA versus a regular deductible IRA measured in purchasing power:

Figure 13

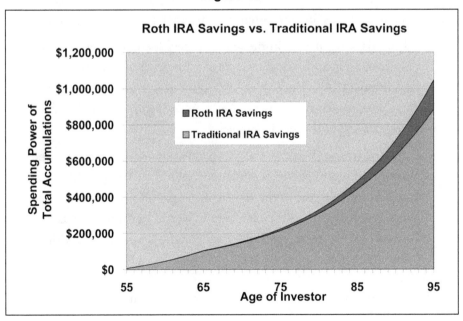

Assumption for Figure 13

- Contributions to the Roth IRA are made in the amount of $6,000 per year, beginning in 2011, for a 55-year-old investor, for 11 years until age 65.

- Contributions to the regular deductible IRA savings are made in the amount of $6,000 per year for the same time period, but because this creates an income tax deduction, 25 percent of this amount, or $1,500, is also contributed into an after-tax savings account.

- The investment rate of return is 8 percent per year.

- For the after-tax monies, the rate of return includes 70 percent capital appreciation, a 15 percent portfolio turnover rate (such that much of the appreciation is not immediately taxed), 15 percent ordinary dividends, and 15 percent ordinary interest income.

- Ordinary income tax rates are 25 percent for all years.

- Tax rates on realized capital gains are 19 percent.

- Beginning at age 71, the required minimum distributions from the traditional IRA are reinvested into the after-tax savings account.

- The balances reflected in the graphs reflect spending power, which is net of an income tax allowance of 25 percent on the remaining traditional IRA balance. If the full amount was actually withdrawn in one year, however, the tax bracket may be even higher and make the Roth IRA appear more favorable.

- The amounts reflected in the graph always show that saving in the Roth IRA is more favorable than saving in the traditional IRA. If tax rates become higher in the future, the overall Roth IRA advantage will appear larger. Given a long enough time horizon (such as when monies are passed to succeeding generations), however, the Roth IRA advantage becomes even bigger.

The spending power of these methods at selected times is shown below.

Total Spending Power of Savings Methods

End of Year Age	Traditional IRA	Roth IRA
55	$ 6,236	$ 6,240
65	102,498	103,868
75	215,146	224,243
85	441,979	484,124
95	882,046	1,045,186

Roth 401(k) Plans and Roth 403(b) plans and the New Contribution Limits

One of the biggest changes in the tax law for employees is how much money can be contributed to your retirement plan. In 2010 you are allowed to contribute $16,500 to your traditional 401(k) plan or $22,000 if you are age 50 or older. The other supreme change that will have an impact on many present workers with existing 401(k) and/or 403(b) plans is the addition of two new types of retirement plans: the Roth 401(k) and the Roth 403(b) plan. This means, assuming your employer offers these plans, you will be able to contribute more money to an expanded choice of retirement plans.

What Are These Roth 401(k) and Roth 403(b) Plans?

The new Roth 401(k) and Roth 403(b) plans are hybrid retirement plans that possess the characteristics of both the 401(k) or 403(b) and the Roth IRA. They allow employees to treat part or all of their own contribution, the amount deducted from their paychecks, as a Roth contribution. This means that the amount treated as a Roth will no longer result in a federal tax deduction as contributions to traditional 401(k) or 403(b) plans do; but the growth of this part and its subsequent withdrawal is not subject to income taxes the way traditional plans are.

In short, if you access to two plans, one a traditional 401(k) and the other a Roth 401(k) with the same amount of money in each, the Roth 401(k) plan will be of greater value since the income taxes imposed on withdrawals from the traditional 401(k) reduce its overall value. We do not mean to imply that these new Roth retirement plans are better than the traditional plans for everyone, but they are for most. The choice is similar to the decision made between making a Roth IRA contribution or a deductible, traditional IRA contribution.

Roth 403(b)s, are similar to Roth 401(k)s, but the Roth 403(b)s are offered to employees of non-profits, such as universities, hospitals, etc. If you work for a regular for-profit organization, you may be offered a choice of a traditional 401(k) plan or a Roth 401(k) plan. If you work for a non-profit institution, you may be offered a choice of a traditional 403(b) plan, possibly using TIAA-CREF or Vanguard as the investment vehicle, or a Roth 403(b) plan, also with TIAA-CREF. Please assume from here on out when I refer to a Roth 401(k), I would mean a Roth 403(b) for employees of non-profits.

Special Note for Teachers and Other Municipal Workers

Most school districts and many government agencies such as police and fire stations offer a 403(b) plan. This is often in addition to a pension plan in which teachers and other employees can participate. I have often heard teachers refer to this 403(b) plan investment as "their annuity."

Some school districts and government municipalities will offer a Section 457 plan that is taxed more or less like a 403(b) plan. What is really interesting is that some districts will allow their employees to contribute to both plans.

For example, Bill, age 51, is a teacher who has access to a 457 plan and a Roth 403(b) plan. His wife, Susan, also 51, makes $200,000 per year as a physician. Susan has access to a 401(k) plan. Neither of them has access to a Roth 401(k) or a Roth 403(b).

They want to maximize their retirement plan contributions. Susan should contribute $22,000 to her 401(k). Bill should contribute $22,000 to his 403(b) and $22,000 to his 457 plan. In addition, they should both be contributing $6,000 each to non-deductible IRAs.

It is important to note, however, that Roth IRAs and Roth 401(k)s and Roth 403(b)s are not exactly the same. The big difference—and it's an extremely important one—is that the new Roth 401(k) and Roth 403(b) plans are available to a much larger group of people. The restrictions on readers with higher incomes (see above) will limit possibilities for Roth IRAs. These restrictive AGI limitations do not apply to the new Roth 401(k) or 403(b) plans, which allow higher-income individuals and couples their first entry into the tax-free Roth environment.

This change provides an unprecedented ability for employees to expand or in some cases begin their tax-free investments. The new 401(k) and 403(b) employee contribution limits will go up to $16,000 (or $22,000 if you are 50 or older) per year. It is important to note that the total employee contribution limit will be $22,000 in 2010 if you are 50 or older. In other words you cannot make a $22,000 contribution to the traditional portion of the 401(k) plan and a $22,000 contribution to the Roth portion of the 401(k) plan

Let's look at an example to clarify.

Joe, a prudent 50-year-old employee, is a participant in his company's 401(k) plan. He has dutifully contributed the maximum allowable contribution to his 401(k) plan since he started working. Until he heard about the new Roth 401(k), his expectation was to continue contributing the maximum into his 401(k) for 2006 and beyond.

Now, Joe has a choice. He could either continue making his regular deductible 401(k) contribution (which has increased to $22,000 for 2010) or he could elect to make a $22,000 contribution to the new Roth 401(k). Or he could split his $22,000 contribution between the regular 401(k) portion and the Roth 401(k) portion of the plan. His decision will have no impact on the employer's contribution, either by amount or the way the employer's contribution is taxed.

With Joe's contribution, however, there is a fundamental difference in the way his traditional 401(k) is taxed and the way his new Roth 401(k) is taxed. The new Roth 401(k) is basically taxed like a Roth IRA. That is, Joe will not receive a tax deduction for making the contribution to the Roth 401(k), but the Roth 401(k) portion will grow income tax free. With the traditional 401(k), Joe would get an income-tax deduction for his contribution to the 401(k). After Joe retires, however, and takes a distribution from his traditional

> For the same basic reasons that I prefer a Roth IRA to a traditional IRA, I prefer a Roth 401(k) and Roth 403(b) to a traditional 401(k) and 403(b).

401(k), he will have to pay income taxes on that distribution. When Joe takes a distribution from his Roth 401(k) portion of the account, he will not have to pay income taxes. When I compare the traditional IRA to the Roth IRA, the Roth IRA usually comes out on top. For the same basic reasons that I prefer a Roth IRA to a traditional IRA, I prefer a Roth 401(k) and Roth 403(b) to a traditional 401(k) and 403(b).

Assuming Joe takes my advice and switches his new 401(k) contributions to the Roth 401(k) portion of the plan, he will have three components of his 401(k) plan at work. He will have the employer's portion of the plan which remains unchanged. He will have his own (the employee's) traditional portion of the plan which consists of all his previous contributions plus the interest, dividends and appreciation on those contributions. Then, starting in 2010, he will have a Roth 401(k) portion.

If Joe is married and his adjusted gross income is less than $177,000, then he may have already been making contributions to a Roth IRA outside of his employer's retirement plan. As long as Joe is working, the Roth 401(k) will remain separate from any Roth IRA he may have outside of his employer's plan. If his adjusted gross income was more than $177,000, he was not eligible to make any Roth IRA contribution, but he will be eligible for a Roth 401(k) for $22,000. He could, however, make a contribution to a non-deductible IRA, but that isn't a Roth IRA. Thus high-income earners will now be offered their first entrée into the tax-free world of the Roth, but it will be in the form of a Roth 401(k) or a Roth 403(b).

Married taxpayers with earned income and adjusted gross incomes of less than $167,000 have been eligible to make maximum Roth IRA contributions outside of their employer's retirement plan. The maximum contribution for 2010: $5,000 for employees under 50 and $6,000 for employees 50 and older. What is much different for these employees who were able to make some contributions to the tax-free Roth IRA is the amount of money that they will be allowed to contribute into the income-tax-free world via the Roth 401(k) or 403(b). These taxpayers could still contribute $6,000 to a Roth IRA outside of work and $22,000 to the Roth 401(k) plan at work.

This tax change could dramatically increase your tax-free wealth. Subject to a few exceptions, if you have access to a Roth 401(k) or Roth 403(b), I highly recommend you take advantage of that option and if you can afford it, contribute the maximum.

Notice, however, there is a caveat. I said "if you have access." Though Congress has now created these Roth 401(k)s and Roth 403(b)s, that doesn't mean your employer will adopt these plans. Previously, a retirement plan administrator had only to keep track of the employer's portion and the employee's portion. Now, the administrator must keep track of the employer's portion, the traditional employee's portion and the employee's Roth portion.

With the advance in today's software, I don't think this is a big deal. The additional cost of changing the terms of the retirement plan should not be significant. The cost of the extra accounting should also not be significant. Many smaller employers may choose not to offer employees the Roth 401(k) or Roth 403(b) options. Many employers will eventually offer Roth 401(k)s and Roth 403(b)s, but will not do so immediately. You may have to wait for your employer to adopt the changes.

If you are an employee who is not given the option of a Roth 401(k) or Roth 403(b), I would gently (or not so gently, depending on your personality and the office politics) suggest your employer adopt the Roth 401(k) or Roth 403(b) plan and allow you to participate.

If you are a retirement-plan administrator or owner of a small business, if you have not already considered implementing a Roth 401(k) or Roth 403(b), I would strongly consider it.

In *Retire Secure!* (Wiley, Feb., 2009) I cover the basics of a Roth IRA, a Roth 401(k), and present good information about all the different types of retirement plans. I also go to great lengths to prove the advice that I am going to present here. I also provide much more detail than this chapter provides. I would recommend you get *Retire Secure!* (Wiley, Feb., 2009) and read the first three chapters if you are in one of three situations:

- You need some basic information about retirement plans, Roth IRAs and Roth 401(k)s and other retirement plans.

- You want proof that my recommended strategies will work for you.

- Your tax rate will change in the future and you want to see the impact of different tax-rate changes on the decision to contribute to a Roth IRA or Roth 401(k).

That said, this chapter will give you the short and sweet version. In general, if you are working and assuming you can afford it, I recommend you accumulate money for your retirement in the following order:

- *Always, always, always* contribute the maximum to your retirement plan at work if your employer is providing a matching contribution or even a partial matching contribution. This is a no brainer.

- Subject to some exceptions based on current and future tax brackets, maximize your Roth IRA contributions and your Roth 401(k) or Roth 403(b) contributions.

- Maximize your traditional 401(k) contributions. This would apply if your company does not offer a Roth 401(k). In that case, you should match what the employer will contribute, maximize your Roth IRA contributions and then maximize your traditional 401(k) contribution.

- If your income is too high (over $177,000) to contribute to a Roth IRA, then make non-deductible IRA contributions of $5,000, or $6,000 if you are age 50 or older.

  With the non-deductible IRA, you don't receive a deduction but the money will grow income-tax-deferred in the account. Please note that a non-deductible IRA is conceptually the same as after-tax dollars inside a retirement plan or IRA. When you make or a family member eventually makes a withdrawal, the principal or non-deductible part is considered a return of capital. The growth or accumulations in the non-deductible IRA is treated as a traditional deductible IRA. Please see Chapter Nine for a discussion of making a Roth IRA conversion of non-deductible IRAs and after-tax dollars inside a retirement plan— without having to pay the taxes on the conversion.

All of the above is critical advice that an amazingly small percentage of people actually follow. If you are married and filing a joint return and your income is under $167,000, you should certainly be making a Roth IRA contribution of $5,000 for yourself and $5,000 for your spouse if you are both under age 50. This applies even if only one of you has earned income. If you are both age 50 or older, you should be contributing $6,000 each to a Roth IRA.

You should also be contributing the maximum to your work place Roth 401(k) plan. A Roth 401(k) is a type of 401(k) plan that is taxed much the same as a Roth IRA but subject to the rules of a regular 401(k) plan. Just like a regular 401(k) plan, you are allowed to contribute $16,500 or $22,000 if you are 50 or over. One difference is that you won't get a tax deduction with a Roth 401(k) contribution. The benefit of the Roth 401(k), like the Roth IRA, is that the money will grow income-tax-free in the future. Please note that the employer contribution to your 401(k) is treated as a traditional retirement plan. You will not have to pay tax on your employer's contribution and the funds will grow tax-deferred, not tax-free like the Roth. You, the employee, can then choose between a Roth 401(k) and a traditional 401(k). In order to contribute the maximum to a Roth 401(k), three things have to happen:

- Your employer must offer a Roth 401(k) plan. At this point in time, most employers don't offer a Roth 401(k)—or in the non-profit world, a Roth 403(b).

- Secondly, you aren't allowed to contribute more money to your Roth 401(k) than you make. Let's do a quick example. George makes $10,000 and his employer withholds Social Security taxes as well as state taxes which total $1,000. The maximum George could contribute to his Roth 401(k) would be $9,000, his net even assuming no federal taxes. The contribution to a Roth 401(k) can't be more than the total earnings after mandatory withholding. Unless you are self-employed and have a one-person 401 (k) plan, you can't write a check for a Roth 401(k) contribution. It must be withheld from your pay.

- You can afford to contribute to maximize your Roth 401(k).

There are two issues I would like to clarify in the accumulation stages. The first is when you should contribute to a traditional 401(k) even though you have access to a Roth IRA and/or a Roth 401(k). The second is the issue of whether you can afford the maximum.

Roth 401(k) vs. Traditional 401(k)

My starting point: given that your tax bracket is the same or going up over time, you should prefer the Roth 401(k) to the traditional 401(k). It is just a matter of math. The trickier issue is when your marginal tax rate will go down in the future. The issue of whether to contribute to a Roth 401(k) or a traditional 401(k) is similar conceptually to the issue of whether you should make a Roth IRA conversion. Please see Chapter Three. The key is current and future tax brackets.

For example, Fred, age 65, is at the peak of his earning power. Fred is married and after all his deductions—but before his retirement plan contribution—his taxable income is $240,000. In 2011, that puts Fred in the 36% bracket. If he contributes $22,000 to his traditional 401(k) as opposed to his Roth 401(k), he would reduce his federal taxes by $7,920 ($22,000 times 36%). He plans to retire in two years. If he contributed to a Roth 401(k) or made a Roth IRA conversion, he would have to pay serious taxes because he is in a high-income tax bracket. If he maxed out his traditional 401(k) instead of his Roth 401(k), not only would he get a significant tax deduction, but he would be getting a tax deduction when his income—and hence tax bracket—is high. Fred should not maximize his Roth 401(k).

What would make more sense for Fred is to maximize his traditional 401(k) contribution and now and then perhaps consider a Roth IRA conversion after he retires. That way he will have had the benefit of the tax deduction when his income was high. After retirement he will have no wages or business income. He will be in a lower tax bracket and he could consider a Roth IRA conversion at that time. Presumably, it would be better if he made his Roth IRA conversion before age 70 ½ because at that time, his income will increase due to his required minimum distribution. The income from the RMD could increase his tax bracket.

For more detailed analysis of traditional vs. Roth 401(k), please see **Retire Secure!** (Wiley, Feb., 2009).

Figure 14

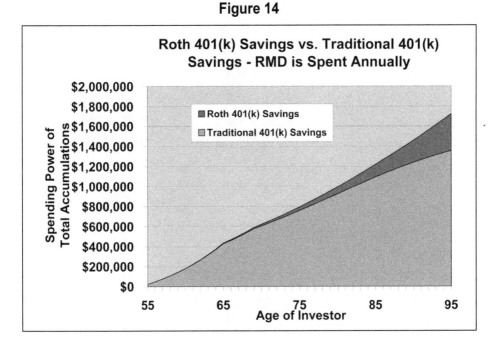

Please note in the original manuscript I included a six page discussion of Affordability of Maximizing Your Roth 401(k). Due to space constraints, I cut that section. If you are interested, please go to www.rothrevolution.com.

—— $$$ ——

Key Lesson for this Chapter

If you are working and have limited funds, try to fund retirement plans as follows: employer match, Roth IRAs and Roth 401(k)s are next, then conventional 401(k) and finally non-deductible IRAs. If your employer now allows you to invest in a Roth Designated Account, you now also have the burden of deciding if you should do a conversion.

Chapter Seventeen

Estate Planning for Roth IRA Owners

"By failing to prepare, you are preparing to fail."
— Benjamin Franklin

Main Topics

- How to spend your assets to maximize your inheritance
- How to plan your estate to maximize the benefits for your family
- Distribution options for spouse as beneficiary
- Distribution options for non-spousal beneficiaries
- Ideas for irresponsible beneficiaries—spendthrift children
- Current state of federal estate taxes
- Lange's Cascading Beneficiary Plan, probably your best estate-planning solution

Key Idea

If you have a traditional family where you are married and you both have the same children, there is an optimal estate plan that you should consider.

—— $$$ ——

One of the interesting facets of being a retirement-and-estate-planner is seeing how clients of different generations look at money. The majority of my clients are 60 and older. The older the clients are, the more likely that they will not spend anywhere near what they could afford to spend given their resources. You may say that living frugally is a habit, or that it is part of their value system, or that they still have a Depression-era mentality. Clearly at age 60 and older, most of my clients are savers, not spenders. The biggest exception is physicians.

Several years ago, I took my mom for a long weekend in New York City. As planned we saw a ballet and a Broadway show, and went to a variety of museums. Before the trip my mother mentioned on numerous occasions that she wanted to go to Saks Fifth Avenue to buy a scarf. The last day we were in New York City, we were cutting it pretty close. We barely made it to Saks Fifth Avenue with roughly five minutes to go before closing. We rushed to the scarf counter, and my mom found a scarf that she loved.

She asked the clerk how much the scarf cost. I desperately shook my head, because I didn't want the clerk to give her an answer. The scarf was $92, but frankly, I was so happy to get the scarf by the deadline that I certainly didn't care. My mother responded in a huff, "$92 for a scarf, why that's way too expensive," and she started to walk away. I told her that I thought the price was in line and anyway I would be more than pleased to buy it for her. In fact, I wanted to do that. She said it's not the issue of who will pay for it; it is just too expensive and that she never has, and never will, pay $92 for a scarf.

I started to walk back towards the counter and she quickly said, "Now don't you go back there and buy that scarf"—which of course was exactly what I was going to do.

Without going into details, my mother can certainly afford to buy a scarf for $92. Particularly because it was a beautiful scarf that would remind her of a rollicking weekend in New York City. But she just couldn't do it. She wouldn't let me buy it for her either. She was the daughter of a physician, she married my Dad who was an attorney and she herself was a college professor. She never knew hunger or even extremely hard times. She did, however, grow up during the Great Depression and was of the mindset that you just don't waste money, even if it is on something that you want.

When it comes down to it, most of my clients have at least a little and sometimes a lot of, for lack of a better term, Depression-era mentality. One of the things that I discuss with my clients is how much money they can safely afford to spend every year without the fear of running out of money.

Typically that amount is way more than my clients are actually spending. I even joke with them and tell them the one area where I'm almost inevitably going to fail is to try to get them to spend more money. They usually laugh. What's also interesting is that, contrary to common stereotypes, it is not always the husband who is the most frugal of the couple. In any case, most clients who think like this also are not tremendously thrilled about the prospect of giving money to their children or grandchildren. Because even if the clients are well provided for themselves, in the back of their mind they worry about a huge change in the market, or the expenses of an illness, or something going wrong.

I have a client that has a $35M estate. I am desperately trying to get him to give some of his money away during his lifetime. I want to minimize—or at least reduce—the estate tax his children will have to pay at his death. In discussing why he didn't want to give away any money to his children, he said "What if I get sick?"

I might think that is irrational.

On the other hand, if I am so smart and he is so dumb, why does he have $35M and I am working evenings and weekends to write this book?

> On the other hand, if I am so smart and he is so dumb, why does he have $35M and I am working evenings and weekends to write this book?

Admittedly, that is the extreme. But even someone who has the normal amount of "Depression-era mentality" is the perfect candidate for a Roth IRA conversion. These types of savers are unlikely to spend the Roth in their lifetime. They don't want to make direct gifts to children, but still want to help their kids out at some point in their children's lives. They are still, despite appearances, more interested in protecting their own futures. Depending on the tax brackets, the clients themselves will have more purchasing power if they make a Roth IRA conversion. Then, assuming they never do spend all the additional money they accrue from all those years of tax-free compounding, the benefit can go to their children, who can also enjoy tax-free compounding for their lifetime.

The individuals themselves, however, see themselves as not liking to waste money. They tell me their old house and their old cars are perfectly serviceable and they have everything they want. They then tell me about the two week vacation they took, etc.

These parents often see their children, who may be between 30 and 50, as spendthrifts. I am not talking about the occasional totally unproductive irresponsible kid who may have a drug or alcohol problem. I am talking about healthy, "normal" children with good educations, jobs, paying their taxes, etc.

The parents finished paying off their mortgage years ago, are on solid footing financially and, when they do need another car, they usually pay cash. Their children, on the other hand, without much savings at all, with a small or non-existent retirement plan, with terrible uncertainty about their job security at work, with the responsibility of raising and educating one or more children of their own, spend way more money than do their parents. They are also more likely to have a beautiful, newly remodeled kitchen. They drive nicer cars than do their parents; of course they buy on credit. The children, both in their parents' view and quite frankly, often in my view too, are spending an inappropriately large amount of money given where they are in their lives. In their parents' and at least to some extent in my view also, adult children often spend too much on housing, too much on cars, and too much on their own children.

If you were to do projections for many of my clients' children, given the resources they have, the work they will do and the money they will earn and, taking into account what they spend, they will certainly not have long-term financial security. Their parents worry about how their children will get by and that is a legitimate worry.

Now—the real bittersweet irony. The parents will spend their lives with extremely conservative spending habits and eventually die with a lot of money. If they become my clients, they are likely to also die with considerable Roth IRAs that will maximize their estates and leave more money and more purchasing power for their children. These assets will bail out their children, who never properly planned for their own retirement and will in effect, be able to retire comfortably because of what their parents left them.

And what is really ironic: I bet if you are 60 or older there is a better than 50% chance you are one of these parents. A similar scenario might be replayed in your family.

One other note about spending: Though in general I haven't been successful in changing clients' spending habits, there is one area where I have made some headway. I have suggested clients take their entire family on a vacation. I learned this from my father-in-law who is a wonderful father-in-law and a kind and generous man. He always has a funny story for you. (He might read this book and I better say nice things about him).

He takes his entire family, including the kids and grandkids and now great grand kids on nice vacations. He has taken the family on cruises and family-resort type vacations. He has one rule: the family eats together for all meals. Other than that, anyone can do whatever they want. It is wonderful and this memory legacy that he is leaving is worth more to him and us than any money he might otherwise leave behind.

My wife, daughter and I go to a family camp, Deer Valley, every year. We go the same week every year and so do the other campers. We get to know the other campers pretty well. Many of the same people have been going every year for 20, 30, sometimes 40 years. Often they spring for their children and grandchildren to go. These memories are also well worth it, even on a restricted budget.

On the other hand, the way I figure it, the parents aren't going to spend their money anyway. If we take that as a given and we want to over provide for a rainy day, the market going down, health care concerns, etc., we might as well be real tax smart about it. Let's make decisions that make sense for the parents (you) but also make sense for the children; and help get the children the most purchasing power we possibly can. The other thing that the parents like about devising these strategies is that the parents do want value. Of course nobody likes overpaying, but if you could take a course of action that will provide your family great value, and it doesn't take you an inordinate amount of time or cost you a lot of money, then why not? Please read the next section on estate planning for IRAs and Roth IRAs with great care.

If you consider wealth in the family, there is no doubt in my mind that the difference financially between people reading this book who properly implement the proposed strategies, and people in their identical financial situations who do not use these strategies, will amount to hundreds of thousands—and possibly millions of dollars.

Which Assets Should You Spend First?

Though again this is primarily a Roth IRA conversion book, I nevertheless feel compelled to present my general recommendation in terms of which assets to spend first. Let's assume that you are retired from your job or your business and you have no earned income. Even if you have some earned income, let's assume it isn't enough to cover your expenses. Let's also assume that you have what I would call after-tax dollars or dollars that no one has yet paid income tax on. Those dollars could be savings, investments, money that you have had for a long time or possibly even money that you inherited. The important part for my purposes is that you never received a deduction for saving that money. You will have to pay income taxes every year on the interest dividends every year that the money earns. In addition, whenever you sell those assets, you will have to recognize capital gains, assuming the value went up from the time you bought the investment.

For tax purposes I would divide after-tax dollars into two basic types of money. Number one would be after-tax dollars that have a low basis. In other words, if you were to sell those after-tax dollars, you would incur a significant capital gain. The amount of money that you paid for them—or perhaps the fair market value at the date you inherited them is much lower than the value today. So if you were to spend those dollars, you wouldn't have to pay income tax on the withdrawal of the money itself, but you would have to pay capital gains taxes on the appreciation of that money when you do sell it.

Another type of after-tax dollars that you are likely to own are dollars that are not highly appreciated, and you would not incur a capital gains tax if you were to sell those investments. They would most likely be CDs, and investments that you have purchased in the last ten years where you don't have any capital gains. Better yet, (not from an investment standpoint but from a tax standpoint) you may have after-tax dollars that are under water or have a fair market value in excess of what you paid for them. If you sold them you would qualify for a capital loss. Without getting in to a discussion of capital loss limitations or tax loss harvesting and what to do with the losers, for our purposes now, let's lump all after-tax dollars that if you were to sell, you would not have to pay taxes as after-tax dollars with a high basis.

The high basis after-tax dollars means the taxes have already been paid on them and there were no capital gains, so if you cash them in, there won't be any taxes.

It is likely in your after-tax portfolio that you probably have some low basis investments and high basis investments. For our purposes, let's assume you have some of each of these types of after-tax dollars.

Let's also assume you have a traditional IRA or retirement plan or 401(k) investments. I would call these pre-tax investments. These dollars were the result of money either you and/or an employer contributed to your retirement plan. At the time you didn't have to pay tax on that money. Or looked at another way: you received a tax deduction for that money. Some day you, your spouse, your children, or your grandchildren are going to have to pay income tax on that money (unless you leave it to charity).

For many of my clients, their IRAs and retirement plans constitute the majority of their money.

Let's also assume that if you don't already have Roth IRAs, that after reading this book and/or consulting with the appropriate advisor, that you will end up with Roth IRAs. It is likely for most readers if you are following my advice, that even if you don't make a big Roth IRA conversion, you will do a series of smaller Roth IRA conversions over a number of years. If you are a high-income taxpayer and have $1 million or more in your IRA or retirement plan, we might recommend the converting and recharacterizing strategies described in Chapter Ten.

Let's also assume that you also have an income source such as a part-time job, Social Security, and or pension, or even a required minimum distribution of an IRA. But, let's assume that the income generated from these other sources is insufficient to meet your spending needs.

Here, subject to exceptions, is the order that I recommend you spend your money:

1. After-tax non-appreciated dollars

2. After-tax dollars that are highly appreciated

3. IRA or retirement plan dollars

4. Roth IRA dollars

Why should you spend dollars that are not appreciated in the after-tax environment before your highly appreciated dollars in the after-tax environment? Because generally, you don't want to pay capital gains tax before you have to. If you don't have to pay capital gains tax, then you only reduce your portfolio for every dollar you spend. If you have to pay capital gains taxes on the withdrawal of after-tax dollars in addition to the amount you need to spend, that reduces the amount of dollars available for interest, dividends and accumulation. One potential exception to this general rule is in the event you think capital gains taxes are going up—in which case it might make sense to lock in capital gains of 15% rather than wait for them to increase in the future.

The choice then between spending after-tax dollars whether highly appreciated or not and IRA or retirement-plan dollars is usually settled by saying (the subtitle of my first book), *pay taxes later.* If you want to spend a dollar, take the dollar from after-tax dollars and your portfolio is reduced only by a dollar. If you want to spend a dollar and take that money from your IRA, you will incur income taxes on the IRA distribution. So, for example, if you're in the 28% bracket, you have to withdraw $1.40 from your IRA to be left with a dollar to spend. In that case your portfolio would be reduced by a $1.40—meaning that the additional $.40 that you paid in taxes is not available for interest dividends and capital gains. If you were to quantify this difference over time given a series of reasonable assumptions, the difference between spending your after-tax dollars versus your pre-tax dollars could look something like the following graph:

Figure 15

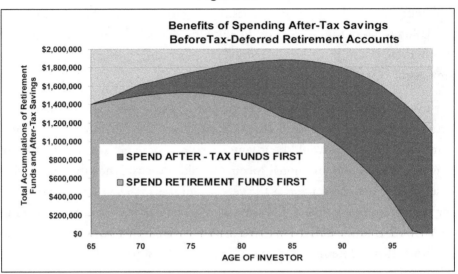

Of course there might be some exceptions to that rule in the environment of increasing taxes which is what we do have for certain taxpayers in 2010 into the future. In general, however, even tax increases would still not justify the acceleration of income taxes and spending IRA or retirement-plan dollars before after-tax dollars.

The next question about which assets to spend first is: should you spend your Roth IRAs or your traditional IRA first? In general I would prefer that you spend your traditional IRA dollars before your Roth IRA dollars. Admittedly, that strategy would be accelerating income taxes. By not spending the Roth IRA, however, you are preserving an asset that will grow income tax free for your life, your spouse's life, your children's lives and the lives of your grandchildren. I also examined when it was appropriate to spend Roth IRAs earlier in Chapter Fourteen.

To be fair, there is some controversy on this issue. I attended a gathering of academics and some practitioners at the 2008 New York University Conference on the Intersecting of Taxes and Investing to examine the question of which assets readers should spend first. I of course argued for the exact case that I just presented and, subject to exceptions, still believe.

One advisor argued he had paid for his children's braces; he paid for their children's college education and he wasn't going to pay for anything else. He was not going to go out of his way or do anything that would cost him money for his children. I don't think he understood my purchasing power paradigm (Please see Chapter One).

Even if he had, in fairness there are some fact patterns where you may be better off spending your Roth IRA dollars before your IRA dollars. The most common fact pattern would be if your current income takes you to the top of your tax bracket and additional income would push you into the next higher bracket. Let's assume you are at the very top of the 15% bracket and you need some more money to spend. Let's also assume your only choices are your Roth IRA or your traditional IRA. In that situation, even I might be tempted to spend my Roth IRA before my traditional IRA. (See the story about that couple in Chapter Fourteen.)

Even more common for lower-income retirees is the taxability of Social Security and its relation to taxable income. For clients who can afford to give up the cash flow, waiting to take Social Security could be an excellent long-term method of insuring your longevity. If you hold up taking your Social Security, you can make a Roth IRA conversion in those low taxable years. There will be no tax on your Social Security during the conversion years because you may choose to hold off on your Social Security.

Later, you will have increased Social Security and a Roth IRA. You might also have taxation on long-term capital gains at higher rates than today. You may be best served by taking some traditional IRA income and some Roth IRA income to keep the incremental tax rate on the taxable withdrawal amounts low. You may reach a point where your incremental tax is 30% or higher when you think you are in the 15% tax bracket. In these situations, it is nice to have a pool of Roth IRA money to take withdrawals from. Remember, the advantages of the Roth are maximized when the conversion tax is low compared to the taxes if you had not done a conversion. So, even if you do not leave a small piece of the Roth to your heirs, saving a lot of incremental taxes yourself is a splendid idea.

In many situations, however, it will be a breakeven or small loss to you by spending your IRA dollars before your Roth dollars. It will be a huge benefit for your children. Most of my clients would be happy to break even or be slightly disadvantaged if it could mean a huge advantage for their children.

One of the points behind these recommendations of which dollars to spend first is to prove the likelihood that you'll end up dying with IRA and Roth IRA dollars.

So now let's take a look at what happens to your IRA or Roth IRA after you die. First we will take the example of your leaving your IRA to your spouse. Then we will take a look and see what happens if you leave your IRA to your children or perhaps to your spouse and then after he or she dies, then your children. Then we will take a look at what happens to your IRA or Roth IRA if you leave it to your grandchildren or preferably a well-drafted trust for the benefit of your grandchildren.

What Happens to a Traditional IRA if You Leave it to Your Spouse?

"Marriage is a wonderful institution, but who wants to live in an institution?"

— Groucho Marx

First let's assume that your primary beneficiary is your spouse. To oversimplify, assuming your spouse is a US citizen, a transfer of any IRA, retirement plan or Roth IRA to your spouse is an income tax-free and estate tax-free transfer. In terms of federal estate taxes and many state inheritance taxes, Pennsylvania is a prime example; there is an unlimited marital deduction. That means that you can leave as much or as little as you like to your surviving spouse and there are no estate or inheritance taxes, otherwise known as transfer taxes.

Spouse as Beneficiary

Your spouse has a number of options. Let's start by assuming your surviving spouse wants the entire IRA and Roth IRA or retirement plan. We will later explore options where the surviving spouse doesn't want all of your IRA or Roth IRA. In that case they can turn down or "disclaim" their interest in your IRA. For our purposes now, let's assume your spouse wants your IRA or Roth IRA. Unless there is a significant age discrepancy, I almost always recommend the surviving spouse complete the trustee to trustee transfer, more commonly known as a rollover, from the deceased spouse's IRA to their own IRA or Roth IRA.

In the case of inheriting a traditional IRA or retirement plan, the surviving spouse will usually treat that IRA as their own. If the surviving spouse is less than age 70 ½, there will be no required minimum distributions on the spousal IRA. After the surviving spouse reaches 70 ½ (or technically on April 1st of the year following the year the surviving spouse reaches age 70 ½), the surviving spouse will have to take required minimum distributions. To calculate the required minimum distributions, the surviving spouse will use his or her own life expectancy.

For example, let's assume Bob, age 80, is married to Sue, age 75. When Bob was alive he was required to take a required minimum distribution on his traditional IRA. His RMD was calculated by looking up his life expectancy factor in IRS Publication 590, Life Expectancy Tables, and dividing that into the balance in the account on December 31, of the prior year.[7] In his case the number was 18.7. Of course an 80-year-old doesn't have a life expectancy of 18.7 years. The factor is calculated using not only Bob's life expectancy, but also

7 These tables can also be found in the Appendix in the back of this book.

the life expectancy of someone that is ten years younger than Bob. Please note that a factor of 18.7 is roughly 5.35% of the balance. To round off, if the IRA was worth $1,000,000, then Bob's RMD would be $53,500.

Even though Bob may die before he has to take his required minimum distribution, his heirs still must take a required minimum distribution for the year that he died, based on that life expectancy factor of 18.7 years.

The following year Sue, who will be 76, will also be required to take a required minimum distribution based on her factor found in Publication 590, which in her case would be 22. So, to calculate her required minimum distribution, you would take 22 and divide it into the balance as of December 31st of the year that Bob died. Since she is younger than Bob and her life expectancy (and thus factor) is larger than Bob's, a higher factor means her required minimum distribution is smaller. This pattern will continue for the rest of her life with her life expectancy and the factor ever decreasing—meaning an ever increasing required minimum distribution.

What Happens if You Leave Your Roth IRA to Your Spouse?

If we were talking about a Roth IRA as opposed to a traditional IRA, Bob would have no required minimum distributions because there are no required minimum distributions for a Roth IRA. In addition, after Bob's death, assuming Sue treats the Roth IRA as her own Roth IRA and does a trustee-to-trustee transfer of Bob's IRA into her Roth IRA, she will have no required minimum distributions on the Roth IRA for the rest of her life. She can allow the Roth IRA to continue to grow and accumulate income-tax free in her accounts for the rest of her life. If she chooses not to spend any of the proceeds of the Roth IRA, then that money will continue to accumulate income-tax free. Since there are no required minimum distributions and there is no income tax while the investment grows, more than any other type of investment, the Roth IRA will grow faster than any other tax-favored environment (like a traditional IRA or after-tax dollars, etc.). Of course when you, your spouse or your children or grandchildren withdraw the money, both the principal and the growth are income-tax free.

What Happens After an IRA Owner Dies and Leaves the IRA to a Non-Spousal Beneficiary?

Now what happens after an IRA owner dies and leaves the IRA to a non-spousal beneficiary? I think this is not commonly understood and in my opinion, it is given an unfairly dismal rap.

When you die with an IRA, you can leave it to someone other than a spouse, a "non-spouse" if you will. Your non-spouse, assuming he or she accepts the IRA, has a new beast called an inherited IRA. The inherited IRA has different characteristics than the original IRA. The non-spouse is not allowed to roll the inherited IRA into his or her own IRA. And, although no one has yet paid income taxes on the balance of the inherited IRA, the non-spouse is not required to pay income taxes on the IRA in the year he or she inherits the IRA.

If the non-spouse beneficiary of the IRA takes my advice and has the paperwork appropriately completed by an attorney or a knowledgeable financial advisor, the inherited IRA can stay in the family for many more years. The inherited IRA, though not immediately taxable for federal income tax purposes, will grow income-tax free for years. Remember, however, that no one has yet paid income taxes on this money; so whenever there is a distribution, the distribution will be taxable. Let's also assume for discussion sake that the beneficiary whom I presume to be an adult child does not have a huge immediate need for the inherited IRA and would like the inherited IRA to accumulate for his own retirement. Unfortunately, the beneficiary of the inherited IRA must take a required minimum distribution. To calculate the required minimum distribution of the inherited IRA, take the life expectancy factor found in the Single Life Table under Publication 590 and divide that into the balance of the inherited IRA as of December 31st of the previous year.

Please note that the child of the IRA owner or spouse of the IRA owner is obviously much younger and has a much longer life expectancy. That also means that the younger beneficiary could have a significantly smaller required minimum distribution than the original owner.

Presumably, the following year, the value of the inherited IRA will have increased because the RMD, based on the longer life expectancy factor will usually be less than the interest or appreciation in the inherited IRA. In the following years, however, the beneficiary of the IRA will have to subtract one year from his life expectancy of the previous year and will have to start drawing his required minimum distribution of the inherited IRA at a slightly faster pace. This pattern will continue year after year; so more and more of the inherited IRA will eventually be subject to income tax by the beneficiary of the IRA. On the other hand this great income-tax deferral for much of the lifetime of the beneficiary of the IRA has been a huge benefit. I spent a whole book with the subtitle, **Pay Taxes Later**, proving that with the exception of the Roth IRA and the Roth IRA conversion, it is usually better to pay taxes later rather than now. That certainly applies to inherited IRAs after death.

This ability to defer your income taxes after the death of the IRA owner is usually called the stretch IRA.

Why Dying with a Traditional IRA is Not So Bad

Leaving money in your IRA to a non-spousal heir has received a bad rap in the financial literature. Authors point out that the heirs will eventually have to pay income taxes on the entire inherited IRA and any subsequent growth of the IRA after the death of the IRA owner.

In addition the entire face amount of the IRA is included as part of your taxable estate for both federal-estate-tax and state-inheritance-tax purposes. Let's assume your million-dollar IRA has an immediate purchasing power of $700,000 because of the income taxes due upon withdrawal. Even though the value in terms of purchasing power may be only $700,000 (as we saw earlier in Chapter One for transfer tax purposes), both the IRS and state inheritance tax offices will count the $1 million IRA as $1 million and will include the $1 million as part of your estate.

You may recall one of the old strategies of which I was never a big fan: as clients aged, they were advised to make withdrawals from their IRA, and pay taxes on that money. After they died, they would in effect get the income taxes on the IRA out of the estate for federal-estate tax purposes.

In addition there seem to be many writers who assume that children will not take required minimum distributions based on their life expectancy: but instead will make withdrawals from the account based on their needs, wants and desires. Please recall that unless the beneficiary is some type of trust, the required minimum distribution of the inherited IRA is just that—the minimum. There is no maximum. Though it would not be wise, the heir could withdraw the entire inherited IRA. Then the heir would have to pay the income tax on the entire amount. Therefore, the idea of the stretch IRA, some of these authors say, is more of a theoretical fantasy than what is going to happen in your own family.

With certain families and certain individuals, they would inevitably be correct. Many heirs would spend the money too quickly, even if the smart thing would be to spend after-tax money or just not spend as much money.

Now, after having given the case for avoiding dying with a large IRA or retirement plan, let me make the case that I prefer. In many—if not most—situations, it's just fine for many estates to have a significant IRA or retirement plan component. First you genuinely do get income-tax-deferred growth over the life expectancy of the beneficiary.

For example, please assume your daughter is 55 years old at your death. Her required minimum distribution will be less than 3% on the first year after your death. She will continue to income-tax defer the remaining balance. Assuming there is growth in the account that exceeds three percent, the inherited IRA is growing, not diminishing. We are still deferring income taxes with at least a portion of the inherited IRA for 30 years. If the end beneficiary is a younger beneficiary, such as a grandchild, we might be deferring income taxes for 70 or 80 years. The value of tax deferral for that amount of time is simply incredible.

What if Your Child is a Spendthrift?

One problem with an inherited IRA is, unless otherwise specified, the beneficiary could withdraw the entire inherited IRA, blow the money, and be stuck with a tremendous tax bill. What if one of your adult children is a spendthrift? Are we not dooming his inheritance by leaving him an IRA?

My answer to the issue of the spendthrift child who will spend the inherited IRA too quickly is the beneficiary for what you were thinking of leaving to the spendthrift should be left in a trust. This would be true whether the underlying asset is IRA money, or after-tax dollars, Roth IRA or for that matter even life insurance proceeds.

If you create a trust and name the trust as the beneficiary of the IRA or Roth IRA, you can in effect have your cake and eat it too. That is, you can have the money protected from the spendthrift child himself as well as the spendthrift child's potential creditors.

Even if your child isn't a spendthrift, said child may develop creditors. Of course in practice the most devastating of the child's creditors is the child's future ex-spouse, who may try to get some of the money that your child inherited from you.

We deal with that specific issue in **Retire Secure!** (Wiley, Feb., 2009) in what we call the "I don't want my no good son-in-law to get one red cent of my money trust."

The third objection to leaving much money in an IRA to the next generation is the increased federal-estate and state-inheritance taxes. Though right now the estate-tax laws are in flux, it is likely that the vast majority of the readers of this book will not end up paying federal-estate tax. Therefore the objection for most readers is not relevant. The difference in state inheritance taxes—though in some cases could be significant—in reality for most readers would not be so significant as to distort the choice of spending IRA dollars before after-tax dollars.

What Happens if You Leave Your Roth IRA to a "Non-Spouse" Beneficiary?

Please note I analyze this issue in quantitative detail in Chapter Two. Your non-spouse beneficiary of your Roth IRA inherits a unique asset called an inherited Roth IRA. Your non-spouse beneficiary must take a required minimum distribution of the inherited Roth IRA. That required minimum distribution is calculated the same way the required minimum distribution of the inherited traditional IRA is calculated. That is, you would take their life expectancy according to the Single Life Table under Publication 590 and divide that factor into the balance of the inherited Roth IRA as of December 31 of the prior year. The resulting amount is the required minimum distribution of the inherited Roth IRA.

The difference between a distribution of an inherited traditional IRA and a distribution of an inherited Roth IRA is that the distribution of the traditional

> The difference between a distribution of an inherited traditional IRA and a distribution of an inherited Roth IRA is that the distribution of the traditional IRA is subject to income tax.

IRA is subject to income tax. The distribution from an inherited Roth IRA is not subject to income tax. That is one of the reasons why by over time you, then your children and then your grandchildren and even great grandchildren will benefit the most from Roth IRA conversions. The younger the beneficiaries, the longer they will enjoy tax-free growth.

Naming Young Children as Beneficiaries of IRAs and Roth IRAs

A young beneficiary has a long life expectancy; and the factor to determine the required minimum distribution of both the inherited Roth IRA and the inherited traditional IRA is large. For example, if your beneficiary is 55 years old when you die, their life expectancy factor would be 28.7 the year after you die. Then, you would have to take out 28.7 divided by the balance of the inherited IRA or Roth IRA the year after you die. That is roughly 3.5%. As time passes, their required minimum distribution of the inherited IRA or Roth IRA will increase. They would get an additional 28 years of tax-deferred growth, or in the case of an inherited Roth IRA, 28 years of tax-free growth after your death.

If, on the other hand the beneficiary was five years old at your death, their factor based on his life expectancy would be 76.7 years. The required minimum distribution for them would be about 1.3 percent the year after you die. That beneficiary would receive an additional 76 years of tax-deferred growth over his life expectancy. If it was an inherited Roth IRA, then they would get an additional 76 years of tax-free growth.

We compared the benefits of naming young beneficiaries of Roth IRA in Chapter One.

Of course if you name a young beneficiary, it is critical that you actually name a well-drafted trust, taking care that the trust meets all the legal conditions to qualify as an inherited IRA or Roth IRA.

The Best Estate Plan for Traditional Married Couples with IRAs and Roth IRAs

Now that we have a background in how the required minimum distribution of IRAs and Roth IRAs works, the next step is to include a discussion of estate taxes and then recommend the ideal beneficiary of an IRA or a Roth IRA. Please note that while this is a Roth IRA book, the following section applies to IRAs, Roth IRAs and after-tax dollars as well.

Estate Taxes

I would like to switch the type of tax we are concerned with at the moment. Up to now we've been talking about income taxes. Let's switch to estate taxes or transfer taxes. One of the critical issues for estate planning for medium and large estates is how much money you are allowed to transfer, at your death, without paying any federal-estate tax. That number has been fluctuating. For years and years, it was $600,000. It was called the exemption amount, the unified credit shelter amount, or the credit shelter exemption amount. It went by different names. It was basically the maximum amount that you were allowed to transfer at your death to someone other than your spouse without paying any transfer taxes.

On top of that, federal law allows the unlimited marital deduction. If you are married to a U.S. citizen, and it is the citizenship of the spouse, not of the citizenship of the person who died, there's no federal estate tax on money being left to your spouse. Pennsylvania recently passed an unlimited marital deduction for PA inheritance tax also.

Let's assume that the exemption amount is $3.5 million when you die. If you die with $4,000,000 and you leave everything to your kids, your kids will have a $3.5 M exemption, and they will have to pay estate tax on the difference. Technically, it works as a credit, but conceptually it is easier to think of it as an exemption amount.

At the time of writing this book in 2010, the estate tax has been repealed. So, theoretically, if you die in 2010, there is no federal-estate tax. Can we be sure that that's going to be the case? No, because they could pass a tax that would be effective retroactively. Would a retroactive federal-estate tax be constitutional or would it be an "ex post facto law" that is, a violation of the constitution? I don't know. If they pass the law retroactively, would there be lawsuits? Almost certainly. Would those lawsuits be cleared up quickly? Almost certainly not. Is it likely that we are going to be in murky waters for at least 2010? Yes.

"Loyalty to the country always. Loyalty to the government when it deserves it."

— Mark Twain

Right now, the law allows you a $1M exemption for decedents dying in 2011. That's a very low amount and last year, I would have thought, "Oh don't worry about that, Congress is certainly going to get it together and they are going to pick some number, maybe three or four million dollars." That will be the exemption amount for 2010 and 2011, 2012 going forward. In fact, recent proposed legislation was going to make the exemption $3.5M, inching its way up to $5M, but that never passed.

The important year, if you are married, is the exemption amount in the year of the death of the second spouse. I think that that's speculative since I don't even know what the estate tax law is today. I don't know what it is today and I don't know what it is going to be in future years. That, to me, is my starting point and is a reasonable starting point for the purposes of estate planning.

There is still, by the way, a million-dollar-gift exemption. So you can't go around and make $2M, $3M, $4M or $5M gifts and expect that that will be free of tax.

The Cruelest Trap of All

Let me tell you what I think is a huge problem for way too many couples. Perhaps this applies to as many as 25% or more of the people reading this book. If you have the traditional A/B estate plan, you may have a big problem. The traditional estate plan that most of my "middle and larger estate size clients" have is called the A/B will or A/B trusts. It's also called the B trust, the unified credit trust, and exemption equivalent trust: it goes by a number of different names. The purpose of that trust is to save estate taxes at the second death. You might have heard of this type of trust. You might even have it in your wills and trusts and not know that you have it! The traditional A/B wills state that all the assets that are pointed to the trust (which for our purposes now includes everything that is controlled by the will or revocable trust) will be distributed as follows:

The income of the trust will go to the surviving spouse as long as the surviving spouse lives. The surviving spouse will enjoy the right to invade principal for health, maintenance and support. There are certain limitations and expansions of the power to invade principal. At the second death, the remainder of what is in the trust goes to the children equally.

Here is an example of the problem the trust is meant to solve. Let's say the exemption amount becomes $3.5 million. Let's say you have $7M that is controlled by your will or revocable trust. You die with $7 million and leave everything to your spouse. She has $7M. Then she dies. The exemption is $3.5 million. Your kids will have to pay estate tax on $3.5 million. That is a horrendous result.

If instead, you have this A/B type trust plan; the will, or revocable trust if you are trying to avoid probate, states "take whatever the exemption amount is in the year of death" and that is how much goes into the B trust—also known as the family trust, exemption equivalent trust, credit shelter trust, etc. That trust provides income and the right to invade principal for health, maintenance and support to the surviving spouse. Now let's assume you have the type of A/B estate plan in place and according to the will or revocable trust, the exemption amount or in our example $3.5 million dollars, goes to the trust. The remaining $3.5 million typically goes to one of two places. The simpler case is that it could go to the surviving spouse outright. That is usually my preference. It could also go into another trust for the benefit of your spouse (the A trust).

For simplicity's sake, let's assume that what your will doesn't create the A trust.

In that case the surviving spouse would get $3.5 million outright; that is, not in trust. He or she could do whatever they want with the $3.5 million. The other $3.5 million would go into a trust that would provide income and the right-to-invade principal if needed for the surviving spouse. At the second death the amount of money in the trust would go to anyone you designated, but typically to the children equally.

The balance of the trust going to the children would not be included in the estate of the second spouse to die. The reason is that it wasn't the spouse's property. The surviving spouse only had the rights to the income. The $3.5 million that went outright to the surviving spouse would be in the surviving spouse's estate. If the surviving spouse also gets a $3.5 million dollar exemption, there would be no estate tax. So, in that scenario the surviving spouse had $3.5 million outright and the income from the second $3.5 trust as well as the ability to invade principal if needed. In other words, the surviving spouse was protected or overprotected, and there was no federal estate tax on the transfer of $7 million to the next generation.

So, before I slam the traditional approach, which is what I am going to do, I have to point out that it does have a purpose. In the example above, it saved estate taxes on $3.5 million.

Sometimes I am accused of manipulating facts to prove my point. The last example was a case where I took an unrealistic fact pattern and didn't take into account many factors. For example, most readers don't have $7 million dollars. Most readers don't even have $3.5 million.

So, for people with very big estates, I found a circumstance where the B trust could be of some value. What about the real world? Let's say you don't have $7 million and let's assume for discussion sake that you have less than $3.5M. Let's also assume everything you have is controlled by a will or revocable trust or even an IRA or Roth IRA beneficiary designation that points to this traditional estate plan.

The language you might see in your will or revocable trust might look something like the following:

> I give, devise and bequeath to my spouse a value equal to the maximum marital deduction; provided, however, that the amount of this bequest shall be reduced by the amount, if any, needed to increase my taxable estate, for federal estate tax purposes, to the largest amount that, after allowing for the unified credit against the federal estate tax and the state death

> tax credit against such tax will result in the smallest, if
> any, federal estate tax imposed on my estate.

If you have this type of language, please note that it directs that the assets passing under your will or revocable trust, up to the maximum applicable exemption amount, goes into the B trust. What does that mean if it were written in plain English? It would mean the exemption amount in the year you die. That is known as the B trust. That trust is not subject to estate taxes at the second death.

So you can end up in a situation where $1.5 M (or any amount up to $3.5 million) goes to the trust and the surviving spouse gets nothing outright. True, the surviving spouse does get an income interest in the trust. The surviving spouse also gets the right to invade principal for health, maintenance and support. That should be enough, right?

No, don't be fooled. Some of the assets such as a house might not be income producing. Even if the entire $1.5 million was income producing, the income might be much less than the surviving spouse wants to spend. The invasion of principal clause isn't much comfort to me. First, the trustee has to approve the invasion of principal. Also, what if the surviving spouse wants more than health, maintenance and support? Tough.

Right now, when the exemption amount is unlimited, there are many attorneys out there interpreting the standard language to mean everything goes to the B trust, leaving the surviving spouse zero no matter how large the estate. This is going to be a huge problem. There are certainly hundreds of thousands of documents like that out there. And, is it what the client really wanted? No, No No. It is almost always the attorney's idea and it is usually a bad one.

Let's say you have a traditional marriage, you and your spouse trust each other, and you have the same children. I call it the "Leave it to Beaver" marriage: husband, wife, and same kids. What do clients in that situation say to the attorney? They say, first, I must be sure we both have enough money to live comfortably the rest of our lives. Then, I want to take care of my spouse if I die first. "Taking care of my spouse is more important than saving taxes, or leaving money to the kids or grandkids. The first thing is you take care of my spouse." That, subject to

> When you are both alive, you both have unrestricted access to all the marital assets. Why would you want to restrict the surviving spouse to income for health, maintenance and support?

rare exceptions, is what people with traditional marriages want.

Do we attorneys listen? No, no, no. We set up these fancy B trusts. "But, gee, Jim, the trusts provides income and the right to invade principal for health, maintenance, and support. Isn't that enough?" No. What if you as the surviving spouse want more than income for health, maintenance and support? When you are both alive, you both have unrestricted access to all the marital assets. Why would you want to restrict the surviving spouse to income for health, maintenance and support?

Restricting the spouse to Income

Maybe your spouse wants to go to Aruba. Maybe he or she wants to help the grandchildren with their education. Maybe he or she wants to buy a second home or update the kitchen. Maybe he or she will take the family on a vacation such as my father-in-law favored. That is, maybe he or she will pay for the entire family to go for a cruise or a vacation. Maybe even pay for the family to come in and attend the funeral!

Most readers with traditional marriages who have the same kids and trust each other should not want to put shackles on the surviving spouse. They should want the survivor to be able to do whatever he or she wants with the remaining money. But that's not what most estate-planning documents do. Instead, they usually have these B trusts. And that ends up being a huge problem.

You end up in a situation where the surviving spouse is limited in what they can do. I will tell you, in practice, this has happened and the surviving spouse is not happy. And there are many people who don't even know what their wills provide. They think they are leaving everything to their spouse—but they aren't.

Then, it gets worse if IRA or retirement-plan money is left to this trust. Then, you have a massive income-tax-acceleration that is too painful to talk about. Naming a B trust as the beneficiary of the IRA or retirement plan accelerates the required minimum distribution for the surviving spouse and for the children. In summary, naming an IRA or retirement plan to a B trust as the beneficiary is an income-tax nightmare.

Many people do not understand what is in their wills, nor do they understand the beneficiary designation of their IRAs and retirement plans, and trusts. Also, many people don't realize that their will doesn't control their IRA at their death. The beneficiary designation of the IRA or Roth IRA is the controlling document for disposition—not the will—at death.

That's one of the reasons, by the way, when we draft wills and trusts, we not only draft the wills and trusts, we also complete all the beneficiary designations for IRAs, retirement plans, life insurance, and anything else that is controlled by beneficiary designation. We also draft a letter that, in plain English, states what the wills and trusts say and beneficiary designations say—which I think is very important.

But do you also remember the benefits of naming a child as the beneficiary of the IRA or Roth IRA? The child has many more years to enjoy the tax-deferred—or in the case of the Roth IRA—tax-free growth. The inherited IRA could be worth more to the child than to the surviving parent.

In addition, it is extremely powerful to leave some money in an IRA—or better yet a Roth IRA and name trust for the benefit of a grandchild as the beneficiary. We saw in Chapter One the opportunity for fabulous wealth for the grandchild without much money left to them in the form of a Roth IRA.

The Best Estate-Planning Solution for Traditional Couples

So, what should you do about this? There are different solutions for different situations, but I want to start with the traditional family unit. I would say that there are four choices. The traditional answer, known as the B trust, is the primary beneficiary. That is, we fund the unified credit shelter amount first, before the spouse gets anything outright. I say no, no, no, no, no. Let's reverse that order. Let's have the surviving spouse be the primary beneficiary of both IRAs and Roth IRAs, and after-tax dollars. If you trust your spouse and you have the same kids as your spouse, then let's start by providing or over-providing your spouse with your assets. But, you protest, what about the case where we needed the B trust to save estate taxes? I admitted I didn't know what was going to happen to the exemption amount. So, I don't want to throw the B trust out the window.

The B trust could save estate tax. Maybe the exemption amount really will go back to $1M. I would have never thought that would happen, but I would also never have thought that it would be unlimited in 2010. So maybe we need this B trust. I want that as an option.

The other one, kids equally. All right? That's a good option. And fourth, trust for grandchildren. Maybe even some money to charity (for our purposes now, let's leave that issue for another chapter).

For most traditional families, would you say that the following are the relevant four choices?

1. Surviving spouse

2. B trust

3. Children equally

4. Well-drafted trusts for the benefit of grandchildren

I'll give you one example of why you might want to have the children get some money at the first death. Let's say that there's a large estate and the expenses of the surviving spouse are fairly predictable. Let's assume there is just way more money than the surviving spouse will ever need. Maybe it might make sense to have the kids get some of the money at the first death. Maybe it is better for the kids to get the money in their 40s, rather than in their 60s—which is how old they might be if they have to wait for both spouses to die before they inherit anything. Even a small amount to the children at the first death might be the difference between their being comfortable or uncomfortable. In addition, the kids are young and they will have a lower RMD than the surviving spouse; so we have income-tax savings for the family too. So we may want some kids to have some money at the first death.

Remember, I showed the benefit to the grandchildren? It might be really interesting to have the grandchild as a beneficiary, even on a $10,000 or $20,000 Roth IRA. That might be an interesting choice.

So let's say you have these four choices: surviving spouse, B trust, kids and trust for grandchildren. Now, we are in a fairly uncertain age. I don't know what the federal-estate tax law is right now, let alone what's going to happen in the future. We're certainly in a volatile era when it comes to investments. We've seen tremendous fluctuations in the stock market, and I suspect we are going to continue to see fluctuations in the stock market. I don't know what is going to happen. Might do very well, might do badly. Your particular investments might do well, might do badly. Some might do well, some might do badly.

You don't know what the needs of the surviving spouse are going to be. Maybe the surviving spouse is going to be perfectly healthy and decide to spend some money. Maybe the surviving spouse will be in a situation where his or her expenses are pretty predictable. You don't know. I don't know. We don't know what the needs of the kids are going to be. We don't know what the needs of the grandkids are going to be.

So any type of allocation that we would choose to make and fix in stone based on today's projections, could very easily turn out to be wrong. In fact, I will tell you in 30 years, I've done a lot of projections, and they have all been wrong. Something different than we expect always happens. Everybody thought the husband was going to die first, and the wife died first. The last ten years have been bad for most investors and the projections I did ten years ago are wrong. Most of my clients have much less money than we would have predicted. We don't know what's going on right now with estate taxes. It's very hard to project, in advance, who should get what.

So, with all this uncertainty in the world, how can we make a decision of who gets what and then fix that decision in stone? We don't. We decide today that we are not deciding today.

We make the conscious decision today not to decide. Rather we drafts wills, trusts, and beneficiary designations of IRAs, Roth IRAs, life insurance, etc. to provide the maximum flexibility for the surviving spouse. We let the surviving spouse decide who is going to get what. The surviving spouse will have nine months after the first death to decide who gets what. I will call that a free second look. Because the surviving spouse is going to know more nine months after you die than both of you know today. The surviving spouse will also have the benefit of getting advice from a trusted advisor; in addition to having his or her children to supply emotional as well as technical support to make these important decisions.

At our office after a death, we meet with the surviving spouse, often accompanied by one of the adult children. I don't like to make the decision of who gets what immediately. There is usually no rush.

Here is what I am going to recommend as to what I consider the ideal estate plan for married couples with traditional families who trust each other. Let's give the surviving spouse the following options.

1. Surviving spouse,

2. B trust,

3. Children equally

4. Well-drafted trusts for the benefit of grandchildren

Any combination of 1, 2, 3 and 4 the spouse wants, including any combination of any asset.

That is the spouse might want to keep all the after-tax dollars, but might want the children to get the IRA dollars—or some of the IRA dollars.

Today, I don't know what is going to happen so I can't recommend who should get what.

That is my whole point. You don't know. I don't know. Let's trust the surviving spouse to make the decision of who gets what after the first death when we will have more information.

You will get optimal results if you set up these options in your wills now, trusts beneficiary designations of retirement plans, etc. Let's assume the documents are prepared properly now, you have appropriate advice now, and you will get appropriate follow-up after the first death. I would submit to you that you can do a much better job of protecting your family by building in this flexibility in your estate-planning documents than the traditional "fixed-in-stone" plan that you may have today. You can find this estate plan in the literature by looking up "Cascading Beneficiary Plan." The choices of who the money goes to cascades from surviving parent, to a trust to a child and to a grandchild (or grandchildren).

I have been constructing these types of plans for my clients for over 25 years. I know they work. If you would like to read more about how I developed these plans, and how acclaimed they are you can find detailed information in my first book *Retire Secure!* (Wiley, Feb., 2009) or visit my website, www.retiresecure.com.

The Cascading Beneficiary Plan was first proposed in the American Institute of Certified Public Accountants' peer-reviewed journal called *The Tax Adviser* in 1998. It was called the Cascading Beneficiary Plan in that article. The reason it was called the Cascading Beneficiary Plan is *The Tax Adviser* would not let me call it what I wanted to call it, which was Lange's Cascading Beneficiary Plan.

The popularity of this plan skyrocketed in 2001 when Congress changed the estate-tax laws as well as the laws regarding disclaimers.

Congress also changed the rules regarding RMDs of inherited IRAs and inherited Roth IRAs. The old law stated that if the surviving spouse disclaimed his or her interest in an IRA, then the next in line—let's assume the children—would have to take their required minimum distribution of the inherited IRA base on the life expectancy of the parent, not the child.

Under the old law, income taxes were going to be accelerated—even if the surviving spouse disclaimed—to the children. The children would be required to calculate their RMD of the inherited IRA, based on the life expectancy of the surviving parent.

The law has always been that if you name your spouse as the primary beneficiary and your spouse says, "I don't want it" or disclaims it or part of it; the disclaimed part goes to whoever is the second or contingent beneficiary of the IRA or retirement plan. There may be a disclaimer so that some IRA or Roth IRA money is left to either children or grandchildren. A disclaimer is accomplished either by a spouse signing a specific form provided by the IRA custodian or the retirement-plan administrator; or a letter giving up a percentage or fixed dollar amount of his or her interest in the IRA or retirement What the new law stated in 2001 was that those children or grandchildren, as of 2001, are allowed to take required minimum distributions based on their own life expectancy—not the life expectancy of mom or dad, who disclaimed it. This is what the law stated before 2001.

So, after this new law passed, the estate plan that I had been using for over ten years in my practice suddenly became tremendously beneficial. Before, since there wasn't an income-tax benefit to the family of disclaiming, there was not nearly as much incentive to disclaim as there is after the new law in 2001.

Of course, I was so excited I couldn't contain myself.

After that new law passed in 2001, I wrote an article called *The Ideal Beneficiary of Your IRA*. The article basically was the Cascading Beneficiary Plan.

I sent the article out to my e-mail list, which consisted of, maybe, 30,000 -40,000 subscribers. Jane Bryant Quinn was one of my subscribers. She called me and after over four hours on the phone over the next two weeks, she wrote an outstanding article in **Newsweek** quoting me. Then the plan became hot news. I did an article for **Financial Planning** which was published. I was interviewed by **The Wall Street Journal**; they did an article on the Cascading Beneficiary Plan. **Kiplinger's Retirement Report** interviewed me and quoted me at length on the Cascading Beneficiary Plan. It was all over the place. I had actually been implementing that plan for years in my practice, but it had received little press before 2001.

In our own office, we have prepared wills, trusts and estate plans for over 1,500 clients over the past 25 years. Most of these plans have some elements of the Cascading Beneficiary Plan. Many of them are the complete cascade. The vast majority of these clients are still alive. We had, however, quite a few deaths and the plan has been well tested.

We typically provide compete flexibility for all of the clients' assets including after-tax dollars, IRA and retirement-plan-dollars, Roth IRA dollars, life insurance (unless we want to keep it out of both estates), annuities, etc.

It creates vast opportunities to optimize the assets of the estate for the family because there are so many decisions that can save the family thousands and sometimes millions of dollars. If the appropriate plan is put in place while both the husband and wife are alive and you have the appropriate follow up after the death, you will get a much better result than would with the traditional estate plan.

A Cascading Beneficiary Story

One example might be helpful. We served a married couple, both in their 70s, who were both retired engineers. They each had about $1M in their IRAs. They lived fairly frugally. They each collected about $25,000 in Social Security.

We implemented the full Cascading Beneficiary Plan while they were both alive. That meant the surviving spouse was going to make the important decisions of who gets what after the first death. After the first death, we looked at the surviving spouse's needs. The survivor was somewhat frail and expenses were fairly predictable. The survivor's needs were about $40,000 per year, and she received $25,000 per year Social Security. They would need to take only $15,000 from their portfolio to meet expenses. Of course you always want to provide a cushion and extra money for "what if."

In this case, the survivor felt she had more than enough funds with her own million, a paid-up condominium, and Social Security of $25,000. She disclaimed the entire $1M she inherited. Next in line was the B trust. She didn't want the income from the trust and therefore the $1M went down the cascade to the children.

There were two children, both doing fairly well. We could have gotten cute and had at least one of the children disclaim a portion of their share to their children. We decided, however, just to be very certain, the children would retain the inherited IRAs in their own name. Just in case Mom ever needed them, they would have paid her expenses.

So, her children split the $1,000,000 inherited IRA. Then, after she died, the children kept a portion of the second million and they further disclaimed most of the second million to well-drafted trusts for the benefit of the grandchildren. Please note we drafted a separate trust for the grandchildren of each child. We wanted each child to keep or disclaim their share of the estate. If they disclaimed their share, we didn't want it going to the nieces and nephews—only to their children. That means to draft properly, you really should have a separate trust for each set of grandchildren.

While they were alive we did a series of annual Roth IRA conversions staying in the 25% tax bracket. We considered going to the top of the 28% tax bracket, but there wasn't very much after-tax assets to pay for a larger conversion.

It ended up working out well for the family. The parents were smart and they understood the benefits. The children were smart and they understood the benefits for them as well as for their children. The grandchildren at this point are still too young to appreciate what we did. They, will, however, be receiving tax-free checks more than 70 years from now on the inherited Roth IRAs.

I haven't spoken much about the mechanics of the disclaimer. For our purposes here, it is critical to have the correct name for the inherited IRA account. In this case, the inherited Roth IRA for the benefit of the grandchildren was called: "Inherited Roth IRA of Joe Schmoe in Trust for Joe Schmoe the third."

Seventy years from now, the grandchild will get a check from an account bearing the name of his grandfather who died 70 years before the check was issued.

A Cascading Beneficiary Story with a Twist

We had a couple who opted to have us draft the full Lange's Cascading Beneficiary Plan. The estate was about $1.6 million consisting of roughly $1,000,000 traditional IRAs, $300,000 in Roth IRAs, and $300,000 in after-tax dollars.

After the first spouse, in this case the husband, died, we went through the analysis of disclaiming assets. The surviving spouse was 66 and more of a spender than was her husband. She wanted to spend $80,000 before taxes per year. Her Social Security was also roughly $25,000/year. Before we met after her husband's death, I was thinking about disclaiming about $300,000 in her IRA and taking everything else. I figured that would leave her $700,000 in IRAs, the $300,000 in Roth IRAs and $300,000 in after-tax dollars. That should have been more than enough for her needs.

She had a different idea. She wanted the ability to spend much more than $80,000, even if she wasn't really going to spend any more. She also figured her children did not need the money now and if they did, she would give them as-needed gifts.

She decided not to disclaim any money. We are, however, making an aggressive Roth IRA conversion strategy. This way, her kids will have to wait, but she feels good that she has control of all the money. The series of Roth IRA conversions will likely be a huge benefit to her children and grandchildren.

I never had a case where someone disclaimed too much. Frankly, I would have yelled and screamed and done everything in my power to make sure that never happens.

Second-To-Die Policies for IRA Owners

The ultimate estate plan combines Roth IRA conversions, Lange's cascading beneficiary plan and second-to-die life insurance.

A second-to-die life insurance policy pays the beneficiaries only after both spouses die. I have been a fan of second-to-die life insurance for couples like Paul and Carol since I became a serious estate planner. In 1986, I presented a workshop to life insurance agents suggesting that IRA owners who were like

Paul and Carol purchase second-to-die life insurance that would go for the benefit of the children. (Technically, we recommend that we create a trust for the children's benefit to keep the proceeds out of the estate). Having the children inherit the insurance proceeds would allow us to leave some of the IRA money to the grandchildren. The grandchildren would get a much longer "stretch" discussed in Chapter One and the family would get an enormous bang for their insurance buck. Our advice in this area hasn't changed. Now, there are actually even greater incentives to purchase second-to-die insurance because the advantages of inherited Roth IRAs for grandchildren are even more compelling than the advantages of traditional inherited IRAs.

One of the reasons I like second-to-die life insurance is that assuming it is structured properly, "when the policy matures," the children get the proceeds income-tax free and estate-tax free. Let's say Paul and Carol buy a policy that costs $11,500/year. Let's assume they live 20 years. The total premium to the life insurance company would be $230,000. The kids get $1,000,000. You would think that the $1,000,000 would be subject to inheritance tax and estate tax. Assuming it is properly structured, the $1,000,000 isn't subject to inheritance or estate tax. In addition, you would expect the heirs to have to pay income tax on $770,000 ($1,000,000 proceeds minus $230,000 cost). They don't. The insurance proceeds are free of income tax. The life insurance lobby is obviously quite effective.

Please note that was before Roth IRAs, another income tax-free benefit, were created. Today, second-to-die life insurance and Roth IRA conversions work synergistically. By providing liquidity and the ability to have the Roth IRA stay in tact and go down at least one and maybe two generations, the family is taking advantage of two income tax-free investments. The life insurance is also estate-tax free.

In the old days, planners used to recommend second-to-die insurance to pay the estate taxes. There is nothing wrong with that, but that isn't reason enough to buy second-to-die life insurance. In today's environment, it is extremely difficult to get a good fixed income-guaranteed investment. Second-to-die life insurance is such an investment. Depending on how long the survivor of the couple lives, your tax-free return on investment can easily be 10% or more.

To compare apples to apples, I think the decision to purchase a second-to-die life insurance policy should be compared with making straightforward gifts to your children. The children would then invest those gifts. That way, you get many of the advantages of the strategy of creating a pool of money for the children.

For example, let's say you made regular annual gifts to children with the instruction they should invest that money in a safe, preferably guaranteed investment. If the children were to successfully invest that money and the second-to-die life insurance was not a good deal economically, you would have some of the same benefits of creating a pool of money for the children. Then, upon the second death, the kids would have some money and some of the inherited Roth IRA could go to the grandchildren.

The non-quantitative advisors would say the insurance provides certainty and liquidity. They would say the idea of giving the money to the kids and having them invest it would never work because the kids would not save the money. They would talk about the children's wives interfering. They would say the second-to-die policy is a forced savings tool. Then they would start about the taxes. Then they would talk about having the money there to pay estate taxes. That is all true and in some people's minds is sufficient reason to buy the second-to-die life insurance policy.

I want to see if the policy itself, forgetting all that stuff, is a good economic decision. Let's say you discount all the advantages listed. Are most second-to-die policies good investments? Our projections say yes. To test the policy economically, we calculate at what point buying the insurance would be a bad deal economically. Obviously, if one of the spouses lives to 120, you would have been better off just gifting the children money and having them invest the money instead of paying insurance premiums all those years. In other words, at what age would the "breakeven point" point be? What is the number of years one of the spouses must survive for the insurance not to be a good economic deal? Our calculations show it is well into the nineties and often late nineties.

What I could never figure out is how the insurance company made money. If it is so good for clients, even taking into consideration the tax savings, how can insurance companies sell the second-to-die so cheaply?

The reason is that the majority of these policies is canceled or sold or exchanged before "the policy matures." This is a little secret the insurance industry doesn't want you to know.

Avery Michaelson, an associate in capital markets with Coventry Capital at the IMN Canada Cup of Investment Management, says that 88% of life insurance policies never pay a death benefit. That creates an incredible amount of value for life insurance companies.

He suggests life insurance companies are charging less than the actuarially necessary premiums because they know there will be so many of these policies that they will never have to pay out the death benefit. Even if the figure isn't that high for second-to-die policies, it is clear that there is a major lapse element taken into account on the pricing of these policies.

In the case of second-to-die life insurance, the numbers are extremely favorable. It is often attractive to the quantitatively oriented member of the couple. In today's age, though I suspect not necessarily in the future, the more quantitative member of most couples is the man. My experience is that the wife says she wants her children to have the money now when they are young, and they need the money. Let's say the husband and wife disagree, but the husband wins and they buy the second-to-die policy. Then who usually dies first? The husband. Then the wife stops paying the policies. This is particularly devastating for the types of policies I like. I like the smallest premium and the highest death benefit. That sounds obvious, but the type of policies I like have some problems also.

The policies I like (partly because I am a cheapskate and partly because I like the math behind them) typically don't have great cash values. In addition, they are never paid up (though some are paid up at 100) which means you have to keep paying for your entire life and your spouse's entire life. If there is a reasonable chance that either of you will stop paying the premium, then second-to-die insurance would be a terrible idea. If, however, you are committed to protecting your family and taking advantage of the tax laws, second-to-die life insurance can be a fabulous tool to accumulate and distribute wealth. There are also safeguards that can be put on that makes certain the policy is paid.

The mistake you don't want to make is to buy too much second-to-die insurance so that there isn't sufficient money for other types of gifting. Therefore, even though I am a great fan of second-to-die insurance for many families, I never want to "over insure." We don't want to create a situation where there isn't enough money for grandchildren's education, as needed gifts, and other forms of gifting. The other thing you don't want to do is to have such a large insurance budget that if there is a downturn in the market, you can't afford the premiums.

To my knowledge, even with the downturn, all the policies in which I was involved remain intact. Second-to-die life insurance policies have probably been the best investment that my clients have made in the last ten years. It has beaten the pants off of most equity investments and will almost always outperform other fixed income investments. In the last ten years, the second-to-die policies that I have been involved with have outperformed other standard investments, including the Roth IRA conversion.

> Second-to-die life insurance policies have probably been the best investment that my clients have made in the last ten years.

Variations on Lange's Cascading Beneficiary Plan

There are many variations where it is wise to include flexibility in your estate planning—even if you don't have a traditional marriage. We have prepared estate plans for many widows, widowers and divorcees. Let's assume you are now single but have children and young grandchildren. You could start a modified cascade by leaving everything to your children equally. But, you include the right for each child to "disclaim all or a portion of what you left them." The money or property would cascade to the next in line which would be a trust for the grandchildren. Perhaps one of your children is doing well and would prefer to disclaim to their children, but not their nieces and nephews. That can be accomplished. The other child might choose to keep their entire inheritance without disclaiming.

If you don't have any children, you can have a cascade starting with your siblings, flowing down to the nieces and nephews, and flowing down from there to grand nieces and nephews. The plan is flexible, and that is its strength.

—— **$$$** ——

Key Lesson for this Chapter

Using Lange's Cascading Beneficiary Plan will give your family huge flexibility to manage your estate effectively, considerately and wisely.

Chapter Eighteen

Roth Conversions Now Possible In 401(k) and 403(b) Plans

Main Topics

- Pending legislation creates Roth opportunities for 401(k) and 403(b) owners

- What it means to convert 401(k) and 403(b) savings to Roth designated accounts

- Making a series of Roth conversions might be the best course of action

- Money converted to the Roth accounts will be considered taxable income

- Not all employers will offer the new Roth designated accounts

- Roth designated accounts offer superior creditor protection

Key Idea

401(k) and 403(b) owners should evaluate making Roth conversions into Roth designated accounts.

—— **$$$** ——

Just on the horizon is a proposed law that once this book is published is likely to have become law. Assuming it does pass, it will have profound implications for millions of employees who are still working. To learn the latest on the status of this law, please go to www.rothrevolution.com.

If and when the new law passes, it will allow employees to make Roth conversions in their 401(k) or 403(b) plans. Plans that include these Roth designated accounts are more commonly known as to Roth 401(k) or Roth 403(b) plans. This legislation will create enormous opportunities for some, but not all, employees with substantial 401(k) and 403(b) retirement plans.

The amount of pre-tax dollars converted will be considered taxable income.

This proposed legislation (actually an amendment to the *Small Business Act*) will create enormous opportunities for some, but not all, working individuals with substantial 401(k) and 403(b) retirement plans. This law will have the biggest impact on employees with significant balances in their 401(k) or 403(b) accounts, little or no balance in their IRA, and who want to make Roth IRA conversions.

The difference between converting a 401(k) or 403(b) to a Roth designated account and a regular Roth IRA conversion is who has control over the investment choices. If you convert an IRA to a Roth IRA, investment decisions are under your control: traditional investments, non-traditional investments, or both, the choice is yours. However, with the Roth designated accounts [your converted 401(k) or 403(b)] are inside your retirement plan at work and your investment options are limited to the investment options within your employer's retirement plan.

Your new Roth 401(k) or Roth 403(b) account within your employer's retirement plan would have the same properties as a Roth IRA in terms of income tax-free growth for you and your heirs. But, as with a Roth IRA conversion, the amount of pre-tax dollars you convert would be considered taxable income.

The previous law prohibited Roth conversions within a 401(k) or 403(b) plan; even if you wanted to make a large conversion, it was not permitted. If and when the new law passes, assuming your employer has added (or will be adding) Roth designated accounts to their plans, you could make a Roth designated account conversion or a series of Roth conversions for amounts appropriate to your situation. The new law is a big deal for employees who have wanted to make a large Roth conversion but who did not have significant balances in an IRA. Now you will be able to make a Roth conversion of your 401(k) or 403(b). Deciding how much to convert from a 401(k) or 403(b) to the Roth designated account [the official name for Roth 401(k) and Roth 403(b) accounts] requires the same analysis as deciding how much to convert from a traditional IRA to a Roth IRA. Furthermore, there is another significant benefit inherent to this law.

These new Roth designated accounts will enjoy ***excellent creditor protection***. For many, if not most employees, 401(k) and 403(b) retirement plans are controlled by a federal law called ERISA. ERISA retirement plans offer better creditor protection than ordinary IRAs or even Roth IRAs. OJ Simpson is actually collecting substantial income while he is in jail because the judgments against him could not penetrate the ERISA creditor protection from his retirement plan.

This new law deserves much more attention than it will receive. When I first heard of the proposed law it seemed only fair; it equalizes the playing field between IRA owners, who were permitted to make Roth conversion, and 401(k) and 403(b) owners who were not permitted access to their 401(k) plan to make Roth conversions. So, while the Roth designated accounts might not offer as many investment options, they do offer better creditor protection—and tax-free growth.

The catch is that your employer has to offer a Roth designated account option, and it is not mandatory that they do so. But, in my opinion, a smart employer will offer all employees access to a designated Roth account. If you are self employed, I would recommend you add a Roth 401(k) or Roth 403(b) option to your retirement plan. It should cost you little or no money. If your employer offers a Roth 401(k) or Roth 403(b), you will be able to make a Roth conversion immediately after the law is enacted.

As with a Roth IRA conversion, if the conversion is made in 2010, the income will be recognized in two equal installments in 2011 and 2012 unless you elect to recognize all of the income in 2010.

The Killer Strategy That Could Make a Tremendous Difference in Many Lives

Employed middle-income taxpayers without IRAs, but with 401(k)s or 403(b)s, and with access to Roth designated accounts, will likely benefit from making a Roth conversion. A too aggressive strategy would be for middle-income taxpayers to convert their entire 401(k) or 403(b) and pay income taxes on the conversion. The best idea would be to develop a long-term strategy involving a series of partial conversions of the pre-tax dollars in your 401(k) or 403(b) to a Roth designated account. This way you can take advantage of converting the money at lower tax rates. (See Chapter Seven and Chapter Thirteen). In Chapter Thirteen, see the subheads: *15 % Bracket* and <u>25%</u> *and 28% Bracket*. If you are a high-income employee, please see Chapter Thirteen's subheads: *For Readers in the 33% Bracket* and *For Readers Who Will Always be in the Top Bracket.*

Age also factors into the conversion decision. If you are in your 40s or younger, it is more likely to be beneficial because you will have many years of tax-free growth. If you are in your 60s and will retire soon to a smaller income, it will not likely be beneficial. Under that circumstance, it would be better to wait until you have retired and then make a Roth conversion while you are in a lower tax bracket. If you are in your 50s, it is a tougher call. Depending on how long you are going to work and depending on your current and future tax bracket, it may or may not be favorable to make a conversion. But, I highly recommend exploring your options with a qualified advisor.

—— $$$ ——

Key Lesson for this Chapter

If your employer offers Roth designated accounts for your 401(k) or 403(b), you would be wise to consider making a series of Roth conversions.

Chapter Nineteen

Combining Different Strategies

"Anyone may so arrange his affairs that his taxes shall be as low as possible;
he is not bound to choose that pattern which will best pay the treasury;
there is not even a patriotic duty to increase one's taxes."

— Judge Learned Hand, American Jurist

Main Topics

- A sample action plan using multiple retirement planning strategies
- Legal recommendations for combining retirement strategies
- Roth IRA conversions for minors, spendthrifts, and disabled

Key Idea

This book covers a lot of strategies that complement a Roth IRA conversion. In practice, we often use a combination of between two and five and sometimes more complementary strategies. This chapter has a story where we combine Roth IRA conversions with multiple complementary strategies.

—— **$$$** ——

I recently gave an eight-hour workshop to a group of financial advisors who really wanted to integrate Roth IRA conversions into their practice. Toward the end of the talk, after I had covered many of the strategies that are in this book, I faced an interesting question. "Jim, of all the strategies that you have gone over, what is your favorite complimentary strategy that works in conjunction with a Roth IRA conversion?"

If I had to narrow it down to one strategy in would be our favorite estate plan, Lange's Cascading Beneficiary Plan. In my practice, however, I typically provide advice that will cover a combination of at least two—sometimes five or more of the recommended strategies that I have covered individually. The way this book is organized is to systematically review a series of topics on an individual basis. In actual practice, we feel the proper approach is to learn all about a family's financial and personal situation. We like to do a complete quantitative analysis, taking into account their personal situation and personal preferences. Then, we typically make a series of recommendations or even a series of alternatives— many of which have been covered separately, but not together—in this book.

Therefore, I thought it would be instructive to tell the story of a client I recently worked with. Our recommendations actually combine many of the strategies that we have included in this book.

There is a complementary strategy, the second-to-die life insurance, which is not covered in this book, but we include some analysis of it since it is included in our recommendations.

The Combining Different Strategies Story

Paul and Carol were brought up with old-fashioned values. Virtues such as hard work, providing for family and giving both time and money to their church—and other worthy charities—were deeply instilled within them.

When Paul and Carol were married, neither of them had significant assets or significant income. Paul pursued his dream and went to school and eventually ended up with degrees in engineering and business. Carol worked when they were first married, but after they had their first child, George, she became a stay-at-home Mom. Then, Susan, their daughter came along. Carol worked part-time after her children were older. Carol knows how to stretch a dollar. To this day, she still clips coupons. It is so automatic now that she can carry on a conversation or watch TV while she is clipping coupons. Though Paul and Carol are thrifty, they still basically have everything they want.

Paul's father taught Paul that if you made money, you should save some, spend some and give some away to charity. Paul also tried to instill those values in his children, George and Susan. Though Paul felt it was okay to spend some of the money you earned, he preferred to get good value for the money spent. He also knew when he had an excellent opportunity to spend his money wisely, even for pleasure.

For example, in 1960 when he was 17 years old, he and a friend had a chance to buy two tickets to the seventh game of the World Series. They used the money they made mowing laws in the neighborhood and purchased two tickets for $11/

> Watching the Pirate's Bill Mazeroski hit a home run in the bottom of the ninth inning to win the seventh game of the World Series 10-9 against the heavily favored New York Yankees was one of the highlights of Paul's life.

ticket, which seemed like a fortune back then. They played hooky from school and took two buses to Forbes Field on game day. Watching the Pirate's Bill Mazeroski hit a home run in the bottom of the ninth inning to win the seventh game of the World Series 10-9 against the heavily favored New York Yankees was one of the highlights of Paul's life. To this day, he likes to bring that home run up whenever he meets a New York Yankees' fan.

But Paul didn't like waste. When he saw waste in his company, he would do whatever he could to reduce it. The waste that he saw in government signaled a huge source of frustration to him. Accordingly, he really hated to pay taxes, almost to the point of obsession. If you want to hear a long monologue, all you have to do is to ask Paul if he thinks taxpayers are getting their money's worth from the government and if the tax code is equitable to the middle class.

Paul and Carol's Family

Paul and Carol tried to instill their values to their two children and were successful with their daughter Susan. Susan was recently named a partner at a prestigious law firm. She is married and has two children of her own. Paul and Carol have a special feeling for their grandchildren. Paul and Carol sometimes watch their grandchildren and the grandchildren love "Pap and Grammie." Haley, their youngest grandchild is a sweet little girl, but was recently diagnosed as having high level autism. Haley is taking part in a program that receives special funding from the state. It is likely that she will receive other state and federal funds over her lifetime. Everyone is trying to make the best of a tough situation. Susan, in addition to her responsibilities as a Mom and a partner in her law firm, is heavily involved with *Autism Speaks*, a non-profit organization that provides education and support to parents of autistic children. In addition, it raises money for research.

Their son, George, however, is a different story. George is somewhat rebellious by nature and has always resented authority. To this day, he still resents his dad and seems to do the exact opposite of whatever his dad thinks he should do.

George took a number of courses at the local community college but never graduated. He goes from job to job and doesn't do a good job of saving any money he does make. George lives with his girlfriend, Dawn, in Chicago. George and Dawn have a pattern of working for a while, losing their jobs, collecting unemployment, and trying to get jobs again. When they get money, the blow it. George and Dawn recently announced that Dawn is pregnant.

Paul and Carol have mixed feelings about providing for George. They don't want to encourage sloth. George, however, is 38.

Carol worries about George and now, the baby. They know as long as one of them is alive, George and the baby will never starve and there will be a roof over their heads. Despite their differences regarding money, responsibility, and appropriateness, Paul and Carol still love their son and don't want him to end up on the street. The fact they are going to have a grandchild by their spendthrift son is really throwing them for a loop.

Paul and Carol's Financial Situation

Paul's company had an excellent retirement plan and he always contributed the maximum that he was allowed. In addition, Paul and Carol regularly made contributions to a non-deductible IRA because their income was too high to contribute to Roth IRAs. In addition, there was a time when Paul was able to contribute more to his 401(k) than he was allowed to deduct. Like the non-deductible IRA, however, that portion of his retirement plan, grew tax deferred. The total of the amount in his retirement plan that he already paid taxes on and the non-deductible portion of his IRA totaled $50,000. By now, all of that money is in Paul's IRA. Paul had a feeling that maybe there was some type of special treatment of this $50,000, but he wasn't sure.

Paul just retired two years ago when he was 65. He might have opted to worked longer but Carol wanted him to retire so they could enjoy their "younger healthy retired years" together. Paul agreed to retire, but he is still at the top of his game and compromised with Carol. He would limit his work to occasional consulting jobs both for his old company and if there was a project that was particularly interesting to him.

As of year end 2010, Paul will be 67 and Carol 65. Paul thought this transition time would be the right time to seek expert advice with his retirement and estate plan.

When Paul first met me, here is a "simplified" list of his assets:

House (no mortgage)	$ 500,000
IRA (includes $50,000 of after-tax basis)	$1,800,000
Non-retirement investments	$ 300,000

If Paul were to collect his Social Security, he would receive $2,500/month and Carol would receive about half that amount. Paul wants to spend about $100,000 per year measured in today's dollars—plus income taxes as needed. This $100,000 included occasional large expenditures such as an occasional new car and an occasional large expenditure for his house—as well as financial assistance to the children. Paul receives a payment of roughly $10,000/year for his consulting. He didn't know how long he would keep doing that, but he liked "staying in the game" and the money didn't hurt. He didn't want to take his consulting into effect for his projections.

Paul and Carol's first concern was providing for their mutual comfort and safety. Then if that could be accomplished, their next concern was to leave a legacy for his family. His goals were not to make any of his children or grandchildren "stinkin' rich" but to make sure all of their basic needs were met. He would help his children and grandchildren if he were confident that he wasn't doing it at the expense of reducing his and Carol's lifestyle. He was also a big believer in education and wanted to find a tax-efficient way to fund his grandchildren's education.

Carol was particularly worried about Haley, her autistic granddaughter, and wanted to leave her money. But she didn't want the government to get any money that she left Haley. She also didn't want to reduce any of Haley's government benefits.

Paul knew from his informal reading that he should consider a Roth IRA conversion. He always made too much money in his job to qualify for a Roth IRA contribution and his company never offered a Roth 401(k) plan. Paul and Carol also knew big required minimum distributions were coming when Paul turned age 70. Paul thinks income-tax rates are going to sky rocket. He had a feeling that a Roth IRA conversion might be a good idea for his family, but his CPA talked him out of it. The CPA was stuck in that old "total dollars" rather than purchasing power analysis and didn't think it was appropriate for people in their mid-sixties to make Roth IRA conversion. Since Paul had a feeling a Roth IRA conversion would be good for him, he sought additional information.

Paul read the second edition of my first book, **Retire Secure!** (Wiley, Feb., 2009) and eventually hired us to make recommendations and redraft their wills, trusts, and beneficiary designations of their IRAs and retirement plans.

They didn't consider themselves big spenders, but they figured they needed $60,000/year including income taxes. That $60,000 would include an occasional large expenditure such as a new car, a new roof, or something "big." However, it did not include any significant amounts for gifts or life insurance premiums.

Paul and Carol were also wondering if there were any other strategies that would help them and their family achieve more value with their existing resources.

Steve Kohman, Matt Schwartz (my esteemed colleagues), and I put our heads together and made the following legal and financial recommendations.

Legal Recommendations for Combining Retirement Strategies

1. Incorporate Lange's Cascading Beneficiary Plan as part of Paul and Carol's wills to provide maximum flexibility to the surviving spouse. We want the surviving spouse to decide whether he or she needs to use the Bypass Trust under the will rather than be forced to receive their inheritance from their spouse in trust. We also want the survivor

to have the possibility of disclaiming directly to children or even grandchildren.

2. Transfer the house and the non-retirement investments from joint names to Carol's name to enable Paul to shelter additional assets from estate tax if Carol dies before Paul.

3. Make direct lifetime annual gifts to pay George's health insurance and rent. We recommended that the best way to help George was to pay expenses directly for him rather than give George money and let George decide what to do with it.

4. Establish a testamentary (it only is funded after death) spendthrift trust for George with Susan as Trustee. The trust would be protected from George's creditors and perhaps more importantly it would be protect from George blowing his inheritance prematurely in a stupid way. There are a lot of variations of what the trust could say, but the important provisions would likely protect George from himself.

5. Since no one enjoys being a trustee for someone like George, consider a bequest in the will that would order the executrix to purchase an immediate annuity for the non-IRA portion of George's share of the estate and life insurance. That way, George will get a regular income for the rest of his life. This will be a simpler solution, and it will avoid putting Susan in a situation of potential conflict with George regarding appropriate distributions for George's health and support.

6. As far as the IRA and Roth IRA portion, I would recommend mandating that the required minimum distribution be paid to George or at least go to pay some of George's expenses on an annual basis so that the IRAs can be stretched over George's lifetime. It is important that the trust established for George meet all the technical requirements to qualify a designated beneficiary.

7. Establish a testamentary (meaning it is funded only after a death) special needs trust for Haley and consider using Roth IRA dollars to fund that trust to minimize income taxes on accumulated income within the trust. As long as Haley's sibling was the beneficiary of the trust after Haley's death, the Roth IRA distributions could be stretched

over Haley's lifetime. It is also important this trust for Haley meet all the technical requirements to qualify as designated beneficiary.

8. Consider leaving some of the Roth IRA dollars to "normal minor trusts" for the benefit of the other grandchildren. Paul and Carol could also purchase a second-to-die life insurance policy in an irrevocable life insurance trust for George's "spendthrift trust" and Susan. By providing life insurance dollars for George and Susan, there would be greater incentive to have at least some of the inherited Roth IRA go for the benefit of the grandchildren.

9. Consider establishing Section 529 plans for the grandchildren's college and post-college education.

Of course the legal recommendations are interwoven and become an integral part of the retirement plan recommendations. Asking our office to do an estate plan without doing a retirement plan is like asking a doctor for advice for the right side of your body but please ignore the left side of your body. Retirement and estate planning should be looked at as an integrated continuum.

Retirement Plan Strategies

1. Have Paul open a one person 401(k) using the current self-employment income. Select the type of 401(k) plan that allows an IRA trustee-to-trustee fund of pre-tax or traditional IRA dollars, but will not accept after-tax IRA dollars. Roll the traditional portion of Paul's IRA into his new 401(k). Make sure the new one person 401(k) has a Roth 401(k) component. This will result in a remaining IRA of $50,000 of after-tax basis dollars. Then, make a Roth IRA conversion of the $50,000 in after-tax basis inside the IRA. No additional taxes will be due on this conversion. Using a 7% rate of return, this will result in about an additional $279,000 of tax-adjusted dollars or an additional $88,000 of purchasing power net of three percent inflation in 40 years. Please see Chapter Three.

2. Maximize contributions to a Roth IRA for Paul and Carol and maximize Paul's 401(k) contribution to both the traditional and the Roth portion.

3. Plan on taking out all spending money from the Social Security income and after-tax dollars in investments and leaving the IRAs alone (except for Roth conversions). We calculated that although they needed only $60,000 of spending for themselves, a maximum spending budget of $100,000 per year is possible. This level of spending would allow for various gifts to the children and grandchildren and still not be so large as to cause more than the required minimum distributions to be taken from the IRA. There is currently $300,000 of after-tax funds and it would be used in a tax-efficient manner to fund their living expenses before the RMDs begin so that lower cost conversions could be made as well as funding Roth and 401(k) contributions.

Though the issue of stopping or returning Social Security was broached, neither Paul nor Carol liked the idea. Also, since there wasn't much after-tax dollars to use to return Social Security as we wanted the Social Security income for other purposes, we just stayed the course with regard to Social Security benefits.

4. Implement a multi-year Roth IRA conversion plan.

After a thorough and comprehensive Roth conversion analysis, it was decided in consultation with Paul and Carol that the best strategy that was comfortable for them was to convert about $110,000 of 401(k) money to a Roth IRA per year over a three-year period in years 2010 to year 2012 before the RMDs would start in 2013. This would be the most they can convert, paying only about 25% income tax on the conversion. Converting more than that would have several detrimental effects.

If they made a Roth conversion of more than $110,000/year, that would push them into the 28% tax bracket, make them lose certain tax credits, cause a higher Medicare tax to be withheld from their Social Security income in the second ensuing year, and even result in some AMT. More importantly, these higher levels of conversion would result in many years without any after-tax savings due to the large income taxes due on the conversion. Paul and Carol did not feel comfortable without an emergency after-tax fund. The smaller 25% level of conversions of $110,000 per year fit nicely into their plan.

After year 2012, they will also have RMD income of approximately $80,000 annually and growing each year thereafter without this plan. With the plan implemented, however, the RMDs start at a lower amount of about $65,000.

By running a series of financial projections and making certain assumptions, we found that they would have accumulations by the time Paul is 87 with and without these first four recommendations of the plan as follows:

	Status Quo	With the Plan	Difference
Roth IRA	$0	$1,659,915	$1,659,915
Traditional IRA or 401(k)	3,026,302	2,485,085	(541,217)
After-Tax Investments	1,095,825	90,497	(1,005,328)
Home	500,000	500,000	0
Tax Allowance – 25%	(756,576)	(621,271)	135,305
Net Assets	$3,865,551	$4,114,226	$ 248,675

The future differences in the value for the children, assuming inheritance at this point, between these two scenarios, with and without the IRA and retirement plan contributions and Roth conversions strategy, can be graphed as follows:

Figure 16

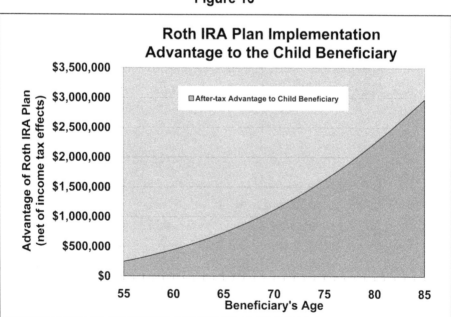

As you can see, by the time the children are age 85, Paul and Carol's family will be $2,966,269 better off measured in after-tax dollars; and if you take 3.5% annual inflation into account, they will still be better off by $513,160 in today's dollars (purchasing power).

Life Insurance Recommendation

Of significant concern, once these recommendations are implemented, is that the after-tax funds are relatively low at the end of their life expectancy. The concern is twofold. First, upon Paul and Carol's eventual death, there may be some significant expenses to deal with in the transition of the estate to the children and grandchildren, which would require the use of after-tax funds. Secondly, the children may decide to make lifestyle changes, such as moving to a new home, which would result in their wanting to spend a significant amount from the inheritance. The problem in these cases is that without a lot of after-tax funds, they might have to withdraw needed money from either the IRA or Roth IRA, which would curtail the stretch value of these savings. Though we feel that it is unlikely with appropriate wills, gifts, etc., there could be an estate tax. There will certainly be a Pennsylvania inheritance tax.

A survivorship or "second-to-die" life insurance policy was found to be of great value in solving this potential liquidity problem for the children and grandchildren. It also served as an excellent fixed income guaranteed investment to make their portfolio more conservative. It was recommended that they invest some of their additional spending budget in such a policy. Our recommendations allow for total spending of $100,000 which includes $70,000 for their own needs and $30,000 for their children and grandchildren. That would give them a $10,000 raise from what they were used to spending. Part of the $30,000 would be used for the children and grandchildren's needs on an annual basis, but some of it could be used for this liquidity fund at their death by a survivorship policy. Paul and Carol felt that using about a third of this budget or about $13,320 for life insurance was reasonable if the benefits were reasonable in relation to the costs.

Since Paul and Carol were in good health and did not smoke, we found that this $13,320 amount of life insurance premium would buy a preferred rate policy that would provide the children and/or grandchildren with $1,167,000.

To allow for the possibility of slightly higher rate class due to their health history, they decided to apply for a $1,000,000 policy which had an annual premium of $11,500.

To verify that the benefits were reasonable in relation to the cost of this policy, we prepared a life insurance break even analysis for them. This analysis calculated the value of a gift fund consisting of the amount of the annual premiums each year with investment growth each year, net of taxes. We would compare the balance of the gift fund with the death benefit on the insurance policy. Eventually if they lived long enough, the gift fund would total the death benefit amount—this would occur about the time Paul turned 99 years old. That this was so far in the future and so much in excess of a normal life expectancy was a clear indication that the life insurance policy was a good deal.

At Paul's life expectancy age of 87, this gift fund would have only amounted to about $452,000. This means that at that time the family would be $548,000 better off with the life insurance policy, which, even accounting for 3.5% annual inflation, is $275,406 bettor off in today's dollars. Plus the insurance provides a significant level of financial security for the family if they would happen to die prematurely before that time.

The life insurance was a good choice for several other reasons as well. For example:

- By using an Irrevocable Life Insurance Trust (ILIT), the policy's death benefit of $1,000,000 could be provided to the children or grandchildren free of any estate-or inheritance-tax.

- George's share of the large death benefit would allow for the funding of an immediate annuity for George that would provide him a guaranteed annual income for the rest of his life.

- By using the life insurance as a form of investment for the children, it acts as a form of forced investment with a very good rate of return. If the children had received the annual premiums as a gift each year, there is no guarantee that they would have saved the money. If Paul and Carol died after 20 years, the after-tax rate of return on the premium payments would be about 12% per year. This is far above any other guaranteed form of investment they had heard of.

- By having the life insurance proceeds as a significant inheritance, Susan will be more willing to disclaim her share of the Roth IRA to benefit her children or trust for her children. The additional life expectancy of the younger generation will prolong the rewards of the tax-free growth and produce even greater longer-term benefits for the family.

The graph above which shows the benefits of the Roth plan for the children through age 85 can be re-done showing instead that the inherited Roth IRA was left for the younger grandchildren. The future additional value of implementing the Plan for the benefit of grandchildren is as follows:

Figure 17

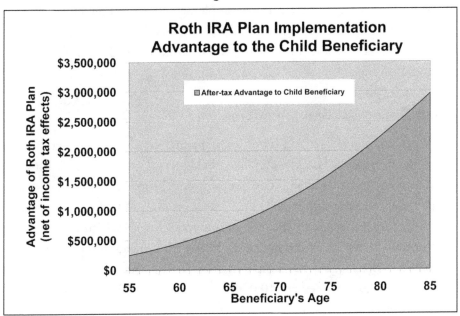

Here we can see how the Plan's advantage grows so much more when we add another 30 years on to the measurement period. The compound growth of the advantage of the Roth plan results in a nearly $25 million advantage by the time the five year old grandchildren are 85 years old. If we allow for a 3.5% inflation adjustment, the advantage at that time becomes an amount of slightly over $1.5 million.

Perhaps even more interesting is the differences in the advantage between the children inheriting the Roth IRA versus the grandchildren. Using the same time period of 30 years after death – age 85 for the children and age 55 for the grandchildren – the advantages are as follows:

	Actual Amount	Amount in Today's Dollars Adjusted for Inflation
Advantages for Children	$2,966,269	$513,160
Advantages for Grandchildren	$3,926,313	$679,246

This shows how much more the benefits of the Roth conversion plan can be for the grandchildren compared to children. This is because the grandchildren have to take so much less in RMDs from the Roth than do the children because of their longer life expectancy. This example demonstrates how having the life insurance for the children's benefit can be such a useful tool in providing money for them so that they feel comfortable with disclaiming the Roth inheritance to the grandchildren.

Other Gifting Recommendations

We talked about Paul and Carol spending more, but we all agreed that was not going to happen. Frankly, they liked being frugal and every idea I had for them to spend money was shot down, except one. I suggested that every couple of years, they take the entire family on a family vacation. Whether it is a cruise or a resort or something more basic, it is great to have the entire family get together. I learned about that idea from my father-in-law. He has had the entire family go on some vacations together and these vacations are the glue that holds the family together. We allowed an extra $10,000/year to cover "family vacation expense."

Our recommendations allow for total gifting of $30,000 for their children and grandchildren. The life insurance would consist of $11,500 and annual— or as needed gifts would comprise the remaining $18,500 per year. This met with Paul and Carol's desires as they knew George needed money and the grandchildren would also. We recommended the gifting budget be put to the most effective use possible.

We recommended the following possibilities for the $18,500:

- Establishing Section 529 plans for Susan's college-bound child and George and Dawn's new child for future college and post-college education.
- Simple gifts.
- Paying for some of George's expenses directly.

Other gifting alternatives, not as effective as second-to-die life insurance include:

- Roth IRAs for the children. The checks for these accounts can be written directly to the broker so that the funds do not get misdirected
- Funding the children's retirement plans at work. If Susan and George and their spouses are not funding their retirement plans at work to the maximum level possible, they should be. As needed, gifts could be made to them to offset the loss in income they face by funding the plans.
- Roth IRA conversion gifts for the children. If Roth planning for the children indicates benefits could be obtained by their doing Roth conversions, they could give them money to compensate for the taxes that would incur. Often a child can convert at a lower tax cost than the parents, although since the children are younger, they also often do not have as much available to convert.

Gifting is one of the simplest and most effective ways to reduce these death taxes. These gifts have the effect of moving money from Paul and Carol's estate into the children's estates. Had the gifts not been done, there would be additional state inheritance taxes and possibly federal estate taxes due when Paul and Carol's estate passed to the children.

By following this gifting plan of $30,000 per year increasing by 3.5% annually for inflation, including the life insurance gifts, the taxable estate would be reduced by about $2,058,000. This represents a potential savings of $92,610 in Pennsylvania inheritance taxes; and if we assume a net 40% federal estate tax on that amount, the potential savings could be $823,200 for a total of $915,810.

Summary of Savings from Recommendations

To this point, the family has been provided with recommendations which would provide financial advantages through the life of Paul and Carol as follows:

Advantage from conversion of non-deductible basis in the IRA
  to a Roth, contributions to Roth IRAs and 401(k)s $248,675
Advantage from using life insurance $548,000
Additional savings in death taxes $915,810

These savings total $1,712,485 in 20 years which is $860,637 in today's dollars accounting for 3.5% inflation. This does not include the additional benefits from the tax free growth of Roth IRA inheritances in the future, which could be an additional $388,000 in today's dollars. Thus the family is over $1 million better off in today's dollars by these recommendations. Even if we assume there will not be a federal estate tax, the potential savings to Paul and Carol's family from a combination of different strategies that we recommended could result in a savings of $889,285 which is $446,925 in today's dollars—plus the potential $388,000 value of future tax-free growth of the Roth IRA inheritance measured in 2010 dollars.

Additional benefits of these recommendations that we did not attempt to quantify but certainly have a benefit for the family:

- Additional flexibility and protection of the surviving spouse

- Feeling of security that George is provided for, but can't blow his inheritance

- Good feeling for providing for Haley in a way that the government can't get her money

- The ability for Susan and her children to receive their inheritance in the most tax-effective manner

- Some, but not all of the grandchildren's college education will be provided for—tax-free

- The reduction of the general anxiety that you are not doing the best thing for your family

- The great feeling you are doing the right thing for your family

—— **$$$** ——

Key Lesson for this Chapter

By combining the Roth IRA conversion and other complementary strategies, you and your family could be better off by over $1,000,000.

"We come to beginnings only at the end."

— William Throsby Bridges

Appendix

Table I: Single Life Expectancy

(For Use by Beneficiaries)

Age	Life Expectancy	Age	Life Expectancy
56	28.7	84	8.1
57	27.9	85	7.6
58	27.0	86	7.1
59	26.1	87	6.7
60	25.2	88	6.3
61	24.4	89	5.9
62	23.5	90	5.5
63	22.7	91	5.2
64	21.8	92	4.9
65	21.0	93	4.6
66	20.2	94	4.3
67	19.4	95	4.1
68	18.6	96	3.8
69	17.8	97	3.6
70	17.0	98	3.4
71	16.3	99	3.1
72	15.5	100	2.9
73	14.8	101	2.7
74	14.1	102	2.5
75	13.4	103	2.3
76	12.7	104	2.1
77	12.1	105	1.9
78	11.4	106	1.7
79	10.8	107	1.5
80	10.2	108	1.4
81	9.7	109	1.2
82	9.1	110	1.1
83	8.6	111 and over	1.0

Additional Resources and Reading

I have a favorite group of IRA and retirement plan experts that I can recommend to you: Ed Slott, CPA; Natalie Choate, Esq.; Bob Keebler, CPA; Barry Picker, CPA and John Bledsoe, CFP.

All five of them have been on my radio show twice. We have the transcripts and the audios of those shows on www.retiresecure.com. The shows are 55 minutes of solid content. I would encourage you to listen to those shows and/or read the transcripts which can be found at www.retiresecure.com. Listening to them will give you confidence that many of the recommended strategies offered in *The Roth Revolution* receive support from the top experts in the IRA and retirement planning field.

I also encourage you to read their works because they all have much to offer.

About the Author

CPA, attorney, and registered investment advisor, James Lange, is a nationally recognized IRA, Roth IRA conversion, and estate-planning expert. His best selling book, *Retire Secure!* (Wiley 2006, 2009), has appeared in two editions and enjoys glowing testimonials from noted financial experts, such as Charles Schwab, Jane Bryant Quinn, Larry King, Ed Slott, Bob Keebler, Natalie Choate, Roger Ibbotson, and dozens more.

Lange wrote the definitive article on Roth IRA conversions for the peer-reviewed journal of the American Institute of Certified Public Accountants, *The Tax Adviser*, in 1998. He has been quoted as a financial expert by *The Wall Street Journal* 30 times. Other notable sources that have quoted him include: *The Associated Press, Consumer Reports, Forbes, Newsweek, Businessweek, The New York Times, New York Post, Detroit Free Press* and *Kiplinger's Retirement Report*. He also developed and published Lange's Cascading Beneficiary Plan™ which is widely regarded as the gold standard of estate planning.

Jim's renowned radio show, *The Lange Money Hour: Where **Smart** Money Talks*, often features the country's leading IRA experts and provides practical financial advice to listeners. He is the president of three interrelated companies. The Lange Accounting Group handles tax planning and preparation for 500 individuals. The Lange Legal Group limits its practice to estate planning and has prepared wills, trusts, and beneficiary designations of IRAs and retirement plans for 1,800 IRA and retirement plan owners. The Lange Financial Group, a registered investment advisory firm, provides long-term integrated Roth IRA conversion strategies and money management assistance. Lange also founded The Roth IRA Institute which educates both public and private groups with keynote addresses.

Jim's website, www.rothira-advisor.com, consistently ranks in Google's Top 10 for a "Roth IRA" search. Overall, Jim's four websites have registered over 25 million hits, offering readers hundreds of pages of analysis, videos, and streaming archives of Jim's radio show.

Jim, his wife, Cindy, and their 15-year-old daughter, Erica, live in his Pittsburgh childhood home. When not devising new tax cutting and wealth accumulation strategies, Jim enjoys bicycling, hiking, skiing, and traveling with his family. For fun, he plays chess and bridge. He also practices the mandolin at night in his office because his wife and daughter can't stand listening to him at home.

The Next Step

Services

Congratulations for selecting and reading *The Roth Revolution: Pay Taxes Once and Never Again* and taking a major step toward long-term tax-free growth. We hope you are now inspired to evaluate your options and take action. As always, we recommend seeking the advice of a trusted advisor or team of trusted advisors with expertise in Roth IRA conversions and estate planning with IRAs. I would strongly urge you to work with a team of trusted advisors until you have a long-term Roth IRA conversion plan as well as a "well thought out" estate plan in place.

Also, consider whether you could benefit from some of the advanced strategies such as making a Roth IRA conversion with after-tax dollars inside an IRA or retirement plan, or a series of conversions and recharacterizations. Consider, as well, whether some of the other strategies which work in concert with Roth conversions, such as when to take (or return) Social Security and making charitable donations, would be to your advantage. It will cost you some time and money, but if you have the right team to help you, your family could benefit by hundreds of thousands—or even millions—of dollars with a long enough time horizon.

After reading Chapter Seventeen, the chapter on estate planning, you should be in a much better position to determine if your wills and/or trusts, and the beneficiary designations of your IRAs and retirement plans are appropriate or whether they need to be reviewed and possibly changed. Please make sure the appropriate estate attorney is reviewing not only your wills and trusts, but perhaps more importantly, the beneficiary designations of your IRAs, Roth IRAs and retirement plans.

For those of you who do not have a trusted advisor or team of advisors who can provide the level of expertise and service that you require, our office may be able to accommodate you.

For a limited number of readers, it is possible that you could work with the same team who put together this book and the two previous best selling editions of **Retire Secure!**

The end result of working with us would be a set of recommendations similar to the recommendations found in Chapter Nineteen but personalized to your situation. We are a small team, however, and will not be able to accommodate many readers for this service. We can be reached at 412-521-2732.

Speaking

James Lange CPA/Attorney, Keynote Speaker
Available for Consumers & Financial Professionals

For Consumers in Western Pennsylvania (or Travelers to Western PA)

If you live in Western Pennsylvania or are willing to travel, Jim holds monthly workshops for consumers at no cost. For additional details, please see www.retiresecure.com.

For Groups & Associations in Western Pennsylvania

If you are part of a group or association that would benefit from a Jim Lange workshop, please contact our office at 412.521.2732 for more information and scheduling options. We also have a speaking section on our website at www. retiresecure.com.

For Those Outside of Western Pennsylvania

Although attending one of Jim's workshops in person is the best course of action, we also offer the next best thing. For those of you who want additional information in the form of a CD or a series of teleseminars, or even advanced training, please go to www.retiresecure.com.

For Everyone

The perfect complement to *The Roth Revolution* is Jim's previous best selling book, *Retire Secure!* (Wiley 2009). *Retire Secure!* has most of Jim's best information that is not necessarily related to Roth IRA conversions.

Financial Professionals

For Wholesalers/Managers--Operation: Territory Growth

Looking to solidify existing relationships and start new ones? Jim is available to speak to your audience of both financial professionals and consumers. We have a system designed to bring you both advisor prospects as well as end consumer prospects. Operation: Territory Growth is a system guaranteed to help you build relationships, credibility, and sales through an easy-to-follow process. Please go to www.retirsecure.com to download our Operation: Territory Growth workshop package.

Free Information

Audio

For a free 90-minute audio ($100 Value), please go to www.retiresecure.com. This audio contains some of the highlights of Jim's popular workshop.

E-mail Newsletter

By signing up for our free e-mail newsletter, you will receive regular communications about not only new laws, but also new strategies and different ideas for cutting taxes and accumulating wealth. You will receive regular notifications of different interviews with IRA and financial experts on the radio which you can listen to with an internet connection.

The Lange Money Hour: Where *Smart* Money Talks

We have a bi-weekly radio show where Jim interviews some of the top IRA and financial experts in the country. Prior guests have included Ed Slott, Bob

Keebler, Natalie Choate, Barry Picker, Bob Keebler, Jane Bryant Quinn and Jonathan Clements—just to name a few.

We have recorded these shows and are making the recordings available by going to www.retiresecure.com. In addition, we are gradually transcribing the shows and offering the transcriptions.

You could also listen live by going to www.kqv.com or if you are in Pittsburgh, listening to 1410am, KQV. The show runs every other Wednesday night at 7:00 EST. For a complete listing of our upcoming shows and the audio archives of the past broadcasts, please go to www.retiresecure.com.

Free Reports

We wrote a number of chapters that could not be included in the book because it is already close to 300 pages. Some of the omitted chapters are most valuable for some, but not all IRA—and retirement plan—owners. We also have other articles and information that we are sharing with our readers. That information can be accessed by going to www.rothrevolution.com and clicking *Book Offers*.